Anne and Martin
with best wishes and
love from
Janet Chisholm

LADYSMITH

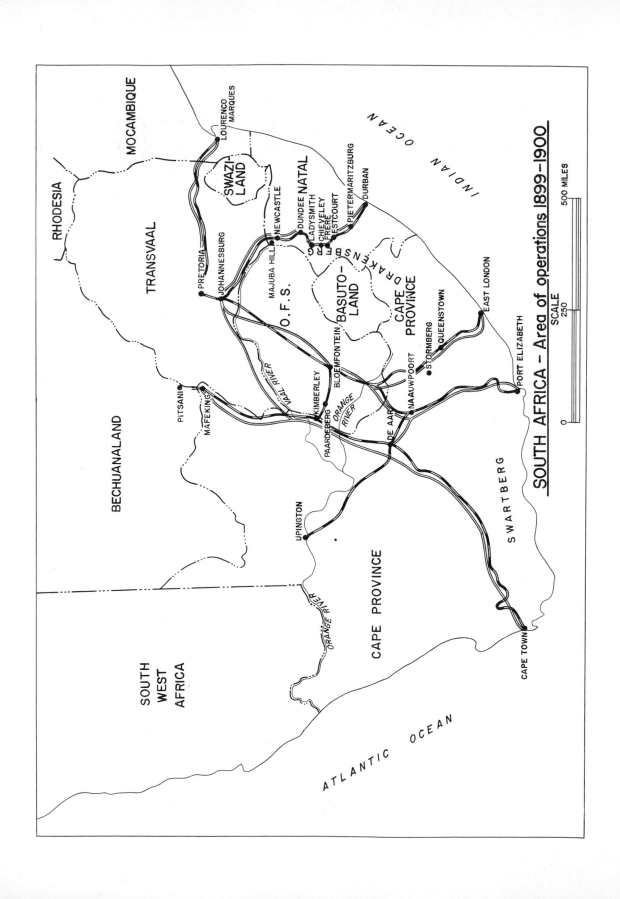

SOUTH AFRICA – Area of operations 1899-1900

LADYSMITH

Ruari Chisholm

Osprey

First published in 1979 by
Osprey Publishing Limited,
12–14 Long Acre, London WC2E 9LP
A Member Company of the George Philip
Group
© 1979 Ruari Chisholm

ISBN 0 85045 312 7

Editor Jeremy Harwood
Designer Mike Rose
Research Marian Eason

Filmset and printed by
BAS Printers Limited, Over Wallop,
Hampshire

Contents

For Janet

Foreword

by Elizabeth Longford

The Anglo-Boer war, as South Africans like to call it, has a perennial interest all its own. Historically, it occurred at the hinge or joint between two different centuries and kinds of warfare—and we all know that arthritis attacks joints. The British Army of 1899–1901 suffered some of the pain and stiffness due to its position in history. The Boer commandos, on the other hand, were individualistic and often indisciplined. At worst they showed the characteristics of spastic limbs that would not obey the brain's directions; at best the loose-limbed ease of a brilliant athlete.

Again, there are many "lasts" and "firsts" in the Boer War story that give it special significance. It was the last occasion, for instance, when a set-piece British cavalry charge took place. And the first time that the British Empire had been pitted against white soldiers in a major war since the Crimea. Between those two landmarks, the Crimea and South Africa, the British had defeated various half-armed natives, including the Egyptian fellahin at Tel-el-Kebir and the Sudanese at Omdurman. How would they make out against the tiny Boer republics? Not forgetting that these Boers had already inflicted an ignominious defeat upon the British General Colley at Majuba Hill twenty years earlier, from which the British had apparently learnt nothing except to wear khaki instead of blue and scarlet. Moreover, the Boers themselves were the descendants of a nation who had built up an overseas empire.

The world watched spell-bound. There were some who hoped that the God of the Old Testament might once again enable little David to slay the giant Goliath. Others felt that the giant empire could not fail to crush its diminutive adversary, as indeed it eventually did. Yet even today, though we know that "little David" has grown into a formidable power, bent on giving the black "Davids" in his midst far less freedom than the British Goliath gave him—even so, the Boers' courageous struggle has not lost the romantic appeal of a small nation defying a great one. "Small is beautiful."

Not that war is ever beautiful or the Boer War any less ugly than all armed conflicts are. But the Boer War offers the added interest of being a key feature in the world game of power politics, with its feedback into the Jameson Raid and its forward impact on the Great War. Some twenty years ago, when trying to unravel the complexities of Jameson's Raid, I quoted Winston Churchill's profound judgment of that disastrous fiasco. Once it had happened, he said, nothing has ever stopped happening since. Certainly since my book was published, much has happened in that part of the world. There is both a real need and a prominent niche for new studies of the great Anglo-Boer war.

Apart from such general considerations, Ruari Chisholm's adventurous account of the siege of Ladysmith has special claims to praise. I use the word "adventurous" advisedly. For in these admirably lucid and pithy pages the famous siege comes through as an adventure story. So much so, that at times the excitement of the conflict is conveyed almost physically, and one's heart beats faster. But Ruari Chisholm's treatment is adventurous in more subtle ways also. He boldly cuts through the strategic meshes of the war to concentrate on what happened at Ladysmith, and at Ladysmith alone. Admittedly this is a large enough canvas in all conscience, treated as it is in depth, and representing as it does the British decision "to cover the vitals of Natal from invasion".

What impresses me is that Ruari Chisholm has resisted the temptation to spread himself on the other celebrated sieges that were taking place in South Africa at the same time: Kimberley, with Cecil Rhodes shut up inside and demanding instant rescue from the Boers and the "raw savages" (blacks) who were inconveniently shut up with him; Mafeking, with Baden-Powell inside but commendably making no imperious demands whatever. Dr. Jameson completed the trio by being shut up in Ladysmith, but as he contracted typhoid his voice is not heard.

The story of the siege presents a wealth of incident, personalities, tragedy and comedy. Ruari Chisholm is particularly skilful at putting a character in a nutshell, or rather in a single paragraph. What a strange display of middle-aged or elderly generals—at once pathetic and heroic—is marshalled for our incredulous inspection, with their odd spelling ("Grenadeers" and a dinner of many "corses"), blue whiskers, skyward pointing waxed moustaches, varicose veins and excessive reactions—either too optimistic like Penn Symons or too self-questioning (but loved by his men) like Buller. On the other side, the pessimistic Joubert, simply too tired at sixty-eight, especially after spending the last twenty years in arguing with British whites and African blacks, to make a great commander. "The age of youthful 'fliers' ", notes the author, "had not yet arrived." No wonder so many of them died or suffered humiliation—a fate worse than death—for war is naturally not kind to the vulnerable.

Beyond the siege itself, Ruari Chisholm has garnered every detail that might and did affect it. We listen to the gossip on board the troopships and the fears of Lord Roberts' army that they will arrive too late for the fun. We follow the streams of volunteers who came from far and near to succour the side of their choice, though the numbers of Irish-Americans and Europeans who supported the Boers were infinitesimal compared with the strong forces of Australians, New Zealanders and Canadians, fired with the Imperial idea. But we are never far from the siege, and as the food situation inside worsens, we watch the typical reactions of the besieged—men being robbed of matches and candle-grease by their friends, girls being tattooed with patriotic slogans, horses being transformed into "Chevril" on the principle of peace-time bulls into "Bovril".

In choosing Ladysmith as his theme, Ruari Chisholm has two immense advantages. One is the dramatic part played by Winston Churchill, and his tragi-comic attempts to relieve Ladysmith on his own. To my surprise, I have learnt that the reward offered by Joubert for Churchill's capture—£25— was not a large one, even by the standards of those days. When Joubert's friends asked why he had not offered more, he replied: "He is just 'n Klein Koerant-skrywertjie"—"A little bit of a newspaper man."

This brings me to Ruari Chisholm's second strong point. He is fluent in the Afrikaans language, familiar with the territory and its present inhabitants, and an expert student of the Boer documents. This enables him to maintain a remarkable impartiality between the two sides, based on intimate knowledge of each. It is my belief that in future no writer on the Anglo-Boer War will be wholly acceptable unless he or she can study the original sources.

One more word on Ladysmith itself. Battles and sieges are the stuff of which war histories are made. By a strange coincidence, the heroine of another famous siege, Badajoz in the Peninsular War, escaped from inside the city and married one of Wellington's officers, Harry Smith. He was to become Sir Harry Smith, Governor-General of the Cape, Ladysmith being called after Juanita his Spanish wife, and the neighbouring town of Harrismith after him. Years later still, the Harrismith commando was fighting for the Boers while Lady Smith, so to speak, was again landed in a siege. When history repeats itself the result is often ironical.

Ruari Chisholm, quoting J. B. Atkins, a war correspondent, speaks of "the two faces of war"; the laughter and the tears. As a historian and vivid story-teller, he himself has shown us the living expressions on each face, as well as penetrating to the thoughts, both Boer and British, behind.

Elizabeth Longford

Author's Introduction

"Probably no single incident in the war has been more determinative of final issues than the tenure of Ladysmith." (Admiral Mahan)

With the eminent American historian Admiral Mahan, I share the view of Ladysmith as the central military event of the Anglo-Boer War of 1899–1902. In this book I seek to unfold the Ladysmith story not only as a military campaign consisting of battles, bombardments, attacks and counter-attacks, but also as a case history in human behaviour, both Boer and British, soldier and civilian.

To locate the siege within the wider context of the war, it seemed to me appropriate to touch upon the root causes of the whole conflict, the disastrous Jameson Raid which heightened irreversibly the tensions between the two White communities in South Africa, the outbreak of hostilities and the battles leading to the town's encirclement. In addition to the thoughts and problems of the army commanders and the battlefield lives of the troops on both sides, I have also dwelt upon the anxieties, the fears and frustrations of civilians inside the perimeter. In the early days, the ladies of Ladysmith gave tennis parties on Sundays when the God-fearing Boers stopped shelling and senior British officers were served strawberries and cream for tea. But later, as things became harder and standards declined, there were stories of officers cheating at cards and gentlemen stealing matches and candlewax. A former mayor incited the public to defy the orders on food control and an irate doctor offered his services to silence a Boer howitzer. On the outside, some unworthy Boers discharged themselves from further duties and others invented trouble at home to get away from the front. All in all, this book is an attempt to bring Ladysmith back into focus.

In acknowledging the part played by those who helped me to write this book I must begin with my own family, above all, with my wife, who scrambled up thorn-covered battlefield hilltops in Natal, typed manuscript drafts and spent many evenings in silent understanding that this or that chapter had to be finished.

The children, whose broken possessions remained unmended for days at a time and whose own creative work was often inadequately admired, showed remarkable forbearance, and occasionally contributed useful ideas.

I am also deeply indebted to a number of friends in Britain for their energy and enthusiasm in pursuit of elusive source material on my behalf. These include, among many, Miss Charlotte Deane, Miss Elizabeth Patterson, Dr. and Mrs. A. Czech, Captain H. Ellis R.N., Miss Ann Carter and Dr. M. Balfour. In South Africa, the tiny Ladysmith Historical Society, notably its organizers Mr. and Mrs. G. Tatham, went to immense trouble making material available and showing me over the ground. Mrs. Shiela Henderson's tour of Elandslaagte was much appreciated, as was Mr. "Pitch" Christopher's piece on Colenso. The *magnum opus* on the Klip River community produced by the Ladysmith Women's Institute was most valuable. I owe a special word of thanks to Professor Johan Barnard of the University of South Africa for his interest and advice and, in particular, for the trouble he took in translating sections of his own book "Louis Botha op die Natalse Front".

Among those who kindly loaned me the private papers of siege participants I have to thank Dr. M. Balfour for the material belonging to his father, Dr. H. H. Balfour of Intombi Camp, Captain M. Hodges R.N., who made available papers and photographs belonging to his father, Lieut. Michael Hodges R.N., commander of the 4.7 gun at Junction Hill and Sir Charles Mott-Radclyffe M.P., who produced the diary of his father, Capt. C. E. Radclyffe, serving in Buller's relief force.

I am especially grateful to Major the Hon. R. W. Pomeroy, who made an uncomfortable cross-country journey in an English winter to bring me the Ladysmith papers of his father, Lieut. the Hon. R. L. Pomeroy of the 5th

Dragoon Guards, and also of Major St. John Gore, who commanded the Dragoons during the siege. The diary of Lieut. Heneage R.N., loaned to me by his grandson (with permission of Lady Heneage-Vivian, the diarist's widow), was most helpful, as were the papers belonging to Lieut. F. Jarvis of the 13th Hussars, provided by his daughter Miss Mary Jarvis. Mrs. Gerald Critchley kindly showed me some letters and other papers belonging to her father, Lieut. A. Tringham, serving with the Devons, and I am also most grateful to Miss E. Serocold for access to the diary of her grandfather, Lieut. E. Serocold of the K.R.R.C., and to Miss A. Currie, who showed me the papers belonging to her father, Dr. N. Currie of the Natal Carbineers. To Mr. B. Franks I am indebted for the material relating to his father, Lieut. G. D. Franks, who served with the 19th Hussars at Ladysmith.

Colonel E. D. Harding and Major D. Metcalfe of the Gloucestershire Regiment were most helpful in making available regimental papers and photographs, as was Miss E. Talbot Rice of the National Army Museum in answering my various enquiries. Other regimental historians who kindly answered my requests for information included Colonel Spencer of the Devons, Major Bartelot of the Royal Artillery Institution, Colonel Nixon of the Green Jackets and Major Blaxland of the Buffs. Also, I felt very honoured to have met two of the veterans who actually took part in the campaign, Colonel C. Jackson, who fought with the Royal Scots Fusiliers in Buller's relief force, and Mr. William Netley of the 13th Battery Royal Artillery, who marched with General Yule to Ladysmith.

On the secretarial side I am indebted to the Misses Rosemary Magrath, Doreen Hutchings and Jean Brydone and, above all, to Mrs. Cherry Fraser. Roland Hiscock showed immense patience in his highly professional interpretation of my map specifications. For their kind permission to reproduce museum photographic material, I am grateful to the directors of the Africana Museum, Johannesburg, the Pretoria National Cultural and Historical Museum, the National Army Museum, London, and the National Portrait Gallery, London. I would also like to thank Mrs. Goldstein for her help in finding my way around the South African War Museum Library and my daughter, Jane, for compiling the index.

To Derrick Olmesdahl of the Ladysmith Historical Society I am most grateful for the enthusiastic help and advice he gave me throughout my researches in South Africa and I would especially like to thank the Countess of Longford for writing the Foreword.

Finally, I wish to thank all those authors and publishers of works in copyright for giving me permission to quote from their books listed in the bibliography.

RWC
Flimwell, Wadhurst
1978

Glossary

Afrikaner A white South African who is by birth or assimilation a member of the Afrikaans-speaking culture group descended from the original Dutch settlers and subsequent French and German immigration

Biltong Dried meat

Boer Afrikaner countryman

Burgher Afrikaner townsman

Donga Dried-up river bed

Dorp Village, small town

Drift Ford, crossing point

Kloof Ravine or gorge

Kop Hill

Kopje Hillock

Krijgsraad (Krygsraad) Council of War

Laager Encampment

Landdrost Magistrate

Nek Mountain pass, saddle

Nullah River bed, with or without water

Rand Reef. Usually refers to the gold-fields of the Transvaal with Johannesburg in the centre

Sangar Stone breastwork erected from loose rocks and boulders

Schanz (Skans) Rampart, trench

Sjambok Leather whip

Spruit Stream

Uitlander Foreigner

Veld(t) Open countryside

Veldt-Kornet Field-Cornet

Zarps Transvaal (lit. South African) Republican Police

B.B.B.	Bechuanaland Border Police
B.M.R.	Border Mounted Rifles
I.L.H.	Imperial Light Horse
N.M.R.	Natal Mounted Rifles
S.A.L.H.	South African Light Horse

THE ILLUSTRATED LONDON NEWS.

REGISTERED AT THE GENERAL POST-OFFICE FOR TRANSMISSION ABROAD.

No. 2177.—VOL. LXXVIII.   SATURDAY, FEBRUARY 5, 1881.   WITH TWO SUPPLEMENTS   SIXPENCE. BY POST, 6½D.

TWO MEMBERS OF THE TRANSVAAL PROVISIONAL GOVERNMENT.

MR. P. J. JOUBERT.

MR. S. J. PAUL KRÜGER.

THE WAR IN THE TRANSVAAL: THE BOERS' METHOD OF FIGHTING.—SEE PAGE 126.

1 The Wilderness Years

"Wherefore come out from among them and be ye separate, thus saith the Lord." (2 Corinthians, 6: v. 17)

Until the beginning of the 19th century, the course of history made almost no impact on the life of the settlers in the Cape. For 150 years they had cultivated grapes and grain, grazed cattle and sheep, fought Bushman rustlers and raiders, and read the Bible, expanding quietly to the north as they did so. They gave little thought to the outside world and received little in return. Their stern Puritan values, their rigorous and dangerous way of life, their special interpretation of Old and New Testaments, leading them to identify white with Christian, and their rejection of Mother Europe became the criteria for a way of life which scarcely changed over the years.

In 1795, however, a British fleet sailed into Simon's Bay to pre-empt French control of the Cape, and southern Africa was thrust inexorably into the mainstream of world affairs. By 1814 the British were firmly entrenched with a two-fold title acquired in the Napoleonic Wars— the somewhat questionable right of acquisition by purchase and the more solid one of conquest.

Seeds of discord between Briton and Boer did not take long to sow. But it was neither British officialdom, interested in nothing much more than the harbours of the Cape peninsula and the sea routes to the Far East, nor the enterprising and industrious 1820 settlers who posed the real threat to the Boer way of life. It was the "meddling missionaries" and the "political parsons", who came to South Africa with the glowing approval of an affluent middle class and the tacit consent of Whitehall, who were the principal cause of resentment. Clashes over land, the inadequacy of the British to protect the Boers against Xhosa incursions, and the creeping advance of the English language were as nothing compared with the libertarian Christian message the missionaries were preaching. Worse was to come, for, in 1833, Earl Grey's Abolition Act was passed by Parliament and official recognition of an unacceptable social order was now ratified. For the Boers, the concept of emancipated slaves being regarded as equal to God-fearing white Christians was intolerable. As one Boer woman, Anna Elizabeth Steenkamp, wrote later, "Wherefore we rather withdrew in order thus to preserve our doctrines in purity."

The mass exodus to the interior started in 1836. In the beginning, it was a conscious escape from British rule. Later, as legend, mythology, real history and time lent stature to it, it was to become known as the Great Trek. Those who took part in it were to become known as the *Voortrekkers* (pioneers). The prestige they acquired over the years in Afrikaner culture was not unearned. For two decades the

Led by Kruger and Joubert, the Transvaal won its independence from Britain in 1881. British imperial pride, however, was mortified by defeat: "Remember Majuba" became a potent rallying cry. (National Army Museum)

seemingly invincible challenges of nature and the Zulu nation were met with great courage and the inspiration of a people who were certain that God was watching over them—not all the time, for they suffered the occasional massacre—but with the assurance of fulfilment in the end.

For the time being, then, the Boers were able to pursue their lives of isolation, with saddle, rifle and Bible close to hand. But, inevitably, the British expanded into the interior. In 1877, the Transvaal was annexed, after 25 years of independent, but, by Westminster standards, corrupt and incompetent government. This move was vigorously resisted by the Boers, and the first Boer War was the result. In it, the British learned the bitter lesson of military complacency. A column under Colonel Anstruther was ambushed at Bronkhorstspruit and would have been annihilated, had not its mortally wounded commander raised the white flag in order, as he put it, "to make sure that some of us live to tell the story." In February 1881, General Colley was thrice beaten in northern Natal—most dramatically at Majuba Hill, where he lost his life and the British army its reputation. The Boers recovered their much cherished independence.

Then came diamonds, gold and Cecil Rhodes. Illness and a Victorian faith in the health-giving properties of the South African climate first brought the 17-year-old Rhodes to Durban in 1870. His real rise to fame began with his move to Kimberley, where, years later, he met Dr. Jameson, another sickly immigrant who had come to South Africa for very similar reasons. Unbeknown to British and Boers alike—both physically vigorous and hardy communities—their lives were soon to be profoundly influenced by a pair of semi-invalids. With the wealth of De Beers behind him, Rhodes rose to become Prime Minister of the Cape, while Jameson became his unofficial political agent in pursuit of the vision of "the North"—the Cape to Cairo route, all under the British flag.

While Rhodes amassed wealth and advanced his political career, a political personage of an altogether rougher and cruder dye looked on, brooding on the gathering storm. Stepahnus Johannes Paulus Kruger, the man who was to become the father figure of Afrikanerdom, was 58 when he was elected President of the Transvaal in 1883. At once he made it his unswerving aim to free the tiny Boer republic of all remaining vestiges of British influence. But the discovery of gold on the Rand and the insatiable lust of overnight wealth which its presence unleashed transformed his pastoral homeland into an Eldorado of sin, sordidness and foreigners. Flora Shaw, a visitor to Johannesburg in 1892, was horrified:

"Johannesburg has no politics. It is much too busy with material problems. It is hideous and detestable, luxury without order; sensual enjoyment without art; riches without refinement; display without dignity."

A contemporary portrait of Dr. Jameson and his staff on their ill-fated raid into the Transvaal. (National Army Museum)

So the Rand in the closing decades of the 19th century became the promised land for two totally disparate and incompatible communities. The *Uitlanders*—mainly British, but also including men from the rest of Europe, the New World and Australia—were chiefly inspired by the quest for wealth, though imperial sentiment, political intrigue, or, just simply, crime also came into their spectrum. Another

characteristic was their determination to accomplish whatever purpose had induced them to come to the Rand, no matter what the cost. The Boers—agrarian, Bible-reading and pious, though not always angelic—resented deeply this intrusion into their newly-won homeland and were not slow to use to the best advantage their political title recovered from the British after the 1880–1881 war. Heavy taxation discriminating against the mining industry, disputes over schooling for English-speaking children in the Afrikaans language, and a point-blank refusal to give the *Uitlanders* votes became the three principal and immediate sources of friction.

By the mid-1890s, feelings on the Rand had reached boiling point. Some 38,000 out of 80,000 *Uitlanders* petitioned Kruger for concessions, and, when these were scornfully refused, they began to count heads. While the more bellicose formed rifle clubs, others took to political intrigue with Mr. Charles Leonard as their spokesman, American millionaire Alfred Beit as their financial backer and Cecil Rhodes as chief patron. The aim was military rebellion with the hope of bringing about British intervention. The leader of the plot was Jameson.

An anti-Boer rising in Johannesburg was to coincide with a dramatic "invasion" of the Transvaal by Jameson and 500 fellow adventurers, mainly ex-members of the Bechuanaland Border Police and the Rhodesia Horse. From start to finish, the affair was a fiasco. Lax security meant that the Boers were aware of what was coming, while the alarmed Rhodes tried to stop Jameson before it was too late. On the afternoon of 29th December 1895, however, Jameson and his men—deaf to all entreaties—set off from their base on the fringe of the Kalahari Desert, determined to celebrate the New Year in Johannesburg. Three days later, cut off and surrounded by Piet Cronje's commandos, they were forced to surrender and the 400 unwounded survivors unceremoniously carted off to Pretoria gaol.

The effect of the raid was catalytic. London had hastily repudiated the raiders, but Kruger's suspicions of British policy—in particular that of Joseph Chamberlain, the Colonial Secretary—were roused to fever-pitch. He was supported in this belief by a telegram from the German Kaiser:

"I express to you my sincere congratulations that, without calling on the aid of friendly powers, you ... have succeeded in defending the independence of your country from attacks from without. Wilhelm IR."

The phrase "friendly powers" was the key one, for the treaty agreed by the British and Boers after the First Boer War specifically prohibited the Transvaal from making any foreign alliances, other than with the Free State. As Kruger moved closer to Germany, British determination to uphold their shadowy rights of "suzerainty" were strengthened. It was clear that the next clash would lead to open war.

In South Africa itself, the two opposing communities closed ranks. On the one side, the two Boer republics enjoyed the support of a now dominant Afrikaner party at the Cape. On the other, the turbulent, cosmopolitan, but mainly British community of the Witwatersrand found common cause with an almost totally British Natal. Together with the highly affluent and influential British minority in the Cape,

An Illustrated London News *artist sketches Jameson in his cell in Pretoria after his capture by the Boers. Although the British government disclaimed all responsibility for Jameson's adventure, the Boers firmly believed that Rhodes and Chamberlain were both involved. (National Army Museum)*

they could count on the active sympathy of Alfred Milner, British High Commissioner in South Africa, and the patronage of Chamberlain in London.

For three and a half years tensions between Boers and British mounted and fissures deepened, while Jameson served time in Holloway jail for his leadership of the raid. He did not reappear on the South African scene until the last months of 1899 when, sick with typhoid, he found himself besieged in Ladysmith—a reluctant onlooker in a war he had helped to precipitate.

2 Confrontation

"England will have to send thrice her Army Corps before she overpowers us." (Commandant-General Piet Joubert)

Commandant-General Joubert and his staff a few days before the Transvaalers began their advance into Natal. Joubert was a national hero to his countrymen, but, soon, his seemingly hesitant conduct of operations was being criticized by some of his younger colleagues.

Despite the visible signs of the war to come, the concept of a siege of Ladysmith seems to have been as alien to British military thinking in South Africa as the idea of a siege of Aldershot. In Natal, no surveys had been conducted nor any maps made of areas south of the town. Colonel Grant, of the Directorate of Military Intelligence, who was responsible for map-making under Major-General Sir John Ardagh, said after the war that, following the Jameson Raid, he had been told to carry out a discreet survey of northern Natal. This he did within three months with the aid of two colonial officers. But their instructions, consistent with all other aspects of military planning for the forthcoming war, had been based on the premise that no Boer advance could possibly reach as far south as Ladysmith.

"Our present strength," wrote Milner quite cheerfully to Lord Selborne, Chamberlain's Under-Secretary, in August 1898, "is rather over 8,000 men. To be really secure we ought to have nearer 10,000."

And it was in Ladysmith that General Goodenough, then Commander-in-Chief, chose to position the main force of 4,500 men available for the defence of Natal. In an act of remarkable complacency, he persuaded Milner to tell the home government that he was completely satisfied with the strength of the British garrison in South Africa and of its ability to contain a Boer attack.

The British military establishment did not lack warning. In September 1898, Major E. A. Altham, a military intelligence officer, produced for the Commander-in-Chief, South Africa, a paper entitled "Frontier Defence in South Africa in a war against the Dutch Republics." In this he drew attention to the massive mobilization programme carried out by the Transvaal government since the Jameson Raid, culminating in the establishment of an impressive arsenal of assorted weaponry—mainly of German origin, but including substantial supplies from British firms in Birmingham. Unfortunately, Altham's superior, Sir John Ardagh, was an extraordinarily modest man for an officer of such high rank, and, despite his direct access to Lansdowne, the Secretary of State for War and a friend from former days, he lacked the persuasiveness and political muscle to impress the findings of his staff on the military establishment of the day. Lean, almost cadaverous, and certainly silent and self-effacing, Ardagh was much too diffident to command the attention of his more ebullient and bellicose colleagues. "The great military officers at the War Office," he wrote, "were as a rule Lieutenant-Generals or of higher rank, while I was a Major-General, and rank goes for a good deal in the confabulations of military people." What chance was there, therefore, for the conclusions of mere majors, however valid and well-documented?

On the political front, 1899 had been a year of polarization. On both sides, attitudes hardened. In London, Milner's impassioned plea for intervention found a receptive audience at all levels of society, and in Pretoria, Paul Kruger, heartened by a massive electoral victory a few months previously and the awareness of substantial military backing in continental Europe, became increasingly defiant.

Negotiations went on in an atmosphere of lessening hope. The Bloemfontein Conference took place in May between Milner, seen by the Boers as an imperial predator, and Kruger, whose "eternal duplicity" was the theme of a letter from Milner to Whitehall. In September, the British played for time. Kruger mustered the Transvaal commandos, while his less pugnacious Boer colleague, President Steyn of the Orange Free State, tried but failed to secure American mediation.

Finally, negotiations came to an end. "They have done it!" exclaimed an incredulous Chamberlain on Tuesday 10th October 1899, as he read the text of Kruger's ultimatum, demanding the withdrawal of all British troops from the Transvaal border and the removal of all reinforcements. Its immediate rejection released in Britain a mood of patriotic headiness, while in South Africa the news induced a more business-like approach, a feeling that the inevitability of strife and all its unknowns was no longer a matter for speculation. War, with the promise of death and destruction, was about to begin.

Kruger's deep-seated conviction that God was on the side of the Boers was a feeling not always so vividly apparent to the equally God-

President Steyn of the Orange Free State. Steyn tried to avoid war, and it was not until after the Transvaal's initial successes that he decided to intervene. (National Army Museum)

fearing Commandant-General Joubert. To him fell the unenviable task of leading a basically undisciplined citizen force, patriotic and totally committed, but unschooled in the notions of military command, submission to strategic plans which were not visibly and dramatically intelligible, or the need to submit personal viewpoints to the authority of an untried stranger.

"Their Council of War is extremely obliging, and the orders are more of the nature of courteous requests," wrote Dr. F. V. Engelenburg, correspondent for the *Volkstem*, who had this to say about the Boer attitude to bravery:

"In general, they have a horror of capitulation, which is their very last resort. Foolhardiness on the battlefield is forbidden; no Boer thinks of risking his life merely from a superfluity of courage. Such rashness in some cases is rewarded by the field-cornet not with a medal, but with an appropriate snub, for every man who falls means not only that a family is deprived of its breadwinner, but also that his commando is weakened and prospects of victory diminish. . . .

In general the critical faculty of the Boer is much greater than that of his opponents. In every Afrikaner slumbers the heart of a general."

No such ambition inflamed the heart of Britain's Tommy Atkins. "The worst paid labourers in England," was how Lord Wolseley described the British soldier when he took office as Commander-in-Chief in 1895. Ignorant, and, for the most part, feckless and lacking in imagination, the average British recruit of the day was not only semi-literate at best, but also not even a particularly robust physical specimen. One of the county regiments mobilized in 1899 could muster only 370 men fit for overseas service out of a total of 950. Before the outbreak of war, there had already been a reduction in the minimum acceptable height for recruits from the norm established in 1897 at five foot three and a half inches for infantrymen and five foot six for cavalry.

In addition, the British soldier was poorly trained. For the most part, military experience was limited to colonial "wars" against crudely-armed tribesmen in Africa, India and China. The last full-scale war fought against Europeans had been in the Crimea in the 1850s; besides this, even the first hapless campaign against the Boers in 1881 counted as little more than a skirmish. From this, too, the only lesson that seemed to have been learned was the need to abandon scarlet and blue in favour of khaki. Still the concept of the impregnable British square and the irresistible collective volley prevailed.

Such training as there was for actual combat was limited in most regiments to the annual manoeuvres. Those lasted for some three weeks in the year, during which time the soldier fired 200 rounds of ammunition—some at targets on a range, but mainly as part of "volley training".

But if professionalism and training were lacking in the British army of the day, the one quality nobody denied it was its bravery. This applied to officers and men alike. There was a spirit, almost a cult, of reckless courage among the regular officer corps, especially in the cavalry, which drove them to pursue military glory at almost any cost. Their code of personal conduct regarded the defiance of danger as wholly honourable and deliberate self-exposure to risk demanded no clear vision of military advantage.

As for the rank-and-file, their courage was of a different order. They seemed to possess a profound and often seemingly invincible fortitude, an almost infinite capacity for accepting suffering and discomfort without complaint. It was as if they were sustained by the notion of imperial grandeur and an unswerving commitment—in adversity, if not always in barracks—to the exercise of the military virtues they were taught to cultivate in the name of Queen and Country. Some of Kipling's poetry reflects this spirit.

The rains started on 4th October and by the time Kruger's

ultimatum expired on the 11th, Joubert's spirits were more than physically dampened. "The English do not have to beat our men," he wrote in a frantic signal to Pretoria, "the rain and the general misery will do it." Deneys Reitz, the son of a former President of the Free State serving with the Pretoria commando, felt much more confident:

"At dawn on the morning of the 12th the assembled commandos moved off. As far as the eye could see the plain was alive with horsemen, guns and cattle, all steadily going forward to the frontier. The scene was a stirring one and I shall never forget riding to war with that great host."

But, for Reitz, the glamour and elation of going off to war, with a sense of purpose that was visibly shared by his 12,000 companions, was dissipated by the dusk and rain and discomfort of the following night:

"We had neither tents nor overcoats, so we sat on ant-heaps, or lay in the mud, snatching what sleep we could. It was our first introduction to the real hardships of war, and our martial feelings were considerably damped by the time the downpour ceased at daybreak. When it was light, we moved out, shivering and hungry, for it was too wet to build fires."

The Natal frontier was crossed and, for the Boers, the war had started. Before daybreak on 12th October, General Joubert's army was well on its way—"an endless procession of silent misty figures, horsemen, artillery, and wagons, filing past in the dark cold night along the winding road that led to where the black shoulder of Majuba stood up against the greyer sky." The guns went first; two batteries of eight Krupp guns each and two heavy 6 inch Creusot guns, making up the much cherished armoury of the State Artillery, the only "regular" unit in Joubert's force. Then followed the riflemen—1,800 from the Pretoria commando, as well as units from Heidelberg, Middelburg, Krugersdorp, Standerton, Wakkerstroom and Ermelo.

But the mood of elation noted by Deneys Reitz among the advancing Boers was still not shared by their commander. "Joubert himself, nosing forward like an uncertain mastiff," wrote Rayne Kruger, "could hardly believe that the British should have thrown away the advantage of their mountain barrier, and be leaving his men to spread over northern Natal, helping themselves to cattle and the booty of farms deserted by fleeing colonists."

Profoundly religious and committed, for that reason, to the notion of Divine intervention even in the strictly terrestrial affairs of men, Joubert was surprisingly irresolute in the pursuit of a cause he so deeply believed in. "I would sooner cut my throat," he said at the last sitting of the Transvaal Volksraad before the war began, "than doubt God's personal support of our cause." Yet he, and his forces, moved exceedingly slowly. One week after the breakout from Sandspruit, his army had covered only eighty miles, advancing unopposed across familiar territory. "Though the mounted patrols of both sides were constantly in touch," wrote General White in his first official dispatch from Ladysmith, "up to the evening of the 19th October nothing of importance took place."

The next day, Friday 20th October, the war and the battle for Ladysmith really began—at Talana Hill.

3 Talana Hill

"You should never have let one single man of the entire army escape that day." (General De la Rey to General Botha on the subject of Talana)

The cruel irony of Talana Hill is that it was one of those battles which, even in military terms, should never have been fought at all. It was a courageous, costly and, in the end, only a temporizing exercise, carried out to dislodge an enemy from a dominant position he should never have been allowed to occupy. And for once there had been plenty of time for preparation. For a whole week, British commanders and troops alike had waited for Commandant-General Joubert's columns to show themselves in earnest—not that they had any particularly clear idea of exactly how many Boers were advancing on them or what their dispositions were. It seemed, furthermore, as though they scarcely cared.

In part, this was due to the low opinion in which the British commander at Dundee, Lieutenant-General Sir William Penn Symons, held his Boer adversary. He rebuffed White's suggestion of withdrawal on Ladysmith by pointing out the difficulties involved, while, in a letter to Colonel Ian Hamilton—dated 17th October 1899 and almost certainly the last letter he ever wrote—he said, "I am more than ever inclined to the belief that the Boers will not attack me here (Dundee) and that we hold the best strategic position to protect the colony and all south of Dundee."

Penn Symons' optimism found very little favour with Hamilton, who had acquired a healthy respect for Boer military prowess at Majuba Hill, nearly twenty years before. "A great deal of the old contempt for the Boer is still existing," he wrote in a letter home. "Symons is very boastful and bad in this way." And Colonel Rawlinson, also on the staff at Ladysmith, noted in his diary the remarkable complacency of Penn Symons and some of his officers. "They speak," he said, "of a British brigade being able to take on five times their number in Boers, which is silly rot."

British complacency at the start of the Ladysmith campaign was well matched by Boer uncertainty. Fearing all manner of guiles, Joubert divided his invasion column into three. The right wing, under General Kock and Commandant Ben Viljoen, consisting of the Johannesburg contingent as well as the Hollander and German corps, was dispatched round to the west to advance via Botha's Pass and attack Newcastle. The left wing, led by General Lucas Meyer, with 4,000 burghers, with Louis Botha and his A.D.C., made a sweep to the east of the Buffalo river and, having occupied Utrecht, crossed the river at De Jager's Drift and approached Dundee from the east. The central column, under the command of Joubert himself and General Erasmus, advanced on Newcastle from the north. It crossed the border at Laing's Nek, where, suspecting a British trap, Joubert sent Erasmus on a flanking movement around Mount Pogweni to the east. Erasmus crossed the Buffalo at Wool's Drift and entered Newcastle unopposed in pouring rain on 15th October. There he waited for twenty-four hours, enforcing with some difficulty Joubert's strict ban on looting, before the Commandant-General himself arrived.

A Council of War was then held at Newcastle and the next move, an

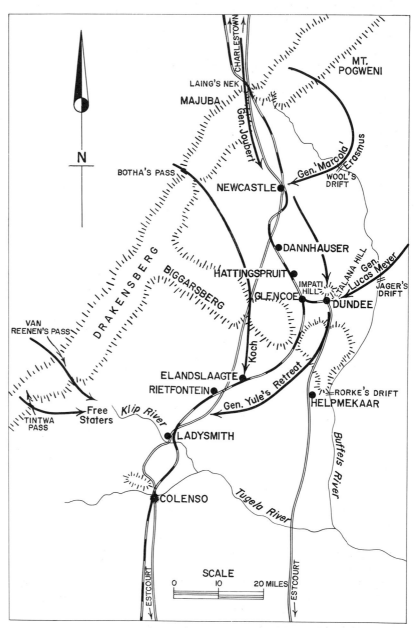

BOER APPROACH ROUTES TO LADYSMITH
October 1899

attack on Dundee, was decided. Responsibility for the attack was given to Lucas Meyer, with Erasmus in support. Joubert then lingered in Newcastle for two days and then set off for Dannhauser, which he reached on 19th October. By this time Erasmus was already in Hattingspruit, seven miles north-west of Dundee, and Lucas Meyer and Botha were pushing out patrols in the same general area.

The Boer strategic plan was simple and obvious—to cut Penn Symons off from White and so isolate his force. But still the British commander did nothing very much, apart from ordering his cavalry to reconnoitre the surrounding country to test the apparent intentions of the enemy. Above all, he did not think it necessary to occupy Talana Hill, and so deny the use of this commanding position, two miles to the east of Dundee, to the Boer artillery. It was up this hill that Lucas Meyer dragged his two French Creusot 75 mm field guns and a pom-pom during the night of 19th October.

According to General White's official dispatch of 2nd November, the first real action of the war began at 3.20 am on 20th October 1899. In the event, it was an accidental encounter between a mounted infantry picquet of Royal Dublin Fusiliers and a patrol of Lucas Meyer's scouts, who opened fire on the dozen or so Irishmen in the pass between Talana and Lennox Hill, less than two miles to the east of Dundee. The night was black and the sky obscured by the gloom of the heavily laden rain clouds of the previous day, so the picquets managed to extricate themselves on foot, their horses having been stampeded by the gunfire. A sergeant brought back the news, while the remainder took up defensive positions in the partly dried-up river bed of Sand-spruit, between Talana and Dundee. On receipt of the news, two companies of Dublin Fusiliers were sent out in support, but no further action seems to have been taken until daybreak.

Then, the swirling mist that had been obscuring the tops of the hills to the north and east of the British camp cleared. Lieutenant R. G. Stirling, of the 1st King's Royal Rifles, was on the spot:

"We paraded as usual in the morning, 4.30. We had dismissed the men, and went back for a cup of tea, when one of our fellows said: 'There they are!' Of course, we all laughed, went and got out glasses and saw them all on two hills, two or three miles away. We were so amazed we must have stood for nearly quarter of an hour, when suddenly a shell brought us to our senses."

It was at 5.30 am that the first shells from the Boer 75 mm guns on Talana plunged into the saturated earth not far from the by now astonished, but in no sense daunted, General Penn Symons. Had it not been for the malfunctioning of the Boer percussion shells, which failed to explode on the soft, rain-sodden ground, he would probably have perished at once, instead of later.

Reaction to the shellfire and the sudden spectacle of the Boers moving on the hilltops between gaps in the dispersing morning mist was swift. The British artillery opened fire at once, but, finding the range too great, Penn Symons ordered the 13th and 69th Field Batteries forward—first at 6 am and later at 8 am—when they were able to engage the Talana positions from a range of 2,300 yards. In the meantime, having deployed the 67th Field Battery and the 1st

Battalion of the Leicestershire Regiment to protect his camp, Penn Symons ordered the main part of his infantry to prepare to take up position for a frontal assault. Colonel Möller, commanding the cavalry, was directed to exercise his discretion and select the right time to deploy his squadrons to cut off the enemy, who, it was confidently expected, would soon be on the run to the north of Talana.

One major obstacle immediately stood in the way of Penn Symons' plan. He seemed to have overlooked completely the presence of General Erasmus, with 1,500 men, on Impati Hill, to the north of Dundee. If Erasmus moved to the attack, the entire British flank would

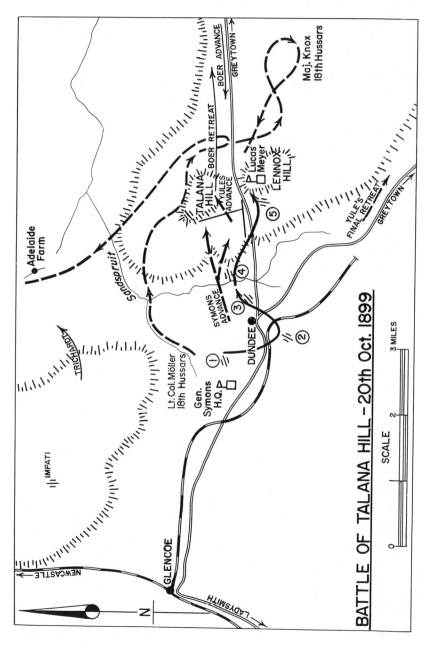

BATTLE OF TALANA HILL – 20th Oct. 1899

be open. But, fortunately for the British commander, there had been some squabbling and misunderstandings among the Boer leaders. Deneys Reitz of the Pretoria commando, which was part of Erasmus' force, recorded his feelings on Impati at daybreak that morning:

"*. . . When it grew light the rain ceased, but a mist enshrouded the mountain top through which everything looked so ghostly and uncertain that we felt more at a loss than ever, and when Maroola (the Boer nickname for Erasmus) was asked for orders he merely stood glowering into the fog without reply. We could not see fifty yards in any direction, but we knew that the English lines were immediately below us, for we could hear muffled shouts and the rumble of wagons, and we expected to be led down the mountain to attack. But General Maroola and his brother made no sign, and when President Kruger's son Caspar, who was serving with us as a private, and who for once in his life showed a little spirit, went up and implored them to march us to the enemy, Maroola curtly ordered him off.*"

Even after the battle was joined, the Boers on Impati played no part. Deprived of a view by the mist and spared the shellfire of the British, still unaware of their presence, they listened and waited. "We fretted at the thought of standing by passively when others were striking the first blows of the war," wrote Reitz.

The British plan of assault was simple enough. The remaining companies of the Royal Dublin Fusiliers were moved forward to join their comrades who had been lurking in the cold, damp bed of Sandspruit since four o'clock that morning. They were followed by the 1st Battalion, King's Royal Rifles (the "60th") and the 1st Battalion, Royal Irish Fusiliers. Eventually, the infantry reached the donga at Sandspruit, and then, following a pause for regrouping after the dash across the open ground to the river bed, they moved to the attack at 8.50 am. A short stretch of gently rising ground yielded to a strip of woodland, followed by steeper rising ground, some stone walls—one parallel to the line of attack and, further up, one at right angles to their front—and finally, the top of Talana.

In a letter to *The Times* of 8th December 1899, Stirling described his feelings as the battle began:

"*When we got the order to advance my heart was rather in my mouth, as I knew then we were under fire, and in a minute or two I might be a corpse. However, I had to get up and give my men a lead. They all behaved splendidly. Bullets came whizzing past unpleasantly. I was dying to run to get to the wood . . . In the wood there were plenty of ditches and at the end of the wood was a wall. We lay there to get breath. Poor Hambro was shot through the jaw, but would take no notice. Then came the bad part. There was a bramble hedge on the top of the wall so one could not get over, but there was a gateway, and through this we all had to go and it was a hot time. When we got under the wall, some heavy firing took place lasting two hours. Then we crossed the road to take the hill; that was the worst place. When I got halfway up the hill I found myself next to Hambro, who had been wounded twice. We lay down under the rocks as the firing had been very heavy.*"

By this time, Penn Symons himself had met with disaster.

A peaceful picnic for General Lucas Meyer, his wife and friends on the battlefield of Talana Hill. It was here that Penn Symons, the British commander, was mortally wounded. (National Army Museum)

Impatient with lack of progress in the battle of the walls, he rode into the wood to ascertain for himself the cause of the delay. Having encouraged first the Irish Fusiliers and then groups of the Dublins, he dismounted to reach the position held by the 60th. Scarcely had he urged them on with the cry of "Forward the Rifles, the gallant 60th, and take that hill!" when he was hit in the stomach and mortally wounded. In full view of the men and conscious of the gravity of his wounds, he struggled back to his horse where, anxious to conceal his true condition for fear of discouraging his troops, he allowed himself to be escorted to the rear, having instructed Colonel (later Brigadier-General) James Yule to take over command of the battle.

By midday, the British infantry's courage and heroism had carried them to the summit, the last ferocious half hour of the battle embittered by the shattering experience of death at the hands of their own artillery. The official dispatch makes no mention of this, but it seems likely that the confusion caused by the fall of Penn Symons resulted in the issue of imprecise and incomplete instructions to the gunners. The consequence of this was that, unnerved by the knowledge of having fired on their own men, the artillery hesitated to open fire on the retreating Boers once they had dragged their guns on to Talana itself.

If 20th October 1899 was not the gunners' day, it was not the cavalry's either. Möller's attempt to cut off the retreating Boers ended in disaster. White's official dispatch records simply that Lieutenant-Colonel Möller and two squadrons "appear, so far as can be ascertained, to have pursued in a northerly direction, to have come in contact with superior enemy forces (those of General Erasmus) not previously engaged and to have been surrounded and forced to surrender while endeavouring to return to camp around the north of Impati Mountain."

Viewing this manoeuvre from the upper eastern slopes of Impati, Deneys Reitz described how 300 British horsemen were seen at midday in the sunlit spaces between the banks of mist in the valley below, seemingly unaware of the presence of 1,500 mounted Boers between them and their base. Finally, harried on all sides throughout the afternoon, Möller's force took up a defensive position in Adelaide Farm, only to have their horses stampeded by the shellfire from a Creusot gun of the Transvaal State Artillery. There was no course open but to surrender.

This provided the rabidly anti-British "Colonel" Blake, an American who commanded the Irish brigade in the Boer forces, with an excellent opportunity to indulge in some divisive propaganda, based on the theme of friction between Irish and non-Irish troops in the British army. "Of the Irishmen captured," he wrote, "eighty-five begged to join the Irish Brigade and fight with the Boers. I wanted to take them on the spot, but the Boer officers did not consider it right, because, they said, if any of them were afterwards captured, the English would surely shoot them." The supposition that any volunteers would have been shot is accurate enough, though Blake's allegation is probably totally slanderous. Certainly, Deneys Reitz, who was on the spot, saw no sign of Irish disaffection:

"*. . . By the time I got there the soldiers had thrown down their arms and* *were falling in under their officers. Their leader, Colonel Möller, stood on the stoep looking pretty crestfallen, but the private soldiers seemed to take the events more cheerfully. I was elated at having taken part in our first success . . . and enjoyed the novelty of looking at the captured men and talking to such of them as were willing."*

By their performance at Talana Hill, the first set-piece battle of the Boer War and of the drive on Ladysmith, neither side did much to command the attention of posterity. For the British, the memory of General Penn Symons, who died in captivity three days after the battle, will survive for his example of immense personal courage, which inspired his men to gallantry and successfully storm a hill they should have walked up unopposed three days earlier—if their general had only thought of it beforehand.

For the Boers, scant respect can be accorded to General "Maroola" Erasmus and Lucas Meyer's performance was also undistinguished. It was the smaller part—some 400 to 500 men—of his own force which actually defended Talana and fought off Penn Symons' brigade with such great ferocity, while he himself looked on with far greater numbers from nearby Lennox Hill. Nor does Commandant-General Joubert emerge with much credit. As the pro-Boer Irish American Michael Davitt wrote:

"It was the first great opportunity which the war had offered to Joubert for the exercise of his generalship in the field, and he was found woefully wanting in the qualities which the occasion demanded. The result of the fight on Friday, which ended at two in the afternoon, must have been known to the Commandant-General that night. The discovery of Impati Hill by Erasmus, and the consequent break-up of the British camp at Dundee on Saturday, could not be concealed from him, even if it were attempted, for he was immediately in the rear of Erasmus' column. He was in touch with Lucas Meyer's men, east of his own position with no enemy in between and yet not a single move was ordered by him, whether to direct a continued and crushing attack on Yule, or to prevent this all but encircled officer from escaping by the Helpmekaar Road to Ladysmith—the only way left for him to retreat by."

Talana was at best a Pyrrhic victory for the British. Their immediate objective was achieved, but at vastly disproportionate cost. The Boers, for their part, must have drawn some comfort from the casualty figures (150 Boers to 500 British) and from the aftermath—the British on the run under General Yule and the well-stocked town of Dundee to plunder.

Perhaps the unsung hero of Talana was Brigadier-General James Yule who, from a position of almost total disadvantage, managed to extricate the exhausted British force in a gruelling three-day march to Ladysmith.

4 Elandslaagte

**"Cavalry scouting,
Artillery duel,
Infantry advance,
Infantry assault,
Cavalry charge and pursuit,
Lost myself and spent day on the veldt,
Probably the prettiest day's fighting
I shall ever see."
(Extract from the diary of Lieutenant
J. Norwood, V.C., 5th Dragoon
Guards, 25th October 1899)**

While General Lucas Meyer's commandos were locked in battle with Penn Symons' brigade at Talana Hill and "Maroola" Erasmus watched from Impati, venerable old General Kock's men—the right-hand column of Joubert's invasion force—were having a much better time out in the spectacular countryside of the Biggarsberg range. Although his rate of progress, approximately 80 miles in seven days from Sandspruit, was hardly "sweeping"—one historian's word for it—Kock's forward patrols under Veldt-Kornets Picnaar and Pot-gieter managed to reach the railway line at Elandslaagte in time to harass a British supply train steaming northwards with stores.

The station master at Elandslaagte described what happened next in remarkably evocative terms:

" 'Pick up the mails and go for all you're worth,' I said to the driver. There was hardly time, however. Loud cries, rattling hoofs, crackling reports from Mauser rifles, and the pattering of bullets all round—the Boers were upon us. Driver Cutbush did not wait. He put on full steam, and amid a shower of bullets the train went ahead. At the moment the van passed me several Boers rode on to the platform and fired over our heads at the train. Others galloped at breakneck speed firing after the train. Two shots from the train killed a horse and wounded his rider, but the train got off with no other injury than broken glass."

A second train was successfully intercepted soon afterwards—the last northbound train from Ladysmith until after the relief. The station master had been severely reprimanded for failing to stop the first train, but the sight of the second's supplies and stores, including a truckful of whisky, must have mellowed his captors, who later apologized for having abused him.

The final British charge at Elandslaagte, "shoving through hell to the throat of the enemy". (National Army Museum)

DR. ILSBURGER   COL. SCHIEL   GEN.

General Kock and his staff before the battle of Elandslaagte. After leading a final counter-attack, Kock was mortally wounded in the last British charge.

Reinforcements soon reached the scene. The first to arrive was Lieutenant-Colonel Shiel, in charge of 300 German volunteers from Johannesburg, and General Kock himself arrived at ten o'clock that night. He at once occupied the station master's commandeered house, which had been set up during the afternoon and evening as a Boer headquarters, but not before the station master had been given a receipt for his rifle. Commandant Ben Viljoen joined his general early the next morning.

The whole of that day was spent unloading the captured train, setting up defences in a somewhat desultory manner and, having mined the railway station, in preparing the Elandslaagte Hotel for a smoking concert that evening, with Veldt-Kornet Pienaar as master of ceremonies. To this evidently convivial occasion—despite unconfirmed reports about the whisky having been destroyed on Kock's instructions—the British prisoners from the train, together with the local railway staff, were also invited, and so were able to share at least some of the captured stores. The station master's account of the proceedings makes it clear that a good time was had by all:

"The concert was opened by a comic song, rendered by a refugee from Newcastle, whose musical abilities proved of great service. He and I then rendered the old duet 'All's Well' and on being encored responded with the 'Army and Navy' duet. A Transvaal burgher sang an Irish song as only an Irishman can. He told us afterwards that this was his eighth campaign, but he did not know then that it was his last. Next day he was dead . . .

A Boer sergeant then played a series of national anthems, including both 'God save the Queen' and the Transvaal Volkslied. They were all played with great taste, and I certainly never expect to hear our National Anthem played or sung again under such apparently impossible conditions."

While Kock's men were carousing with their captives in the Elandslaagte Hotel, seventeen miles away in Ladysmith General White and his staff were in a far less festive mood, busily planning an attack for the following morning. Major-General French's reconnaissance of the Boer positions at Elandslaagte during 20th October, combined with his knowledge of Yule's position following Talana, made it only too clear to White that the escape route for the Dundee force was in danger of being cut. The Boers would have to be dislodged.

For the second morning in succession, French, in command of the cavalry at Ladysmith, had to get up early—this time at 4 am on 21st October. His orders were to proceed with five squadrons of Imperial Light Horse and the Natal Field Battery to the Elandslaagte area, clear the railway of the enemy and thus secure both rail and telegraphic communications between Dundee and Ladysmith. The task was clear enough, and judging from the writings of the Elandslaagte station master, French certainly achieved the element of surprise:

"Next morning about 9.30, bang, shriek, crash and a shell burst in the goods shed not fifty yards from where we were. Consternation is a mild term to apply to the feeling which prevailed. When I got into the open air, and found the British artillery pounding away in our direction, such a scene of confusion met the eye as is seldom witnessed."

In fact, the confusion was not as acute as all that and the Boer recovery was evidently swift enough. As General White put it in his official dispatch: "The enemy at once replied with artillery, and thus disclosed his main position on a commanding group of hills about a mile south-east of the railway station." Here, the configuration of the land was roughly that of a huge horseshoe, with the leading edge facing south-east and the two arms running south-east to north-west, about three miles apart at the open end. The more easterly of the two features was where Kock positioned his forces.

By midday, French assessed his opposition to be in the order of 1,000 men, an unusually conservative estimate for a British general facing such elusive adversaries as the Boer commandos. Conscious of White's desire to inflict a real trouncing on the Boers, French had no hesitation in asking, somewhat extravagantly, for three infantry battalions, two batteries of artillery and extra cavalry. What he got was even more generous—seven companies of the 1st Battalion, Devonshire Regiment, under Major Park; five companies of the 2nd Battalion, Gordon Highlanders, under Colonel Dick-Cunyngham; and the 1st Battalion, Manchester Regiment. In addition, White dispatched the 21st and 42nd Batteries of Field Artillery, a squadron of 5th Lancers and one of the 5th Dragoon Guards, making a total force—including the original contingent—of about 3,500 men under French's command.

By 3 pm on Saturday 21st October, the reinforcements had arrived and de-trained some four miles from the Boer position. In command of the infantry was Colonel (later General) Sir Ian Hamilton, who, like many a younger Boer War officer, was to have a distinguished World

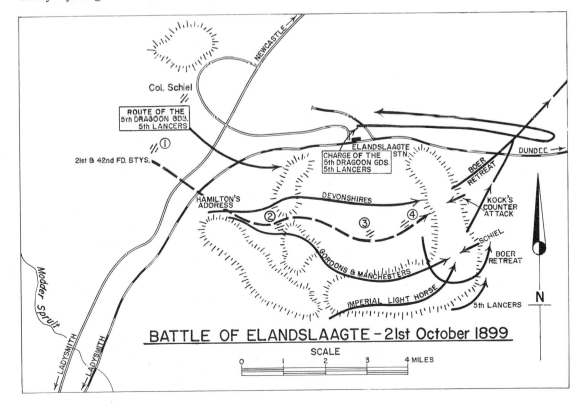

BATTLE OF ELANDSLAAGTE – 21st October 1899

War One military career. He was brave, good-looking, popular and immensely well connected, with considerable gifts both as a writer and as a romantic. The latter trait was vividly expressed in his *Introduction to War Songs*—"the clash of sword and hollow reverberating clang of brazen buckler, the storm and wild joy of battle ..."—but his own memories of battle were not all joyous. At Elandslaagte, his command included his own Gordon Highlanders, whose humiliating defeat he had shared in at Majuba nearly twenty years before, and which he was now determined to avenge.

The British battle plan was simple enough. The Devons, widely extended, were to demonstrate against the northern end of the Boer position, while the Manchester Regiment attacked the southern end and the Gordon Highlanders moved to their right and turned the Boer left flank. At this point, the Devons would move into the attack. The 5th Dragoon Guards protected the British left flank and the Imperial Light Horse, supported by a squadron of the 5th Lancers, secured the right.

Shortly before four o'clock that afternoon, as the rain clouds gathered in the sky, General White himself rode out from Ladysmith to confer with his subordinates and check their dispositions. Having done so, he turned over command entirely to French. Melton Prior, a war correspondent on the scene, reported on the exchange between the two men:

"Then soon the troops began to arrive, the infantry regiments by train ... and Sir George White then met General French. During their consultation as to the position of affairs, I heard General French say, 'I hand over command of this to you, sir', but General Sir George White, with his usual charming manner, replied 'Oh no! You commenced the show, you carry on.'"

Hamilton then made his famous speech of exhortation, apprising the men of the battle plan and assuring them of a victory which the newsvendors would acclaim in the streets of London the following morning. A measure of the effect of Hamilton's oratory was the lusty euphoria he provoked among his troops who, breaking ranks, shouted and cheered, waving their helmets in the air, "We'll do it, sir, we'll do it!"

As the British bombardment and the Boer counter-fire reached a peak, the order to advance was given and the Devons, under Major Park, moved forward. But they did so in an open formation quite unlike that normally used by the British army of the day—a tactic which undoubtedly saved many lives. They advanced across the open grass plain, keeping a yard apart from each other, until they reached a position only 900 yards from the Boer defences. There they were halted, and, on the right, the Manchesters moved to the attack. What happened then was vividly described by Captain Paley, who gave an account of the final assault in a letter published in the London *Times* on 9th December:

"... As we crossed the skyline we were met by a perfect hail of bullets and the Gordons began to reinforce us.
The men had all thoroughly got their blood up by this time, and they

went at the last hill in splendid style. It was very steep and broken and covered with rocks and stones. As we went up it we saw the Boers gradually begin to leave their sangars and retire. Then our drums sounded the 'Charge', it was taken up by the Gordons' pipers, and we dashed in with a tremendous cheer. I jumped a sangar wall, and I believe that I was the first man into their main position (this is probably claimed by at least a dozen others). Very few of them waited for the bayonet."

G. W. Steevens of the London *Daily Mail* also recorded the last stages of the battle, his account being widely acclaimed at the time as a model of war-reporting:

"The merry bugles rang out like cock-crows on a fine morning. The pipes (of the Gordon Highlanders) shrieked of blood and the lust of glorious death. Fix bayonets. Staff officers rushed shouting from the rear, imploring, cajoling, cursing, slamming every man who could move into the line. Line—but it was a line no longer. It was a surging wave of men—Devons and Gordons, Manchesters and Light Horse (by now dismounted) all mixed inextricably; subalterns commanding regiments, soldiers yelling

advice, officers firing carbines, stumbling, leaping, killing, falling, all drunk with battle, shoving through hell to the throat of the enemy."

Paley's account, however, underestimates the fierceness of Boer resistance. At the climax of the battle, General Kock himself led a counter-attack, and it was only the presence of Hamilton—and French, too—in the firing line that staved off a British retreat. A last desperate charge—the one described by Steevens—overwhelmed the surviving defenders. Among them was General Kock, who fell dying on the field.

It was about 4.45 pm—still pouring with rain and the cloud base no higher than 500 feet—when Hamilton observed a white flag fluttering on the Boer side and ordered "Cease Fire". In the moment of hesitation resulting from an almost certainly unauthorized surrender signal and only partially recognized by the British foe, lives were lost and feelings embittered.

The battle was over for the men of the Devons, under Major Park, for the Gordons, whose commander, Colonel Dick-Cunyngham, had fallen wounded—among many—with oaths and exhortatory invective

A group of Irish-American volunteers fighting for the Boers. Their commander, "Colonel" Blake, is standing seventh from the left. On his left, in the bow tie, is B. Webster Davis, a pro-Boer U.S. official.

Boer prisoners captured at Elandslaagte on their way to the station, and a train to captivity. Behind follow wounded in Red Cross waggons.

on his lips, for the Manchesters and for the Imperial Light Horse, whose leader, Colonel Chisholm, lay dead upon the crest. Now it was the turn of the cavalry.

"The cavalry squadrons on our left, who had been closely watching the course of events, now charged through and through the enemy, inflicting much loss and capturing many prisoners," is all that General White's official dispatch had to say on the part played in the battle by Major St. J. C. Gore and his two squadrons of cavalry who, up to this moment, had stood concealed to the east of Elandslaagte station—waiting. In the USA and, more strangely, in Britain itself, certain sections of the press embarked on a sustained, if not actually co-ordinated, campaign of vilification, drawing upon stories of excessive brutality by the cavalry at Elandslaagte to support their case. There were countless extracts from letters from participants in the battle, often Irish Americans fighting for the Boers and sometimes from Lancers themselves. In this way, for many, Elandslaagte came to be remembered as the occasion when the British 5th Dragoon Guards and the 5th Lancers behaved with the utmost savagery in slaughtering small parties of helpless and terrified Boers.

The *Cincinnati Enquirer* published a letter sent to Mrs. Adelaide Weller by her nephew, an 18-year-old American on the Boer side, who described with some extravagance how his party of about 1,000 men were pursued by Lancers who outnumbered them six to one. In fact, Major Gore's two squadrons totalled under 200 men, but they doubtless seemed like thousands to the young American crouching in a foxhole. J. G. Dunn, an Irish American from Lowell, Massachusetts, serving with the Irish Brigade under Joubert's command, also had a letter published on 29th November 1899. In this, he wrote:

"The Lancers acted as if fighting Indians, and gave no quarter, stabbing and murdering prisoners and wounded in a horrible fashion, just like a lot of Sioux. It is said that officers are responsible for this dastardly work, but it makes little difference to us. That lot of gentry are down in our black book, and if the opportunity presents itself—and I know it will, since there are some of them in Ladysmith—we will wipe that regiment off the rolls."

In fairness to the cavalrymen, it has to be recognized that, in warfare, their role can never be a genteel one, and the notion of men on foot being overrun by galloping chargers bearing soldiers astride them with sabre and lance at the ready is particularly horrifying. Each generation has different norms in the standard of callousness and violence it finds acceptable. When General French said to Gore the day after the battle, "You have had the honour of commanding the first real cavalry charge since the Crimea," he could not have known that it was also one of the last ever by the British army in a set-piece battle.

The testimony of Gore himself should not be left out of account, particularly since he spent such leisure time as he had during the Ladysmith siege documenting the battle for the regimental records. For this purpose, he assembled contributions from about half a dozen officers and NCOs and there is no evidence of collusion between them. His own formal report to the Brigade Major of Cavalry at Ladysmith, dated 23rd October, offers a vivid account of that horrendous occasion, presented in remarkably restrained language.

"At 5.20 pm the enemy were seen coming out of their position into the open plain, and taking a line of retreat in the direction of Glencoe. I then gave the order to advance. My two squadrons were formed in line at extended files, and charged right across the line of retreat which the enemy were taking. The latter were going away quietly at a trot, till our men's heads appeared over the crest of the hill; they then changed their direction and galloped straight away in front of us and in all directions. Their ponies, however, were no match for our horses, and we rapidly overhauled them. Those men who still tried to escape were attacked with the lance or pistol and those who jumped off their horses and threw down their arms were made prisoners of. Unfortunately, it was now quite dusk, and it was extremely difficult to see where the enemy were. The first charge was from a mile and a half to two miles in length. The two squadrons were then halted, faced about and reformed. They then charged back again over almost the same ground, and encountered a good many more of the flying enemy."

Whatever the brutality of the Saturday evening and the allegations of subsequent robbing of the dead—and perhaps even the wounded—mercy was also present. Sergeant Savage of the 5th Dragoon Guards records his hand-over of prisoners to Major Gore at Elandslaagte station and Captain Reynolds' appeal for volunteers to go out in the rain to look for the wounded. "Several were ready at once," he said, "though the tea was still being made." He went on to describe his experiences:

"The lamps of the search parties—Boer and Briton—flickered out in many places, and the calls to attract the attention of the wounded could be heard in every direction. We had a whistle, and blew it occasionally, then listened; we were some time before we found anyone, and then near a wire fence we came across a few who had fallen quite close together. All the wounded had been attended to (presumably by the medical orderlies of both sides) so that we could do no more than give them a drink, and if possible cover them over . . . We did all we could which was, I'm afraid, very little, and made our way back to the bivouac where a concoction, consisting as near as I can say, of five parts water, three condensed milk, one of tea, and the other one something strongly suspected of being brandy, was served out. As we came in, Captain Reynolds asked me to get him some tea, and I managed a mess-tin full of this mixture—I think he liked it."

The requirements of the British army had not changed much by the time of El Alamein nearly half a century later.

The tragedy of Elandslaagte lay in its dramatic presentation of what J. B. Atkins described as "the two faces of war so close together. One face is a mask which has been thrust upon it and this face is all laughter"—the flippant, buoyant bonhomie of Major Gore who, on arrival at General French's forming-up point, was delighted to see "old 'Jabber' Chisholm at the meet," and the laughter of the Anglo-Boer revellers carousing on captured whisky on the Friday night. The other is "the natural face of war, and it is all tears. The two are not seen as alternatives, but always side by side"—the tears and anguish of the bereaved and the suffering of the wounded, 200 or so on either side lying in the rain scarcely a mile away from the Elandslaagte Hotel the night after Veldt-Kornet Pienaar's party.

5 Yule's Retreat

"I cannot reinforce you without sacrificing Ladysmith and the colony behind. You must try and fall back on Ladysmith. I will do what I may to help you when nearer." (General White's message to Brigadier-General Yule at Dundee, 22nd October 1899)

On Saturday 21st October—the day of Elandslaagte—the situation in Natal looked much less promising to those on the spot than it did to the British press in London. Lucas Meyer's Boer commandos had indeed been driven from the summit of Talana Hill and had last been seen heading northwards at high speed. By Saturday night, the news of the Boer withdrawal from Elandslaagte, followed by their rout at the hands of the cavalry, was well known in Ladysmith and buzzing over the wires to London. But the value of these successes was more symbolic than strategic.

In Dundee, it poured with rain through the night of the 20th/21st October. Nothing could have been less conducive to a sense of triumph among the troops, who were physically tired, not a little bewildered by the unexpected quality of Boer opposition and who mourned their commander as well as their fallen comrades. Penn Symons was not yet dead, but the severity of his wounds was by now known to all ranks. The hours-old memory of a hill taken at bayonet point and then abandoned seemed cold comfort.

The army slept in peace that night but, by dawn, the Boers had returned. Some drifted back singly or in small, unorganized groups, others in a more orderly fashion in units, but all were probing forwards in the right direction—southwards again to the hills around Dundee. By mid-afternoon, they had opened up on the British camp with their heavy artillery. For two hours the giant Creusot bombarded the Dundee camp from Impati Hill where, twenty-four hours previously, "Maroola" Erasmus had stood brooding and impassive while the British stormed Talana.

Yule now pondered his next move. Hearing on the Sunday morning, perhaps in somewhat crude and simplified terms, of the British success at Elandslaagte, it may well have crossed his mind that a link-up with French and Hamilton was a distinct military possibility. Accordingly, he set off once more in the direction of Glencoe Junction after breakfast that morning, but he soon came under fire from the Boer artillery on Impati. Although the descending mist enabled him to extricate his force with very few casualties, it now became clear that there was little prospect of intercepting at Glencoe the Boer fugitives, who, he calculated, would be coming northwards up the railway from Elandslaagte. The question now resolved itself into two possible alternatives—holding Dundee itself or of adopting the unwelcome course of withdrawing to Ladysmith. After an agonizing hour or so of debate, Yule decided on the latter, and scarcely had he done so when a message from White arrived ordering immediate retreat.

The three immediate problems for Yule and his staff to resolve were route, provisions and timing.

The Boer dispositions ruled out the main north-south road and rail routes to Ladysmith. This left only the Dundee–Helpmakaar road as far as Beith. There, the column would turn south and make its way through Van Tonders Pass. After this, three rivers—the Waschbank, Sundays and Modder Spruit, each in an unknown state of flood—would have to be crossed at approximately twelve-mile intervals before Yule's force sighted Ladysmith.

It was estimated that the march would take at least three days. This was clearly unthinkable without adequate provisions—food, ammunition and clothing. These lay two miles away in the now deserted main camp of 19th October, within easy range of the Boer artillery dominating the position.

Yule's first priority was obviously to recover at least some of these stores. The task was entrusted to Major Wickham of the Indian Commissariat, who successfully—and, in the circumstances, rather surprisingly—carried out an undetected raid that Sunday night. Protected by two companies of Leicesters, 33 wagons were taken back to the original camp and loaded with as much material as pitch darkness, the general scramble among collapsed tentage and the limited time available would permit. By 9 pm Wickham's column was ready at the agreed rendezvous on the southern outskirts of the town and the main force formed up. It was a measure of Yule's powers of command and control, as well as those of Colonel Dartnell, leading the Natal Police detachment, that 4,500 men from four infantry regiments, three field batteries and the cavalry could be organized in the dark and on their way within half an hour.

Now was the time Yule put into operation the first of a few simple deception tactics. Private Allen, one of the Leicesters escorting Major Wickham's party, wrote in a letter to some friends in Spalding, Lincolnshire:

". . . General Yule sent some men down to the camp to light candles in the tents to make believe that they had retired into camp, and while this was going on we were on the move. The Boers woke up the next morning, and shelled the camp and town, only to find the troops had gone ; so they gave chase, but went the wrong way."

It also seems from the testimony of Mr. H. H. Paris, the postmaster at Dundee, that he personally was the unwitting instrument of another rather more subtle ploy by Yule, again designed to ensure that the Boers were looking the wrong way at the appropriate time. He described how Yule sent for him at the last of his three camps—Rowan's Farmhouse, about four miles to the south-east of Dundee. It is not entirely clear precisely when this meeting took place, but it was almost certainly either on the Saturday evening or very early the following morning:

"Major-General Yule sent for me and asked me to go to the office with a message stating that the Boers had surrounded us. He required reinforcements from Ladysmith, and expected that they were near at hand; in fact, he was going to Glencoe Junction to meet them.

I rode in under the whizzing 40 pounder shells. I ascertained that no reliefs were being sent, which surprised General Yule very much. At 7 pm (on Sunday 22nd October) the General asked me to go in with another telegram, adding that he wished us to destroy all military messages that had been sent.

As we could not get horses we walked into the town, and we did as requested. At 11.30 pm a friend, who is guide to the military, rode up very excitedly, saying that he had come to inform me that the troops had gone, and that their last wagon was then moving down the street. The General had forgotten all about us!

Needless to say, we soon had our lights out and after cramming the registered letters into the safe, and carrying away what office cash and stamps we could, amounting to £200, we soon caught up with the last wagon, and walked through the night, toiling through slush, mud and rain, over a very bad, hilly road. We caught up the camp a mile and a half past Beith where the artillery had drawn up into position to cover us."

The programme was completed when a signals officer on Yule's staff cut the telegraph wire to Greytown.

Seven hours later, in the small hours of Monday morning, the leading files of the column had covered fourteen miles since leaving their starting point, and there was still no sign of Boer pursuit. This, however, was not entirely due to Yule's modest programme of deception and misinformation. The Boer leadership itself was to blame—a fact soon pointed out by Commandant-General Joubert in a series of angry telegrams:

"From Commandant-General, Dannhauser
To Assistant-General Meyer, Vryheid, begins
10 am. I have telegraphed and written to you so often that I really think it is useless to persevere. I hear of your readiness, I hear of your coming, but I see nothing. You are no longer needed for an attack on Dundee but for a combined attack on the enemy. What hinders you? In heaven's name let at least Schalk Burger come up . . . The troops have fled from Dundee, it is true, but only to gather strength for a counter attack. Come then without any delay at all. Your immediate answer please. Punish all laggards according to martial law. Ends."

At 7.30 the same evening:

"I saw today the telegram sent by you to the government wherein you state that you have been all set to attack Dundee as from noon yesterday; but since Trichardt and Erasmus's men have already occupied Dundee and been in it since yesterday morning, there are no longer troops there to attack. No one quite knows where they are now, but it is reported today that they have fled past Helpmakaar . . . We must get moving or great harm will ensue. So hurry forward all of you. Ends."

No Boer commander ever explained why nothing serious was done to harass General Yule's forces. Even given their late awareness of the retreat, Erasmus and Meyer were only twenty miles behind the British at this point, and, between them, certainly capable of mustering sufficient strength to at least impede, if not halt, Yule's forces. Perhaps the degree of tenacity and sense of military purpose displayed by the British at Talana had, for the time being, dissuaded the Boers from further military encounters.

As far as Erasmus was concerned, an equally powerful deterrent to close pursuit was the problem he had in maintaining even the most basic semblance of discipline and order among his commandos after they had discovered the booty that lay in Dundee and the deserted British camp. According to Deneys Reitz, Erasmus' task was hopeless. "The men went whooping through the town and behaving in a very undisciplined manner. Officers tried to stem the rush, but we were not to be denied, and we plundered shops and dwelling houses . . ."

While this orgy was in full spate, Yule and his column rested during the afternoon of Monday 23rd October, having reached the approach to Van Tonders pass, twenty miles from Dundee, at noon that day. They marched through the six-mile pass that night and, the following morning, arrived at the Waschbank river. Intent on spending the daylight hours at rest—his force having been fighting or marching for five days and nights—Yule prepared to camp until dusk, but suddenly, he heard the sound of artillery at Rietfontein, fifteen miles to the west of his present position.

The object of White's demonstration, which Yule could hear from Waschbank was to stop the Free State commandos, led by General Cronje, from crossing the Newcastle road and so falling on Yule's unprotected right flank. Five thousand troops took part in this "excursion", of which a dozen perished and just under a hundred were wounded. Having done what he could to aid the retreating column, White fell back on Ladysmith again.

Yule, for his part, correctly deduced what his superior was up to and, although ill and spent with fatigue, he led his men out dutifully to see if he could co-operate. However, the firing died away, and he returned to his camp. The column set off again the following morning, Wednesday 25th October—still unopposed. Another twelve miles were covered before Yule gave the order to set up camp for the night again. It was at this point that the retreat turned into an endurance test, for Yule then received orders from White to march on without delay and join up with a column sent out from Ladysmith under Colonel Royston. White must have calculated, as indeed Yule had, that Erasmus' force—now replete, gorged and rested after a day or two in Dundee—could not be far behind.

It was this last part of the march, so demanding of those who took part in it, which remained as the abiding memory of the whole four day and night experience. One of the walkers, a colliery manager from Dundee, recorded his feelings:

"We were dead tired and hungry, and footsore, but on we went until four o'clock in the morning, and then we knew that we were retreating on Ladysmith. I cannot go into the awful hardships we encountered, walking seventy miles in horrible storms of rain and thunder. Suffice it to say, we walked for five days with not a dry thread on us, and nothing to eat except

hard biscuits and bully beef. The last mile I walked without boots; they had fallen off my feet."

Regardless of the well-recognized need for haste, it took Yule and his officers six hours to muster the straggling, squelching army of over 4,000 men for the final effort. Yule's troops set off in torrential rain and total darkness, floundering in mud and stumbling over exhausted and starving oxen and horses, scarcely conscious of the exhortations of their own officers and Royston's cavalry escort. But daybreak on 26th October revealed to them across a short expanse of plain the exciting and reassuring glimpse of Ladysmith. Caked in mud, saturated and not a little bewildered, they marched in on to the harder road surface of the town's approaches. The entire garrison came out to meet them, when, according to one account, "they picked up step, straightened their weary backs and swung into Ladysmith with that touch of unaffected swank which is the copyright of the British soldier." After all, they were the victors of Talana—and they were safe.

Yule's unswerving commitment to an excessively arduous task has never been fully recognized. The extraction of an army of over 4,000 exhausted men from impending disaster, followed by a 60-mile forced

march over difficult terrain and in hostile weather, with the ever-increasing risk of pursuit and ambush, was a major achievement of leadership. It was a feat out of character with the times—neither spectacular, successfully bellicose or in any sense glorious. But, in conducting the operation in the way he did, Yule accepted an additional and special kind of personal challenge, from which many of his contemporaries would have shrunk. For the sake of military expediency, he shrewdly calculated that deception would be a vital contributory factor to success. Not only did he deliberately abandon the populace of Dundee to the enemy, but he left behind the wounded, including his dying general, Penn Symons, to fall into their hands. By making these decisions, Yule transgressed some features of the accepted code of honour of a Victorian officer and gentleman. There were those who never forgave him for it.

Nevertheless, on practical grounds, Yule's logic could not be faulted. The retreat cost him his health, but it saved his army—not a single man of which fell to enemy action. Within days, his troops were to become an indispensable component of White's Ladysmith garrison, making up about a quarter of the total force. Some would argue that Ladysmith could not have held out without them.

Mounted infantry, members of Yule's column, pictured during the retreat to Ladysmith. Over 4,000 men withdrew for 60 miles without a single casualty from enemy action.

6 "Mournful Monday"

"It is doubly sad that the blow of my life has fallen upon me this day." (General Sir George White, 30th October 1899)

Well into the night of 30th October, the eve of his wedding anniversary, General Sir George White was still drafting a final letter to his wife, convinced by now that this was likely to be the last news that would get through to her from Ladysmith. "The newspaper boys are now calling in London the terrible disaster that I have only heard of two hours ago," he went on. "I must tell you the history of it." White was referring to the disaster that had befallen what he called his "reconnaissance in force"—first, at Lombard's Kop, where he had hoped to inflict a crushing blow on the Boers, and secondly, at Nicholson's Nek.

With General Yule's force now safe in Ladysmith and reasonably rested after the rigours of the retreat, White was convinced that the moment had come to launch an attack on the Boers. While the Dundee column was nursing blisters and soaking up sunshine, General French's cavalry, in fierce competition with the new-fangled observation balloon in Ladysmith, were busily counting Boer heads. As the hours advanced, more and more of them appeared on the summits of the hills surrounding Ladysmith, their ponies tethered by the hundred in the laagers on the reverse slopes. "A collision with the British was imminent," wrote Deneys Reitz, then with the Pretoria commando at Pepworth Hill. "They had ten to twelve thousand men, including those who had retired from Dundee, and we had fourteen to fifteen thousand, so that something was bound to happen."

For several days White had observed with anxiety this massing of the Boer commandos on Pepworth Hill to the north, on Long Hill and on Bulwana, to the east. Now, on Saturday 28th October, he was ready to strike, but his staff persuaded him that it would be folly to engage the Boers on a Sunday, when their already strong propensity for thinking that God was their ally would be further intensified. The attack was thus set for dawn on Monday, 30th October. Preparation for it began the day before. An entry in the diary of a young woman living in Main Street bore eloquent witness to the bustle:

"The long Ladysmith street just looks one moving mass, and then the mule wagons clattering and tearing along makes one wonder that there are not more accidents. You can't help wondering how many of them will return. Now I am off to bed. What will have happened before this time next week?"

White's plan was to lead off with an attack by a major formation, designated the 8th Brigade, consisting of five battalions of infantry and supporting artillery, all under the command of Colonel G. G.

Grimwood. Their purpose was to dislodge Lucas Meyer's commandos from Long Hill, five miles to the north-east of Ladysmith. While this was going on, a second column—the 7th Brigade, consisting of four infantry battalions, cavalry and artillery, under Colonel Ian Hamilton—were to contain the Boers on Pepworth Hill to the north. After Grimwood had succeeded, they, too, were to move to the attack. French's cavalry was to protect Grimwood's right flank. In addition, a third infantry column of two battalions and artillery, under Colonel F. R. C. Carleton, was to make a seven-mile night march to Nicholson's Nek. There, Carleton was to hold the stage securely for the British cavalry, who, White hoped, would be pursuing the routed burghers after the success of the two main British attacks.

The plan was an ambitious one, and things soon started to go wrong with it. The unfortunate Grimwood, inexperienced in handling large formations, quickly began to regret the chance he had been given to do so. At midnight, his troops moved off and by dawn they were in position facing Long Hill. Or at least some of them were, for it was at this point that Grimwood discovered that he had neither enemy in front of him nor half his own force alongside him. The Boers had slipped away under cover of night, and the same darkness had misled two of Grimwood's five battalions into following the artillery to a totally different objective. And of French's cavalry there was simply no sign at all.

There was soon plenty of evidence of Boers, though, and from a totally unexpected quarter. Across the Modder Spruit, a sick and exhausted Lucas Meyer relinquished command of 4,000 commandos to a man destined to become one of the great names in South African history—Louis Botha. Seizing the opportunity to demonstrate his exceptional powers of leadership, Botha directed a withering fusillade upon Grimwood's 8th Brigade.

Botha's dramatic intervention provoked a chain of tactical military developments which were not provided for in White's plan, were wholly disadvantageous to the British and led finally to the total failure of the operation. Far from proceeding with the attack on Pepworth, White was now obliged to utilize Hamilton's battalions to support Grimwood, whose units were in some disarray by mid-morning. At midday, the 8th Brigade was withdrawn before it was defeated. As if to inject further gloom into an already sombre picture, Colonel Knox, commanding the small reserve force left in Ladysmith, now announced signs of a gathering threat to the town from the Free Staters to the west. Whether or not this was a piece of Boer disinformation, White had little alternative but to hurry his main force back to camp.

The artillery, whose performance in the battles of the past ten days had been unremarkable, now excelled itself. The retreating infantry would certainly have suffered far more heavily, had not the 13th Field Battery, followed after an interval by the 53rd, galloped forward, firing shrapnel at short range, to cover the withdrawal. Having accomplished this successfully, the batteries then covered each other in alternate retirements. The 21st Battery, too, distinguished itself by its staunchness in covering the retirement of the cavalry. Such battle honours as were salvaged by the British army that day unquestionably went to the gunners.

To many Boer eyewitnesses, however, there seemed to be very little glory about the manner of the British withdrawal. Indeed, it sparked off another debate in their ranks about a further missed opportunity to turn a reverse into complete defeat. Looking down on the army retreating across the plain to Ladysmith, Deneys Reitz overheard a memorable exchange between the ageing and gentle Commandant-General Joubert and his more pugnacious lieutenant, Christian de Wet:

"Great clouds of dust billowed over the veldt as the troops withdrew, and the manner of their going had every appearance of a rout. There were about 10,000 soldiers, but General Joubert had far more than that number of horsemen ready to his hand, and we fully looked to see him unleash them on the enemy, but to our surprise there was no pursuit. I heard Christian de Wet mutter 'Los jou ruiters; los jou ruiters' (let your horsemen loose), but the Commandant-General allowed this wonderful opportunity to go by—a failure that cost us dear in the days to come."

It was about this moment that Joubert made his famous remark, "When God holds out a finger, don't take the whole hand."

Throughout the battle, too, White also had another worry to distract

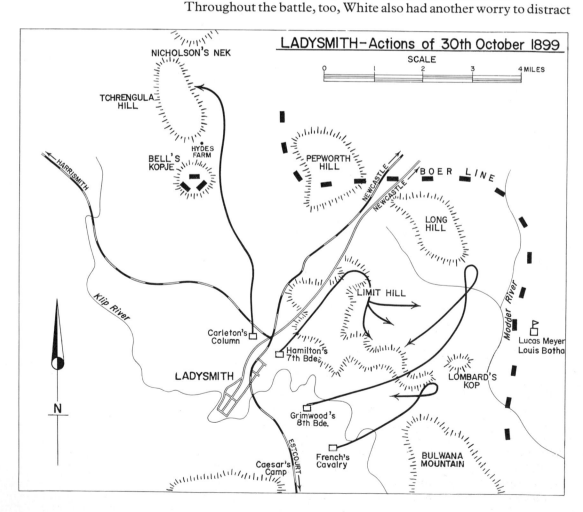

him—what was happening to Colonel Carleton's column at Nicholson's Nek. Occasionally, the sound of distant firing was heard, but apart from that, White was completely in the dark.

The first few hours of Carleton's expedition were uneventful enough. Devoid of adequate maps, but supported by an able and energetic intelligence officer, Major Adye, and Mr. Hyde, a gentleman-farmer from Nicholson's Nek itself, he set off northwards along Bellspruit with a force of 1,100 men. Very few of them could have realized, as they exchanged jests in Cork and Bristol accents with the outlying picquets, that very few of them would see their comrades-in-arms again in this war.

It was not an easy march, for the night was moonless and the road surface irregular enough to cause much stumbling over unexpected stones and potholes. The Irish Fusiliers were in front, followed by the 10th Mountain Battery and the Gloucestershire Regiment. From time to time they shuffled to a halt for the officers to check their position.

Just before reaching his target of Nicholson's Nek, Carleton became apprehensive of a large hill which had become visible on his left during the middle stages of the march. This was Tchrengula, and Carleton's instinct, as well as Hyde's advice, persuaded him to occupy it. The Fusiliers led the way and set off in single file up the slopes. Just as the leading files were reaching the top, with some of the pack-mules not far behind, one of those unexpected phenomena of war occurred. Somebody—or some animal—seems to have dislodged a rock. This, in turn, started a cascade of alarm, falling stones, rifle shots and general panic. Several eyewitnesses, including Captain Rice, the adjutant of the leading battalion, the 1st Royal Irish Fusiliers, speak of a runaway Boer picquet adding to the general, though happily only temporary, pandemonium:

"It was pitch dark and nobody could see an inch in front of them. Suddenly, as we were going through a defile, a dozen or so of boulders came crashing down the hillside. We shouted to our men to lie down, and they obeyed at once. The Battery men followed suit, holding the halter of a mule in each hand. Then, after the stones, some half dozen of the Boers dashed right through us. It was probably a picquet which came down by accident and had no idea they were coming full upon us.

That started the mules; and the men, being in a prone position, were quite unable to hold them, and they all got away. After lying close for a bit, we took our dispositions as best we could in the darkness. We could not see much but we took up a position on a likely-looking hill. It turned out afterwards to be Nicholson's Nek."

Carleton's predicament was indeed unenviable. All his artillery and shells were bolting piecemeal back to Ladysmith and his small arms ammunition was strewn all over the countryside. The men had only what was in their pouches—about twenty rounds each. With commendable devotion to duty and that touch of fatalism which is part and parcel of soldiering, Carleton decided to stay where he was, aware that the success of the forthcoming dawn battles to the east might depend upon him. Not the least of his anxieties was his inability to communicate with White, as both his heliographs had also been lost.

Until dawn, the British remained safe from Boer observation, even though the noise of the stampede had been overheard by Deneys Reitz:

"All remained quiet until three in the morning when out of the darkness there came the sound of shots followed by confused shouting and trampling, but as the noise died down, after a while we let things be. Shortly before day-break, when it was growing light, two large mules came trotting up from below, their head-ropes trailing upon the ground, and on bringing the animals to a halt we found that one of them carried on his back the barrel of a mountain gun, and the other a leathern box containing shell ammunition."

But, although Reitz and his companions correctly deduced that the animals came from the British lines, they clearly had no idea of the size of the calamity which had befallen Carleton's column, or that such a force even existed. Things changed with first light, however:

". . . we could now make out this force on the level top of Nicholson's Nek across the valley. The soldiers were working like ants building sangars of stone, and we could see a knot of officers, standing around what looked like an outspread map, while other men were pulling a tarpaulin over a tree for shade."

Unfortunately for Carleton, other eyes were watching too. The implacably bellicose, crafty and soon to be renowned guerrilla leader, Christian de Wet, was located in a nearby laager. Also close to the scene was the Heilbron commando, under Commandant Mentz, and, very soon, van Dam's ZARPS.

Nevertheless, it remains a matter of some astonishment that the general clatter of Carleton's column on the move, the stamping and shouting of soldiers trying to keep pace with invisible comrades in the dark, the jingling of chains and finally the stampeding mules was not detected by the Free Staters at the time. And yet, not only Reitz but de

British troops returning to Ladysmith in some disarray after the defeat at Nicholson's Nek. The events of "Mournful Monday" made the investment of the town a near certainty.

Wet himself makes it clear that it was not until dawn that the Boers were aware of the British force on Tchrengula. Pressing on to join the Transvaalers at Lombard's Kop, de Wet described how Commandant Steenkamp's commando, of which he was a member, came upon them. "We made our way past the kop to the south of Nicholson's Nek. What a sight met our arrival there. The kop was occupied by the English."

However, it was soon the turn of the British to be surprised. Rice recorded:

"When it began to dawn we saw that our hill was completely surrounded by other hills, which towered above ours, and, although we could not see a single Boer the enemy kept pounding us from every side.

As time went on the rifle fire became terrific, and our men began to drop on every side. The worst of it was that, of course, we had lost every gun, and had no ammunition but what is in our pouches.

We tried putting the best marksmen on to volley firing, but that did not seem to even shift the Boers. Then I was hit in the ankle and compelled to lie down. My sergeant piled big stones round me to give some sort of shelter, but the bullets were plunging all around."

Twenty years after Majuba, the British army still found an adversary who dodged from boulder to boulder and declined to expose himself to decently directed rifle-fire almost as baffling and militarily unfamiliar as the sight of a dog-collared parson wielding a machine gun. "You don't know what it means shooting at a Boer," wrote Second Lieutenant C. Kinahan of the Royal Irish Fusiliers to his father. "He is behind a rock and all you can see is his rifle sticking out."

As if to augment the cheerlessness of occupying an unreconnoitred, and by midday surrounded, rocky prominence, with no reserves of ammunition and no entrenching tools, Carleton and his men were also able to witness the far from orderly withdrawal of the main British force on the plain below. The momentary glimpse of progressively encroaching dark figures—400 of them dodging from rock to rock—falling comrades hit as though by invisible snipers, the artillery cannonade below them, and the demoralizing effect of a steadily dwindling supply of ammunition must have been enough to daunt the most steadfast of soldiers.

Yet, the story of how Colonel Carleton's force surrendered is still not quite clear. Some on the Boer side held to the view that the men were only too happy to quit the war. The war correspondent E. W. Smith reported that the Boers ". . . challenged the statement that our fellows ran out of ammunition and offered to show me piles of it with the thousand rifles they captured from the prisoners and wounded."

But Smith does not report that he was actually shown these "piles of ammunition" and if the Boers did find it—which is not impossible—it is more than likely to have been some distance away from the soldiers who, twelve hours earlier, had every expectation of having it to hand.

De Wet mentions twenty cases of ammunition as being among the day's booty, but he, too, neglects to say precisely where it was found. Much more plausible, and quite heavily documented, as an explanation of what happencd, is a time-honoured wartime phenomenon: misunderstandings stemming from poor or, in this case almost non-existent, communications between every echelon involved—White to

Carleton to company commanders to individually embattled sections and platoon officers.

Forward of Carleton's main position, Captains Duncan and Fyffe (Gloucestershire Regiment)—finding themselves surrounded, wounded, almost out of ammunition and accompanied by only eight men—hoisted a white towel on the end of a sword. It could hardly be held to Captain Duncan's discredit that the Boers emerged from their sangars, cheering and waving their jubilant acclamation of what they assumed was a total British surrender. Nor could Carleton be blamed for not carrying on the fight against men who had now come into the open, genuinely convinced that the battle was over. The age of total war had not yet arrived, and Carleton handed over his sword along with 37 officers and 917 men.

General White was overwhelmed by the enormity of the disaster, and, in the final lines of the letter he wrote to his wife that night, said, "I don't think I can go on soldiering." In more official language he telegraphed to the War Office:

"I have to report a disaster to a column sent by me to take a position in the hills to guard the left flank of the troops in their operations today. The Royal Irish Fusiliers, the Gloucestershire Regiment and No. 10 Mountain Battery, were surrounded in the hills and, after heavy losses, had to capitulate. Losses not yet ascertained in detail . . . I framed the plan in carrying out which this disaster occurred, and am alone responsible for that plan. No blame whatever attaches to the troops, as the position was untenable."

It was a generous telegram, for in it White accepted the blame for a military disaster even before establishing its precise cause. In the event, he could not have chosen his words better, for the following day he received a reply from Lord Lansdowne conveying a most reassuring message from Queen Victoria:

"Am much distressed to hear of this sad news. Trust it will not dishearten the troops at Ladysmith. We feel every confidence in Sir George White, although he naturally takes all the blame upon himself."

The Queen's confidence accurately reflected public reaction in the streets of London to the events of what soon became known as "Mournful Monday." J. L. Garvin and Julian Amery later recorded it:

"The news was published on a grey raw day. In London people bought up the early editions of the evening journals. The placards caused the horse-omnibuses of those days to stop that passengers might buy the papers. There was neither noise nor gesture. The news was read, the journals were not flung down, but folded and kept; few men desired speech with their neighbours. It was certain from then, whatever this war might bring, that national will would never give in."

National will was probably far from the thoughts of General White that night. For him, the overwhelming and immediate consideration was that the investment of Ladysmith was now almost a certainty.

7 White's Dilemma

"Surrounded on all sides by tiers of hills, an outer tier too wide to defend, and an inner tier still too extensive for defence by a comparatively small army, and commanded by the outer tier, Ladysmith invited a siege and was ill-adapted to sustain it." (J. B. Atkins, *Manchester Guardian*)

To others—notably Milner, Hely-Hutchinson (the Governor of Natal) and General Goodenough—fell the main responsibility for establishing the British garrison at Ladysmith, but the decision to stay there after the reverses of "Mournful Monday" and the near completion of the Boer encirclement was White's alone. Three months before he made it, George Stuart White had celebrated his sixty-fourth birthday. The age of youthful "fliers" had not yet arrived, and those who considered him rather old for command of the Natal Field Force might have been reassured by the thought that his adversary, Commandant-General Joubert, was four years older and physically a good deal less robust.

White had always set great store by physical fitness. His biographer, Sir Mortimer Durand, seems to have had some difficulty—even at a time when many of White's contemporaries were still alive—in finding any noteworthy reminiscences from Sir George's schooldays, except that he was always a "young gentleman, a beautiful cricketer and a strong swimmer". By the time he was 18, and leaving Sandhurst for the Inniskillings in 1853, White still only commanded attention for physical and sporting attributes—"a striking boy, tall and strong for his age, with the makings of a very fine horseman." It is fair to add that one of his contemporaries also spoke of his "affectionate and sunny nature."

Letters home during his early years in India bore witness to White's preoccupation with the physical side of life—pig-sticking, athletic fitness and a sneaking admiration for the drinking prowess of a fellow officer, sent home for persistent drunkenness. White wrote of this to his brother, exaggerating wildly the capacity of his wayward comrade-in-arms:

"I have known him drink 43 glasses of brandy 4 bottles of beer a bottle of sherry and 10 bottles of soda before 12 o'clock noon in one day and then crawl without a hat under the awful sun on his hands and knees to his own Bungalow this appears fabulous but I can assure you that it is not even an exaggeration."

General Sir George White, commander of the Ladysmith garrison, as depicted in a Spy cartoon of the period. (National Army Museum)

White's total disregard of punctuation was never completely corrected and his dispatches at no time reached the literary standard attained by his younger fellow officer, Ian Hamilton. He described a mess dinner with Hamilton's regiment, the 92nd, as "a very heavy night. I never saw so many corses in so short a time." The effects of an evening's carousal may have caused this slip of the pen, but it is unlikely to account for White's frequent mis-spelling of the word "Grenadeer."

As a young man, White also seemed to show more than a touch of uninhibited narcissism and bombast. In one of his first letters from India in 1854, he wrote:

"I measured myself for curiosity when I arrived here. I stood in my stockings 5′ 11¼″—on parade about 6′ 1″ measure without anything on 41 inches round the chest—13 inches round the left arm—and held out 5 stones at right angles to my body with one hand—a feat I don't believe another man in Bengal could do and altogether about as fine a specimen of what a soldier should be as one would wish to see."

To his brother, John, he wrote in 1857:

". . . the first fellow said to me 'By George you are the personification of health and strength!' My breadth is now nearly as great as my height which is six feet and I have cultivated a very big pair of whiskers since I was last with the Headquarters of the regiment . . . I hear it reported that you are growing like me, or rather like what I used to be; if so you must be a good looking fellow . . ."

Even allowing here for a somewhat heavy-handed attempt at levity, it is unlikely that White was being anything other than serious when he wrote to his mother two years later saying, "I have nobody or nothing on earth that I care for except my own family and it is a real pleasure to know that I have never given them a pang of regret."

Although his sense of bravado and self-esteem seem to have been a little over-developed in his youth, White had no chance to put his physical courage to the test on the battlefield until he was 44. The battle of Charasiah in the Afghan War of 1878–1880 earned him the Victoria Cross. There apparently in total unawareness of any personal danger, White scrambled upwards among rocks and boulders, hell-bent upon the dispatch of large numbers of well-concealed Afghan tribesmen before his two companies of Highlanders could catch up with him. This they eventually did, and the position was overrun. A year later, he led another assault against an Afghan fortified post, calling to his men—almost as if appealing for another rubber of bridge—"Just one more charge to finish the business." This led to promotion, further service in Egypt and India, recognition by the Viceroy, more promotion and eventually a general's insignia.

As he grew older, White began to transfer to others the somewhat exaggerated assessment of personal qualities which, in youth, he had ascribed to himself. Thus, Penn Symons, who had served under him in Burma, became the beneficiary of some highly extravagant tributes shortly before the outbreak of the Boer War, and remained high in White's esteem until his death at Talana.

Milner and his staff. A convinced imperialist, Milner was as mistrusted by the Boers as was Chamberlain himself. (National Army Museum)

The two generals met each other for the last time at Pietermaritzburg on 8th October 1899. Penn Symons was now a Major-General, with three months' service in Natal, and White a Lieutenant-General, with less than three days' experience of South Africa.

The major decisions had already been made in Capetown, where White, Milner and General Forestier-Walker, commanding general in the Cape, had conferred the week before. Milner was acutely conscious of the need for a strong military presence in the colony, strong enough to subdue the gathering spirit of aggressiveness among the Cape Dutch and the rebellious exodus of men and arms to join their kinsmen in the Boer republics. But he appreciated that it was impossible to be strong everywhere and that a policy of dissemination of forces would probably be fatal. All three men, however, agreed that the military centre of gravity was in Natal, where the main forces for the forthcoming Boer attack were being concentrated.

Milner therefore agreed that all British troops arriving in Durban from India should be placed under White's immediate command. With that commitment secured, White cut short his stay in Capetown and hurried to Port Elizabeth by train. From there, he took ship to Durban and then went on by train again to Pietermaritzburg to meet the by now highly anxious Hely-Hutchinson as well as the much more relaxed and confident Penn Symons. But, in his analysis of the immediate military dilemma, White found his own judgement in conflict with the political considerations outlined by the Governor and with the soldierly self-confidence exuded by Penn Symons.

The troops available to White on his arrival in Natal consisted of a force of 8,000 at Ladysmith and 4,000 located 40 miles further forward at Glencoe, to protect the coal mines of northern Natal and the towns of Dundee and Newcastle. Hely-Hutchinson argued that this division of forces must stand. Any withdrawal, he believed, might have an inflammatory effect upon the Zulus, the sons of Cetewayo who had massacred a British column 20 years before at Isandlwana and who might be encouraged to try the same again. White, on the other hand, wanted to concentrate his forces on Ladysmith, but, in the end, gave in to Hely-Hutchinson's pleading. The balance of judgement, including Lord Roberts' subsequent appreciation, was that White's hunch was right and his decision wrong.

However, White might have argued more strongly had he been fully convinced in his own mind that Ladysmith itself was the right place to make a stand. On his journey out to South Africa, working on the basis of maps and papers, he had selected the east–west range of the Biggarsberg hills to the north of Ladysmith as a possible line of defence for Natal. This, he considered, might become a salient from which to launch attacking sorties upon individual Boer forces, but he wisely deferred the final decision until arrival on the spot. The idea then turned out to be untenable, partly because the hills were found to have inadequate sources of water and partly because they were too far north to prevent flank attacks on Ladysmith from the Drakensberg passes.

Against this theory, too, there was another concept, subscribed to by Colonel Rawlinson and other officers of White's staff on the spot as well as by Wolseley back in London. This was to withdraw behind the Tugela river and simply abandon Ladysmith completely. Mindful of what would be the certain reaction in Whitehall to this latter proposal, and with a thought to the substantial arsenal and 60 days' worth of provisions contained in the town, White came to the conclusion that Ladysmith must be held—though he certainly did not envisage a siege lasting four months. Subsequent events changed his mind.

Later critics, notably Conan Doyle in his *Great Boer War*, have ascribed a fair measure of blame to White for the generally unfavourable predicament the Natal Field Force found itself in at the end of October 1899. Conan Doyle condemned White's invincible optimism as at least partially responsible for landing him in trouble. He also drew attention to what he considered to be three specific errors of judgement by White—the failure to blow up the Newcastle–Ladysmith railway, his complacency in submitting to the occupation of Dundee, and his "retention of the non-combatants in Ladysmith until it was too late to get rid of their useless mouths." He also particularly criticized White for his handling of the events of "Mournful Monday" and, had he pronounced that night, White would probably have been the first to agree with him. British prospects in Natal looked very grim indeed.

At this point, White found new reserves of inner purpose. The decision he now made was right—and, strangely enough, it coincided with the thoughts of his Boer adversary. Joubert, resisting pressures from his more venturesome and bellicose subordinates, decided to besiege Ladysmith, rather than attack the town. To White "a siege so far from appearing a calamity, seemed now to be the best, if not the only means by which to 'cover the vitals of Natal' from invasion." On the evening of 31st October, after a day of consultation with his staff, an exchange of telegrams with Buller—scarcely ashore at Capetown—and the comforting sight of the Royal Navy's heavy artillery digging in, White had made up his mind and said so in a telegram to Hely-Hutchinson:

"31st October. My intention is to hold Ladysmith, make attacks on the enemy's position whenever possible, and retain the greatest number of enemy here."

In fact, White had very little choice left, for, on the following morning, Commandant-General Joubert called a council of war which settled everything for him. While the Free State forces, under General A. P. Cronje, would seal off the southern, western and northern approaches to Ladysmith, the Transvaalers would occupy the ground to the east. The meeting points were to be the Klip river on the north and Nelthorpe to the south.

These decisions were set in motion at once and, early in the morning of 2nd November, a mounted reconnaissance force from Ladysmith—sent out partly in deference to Buller's suggestion that the cavalry might be better employed covering Pietermaritzburg—came under heavy fire. The cavalry scampered back to Ladysmith and the following day the Boers linked forces at Nelthorpe. The last train from Ladysmith, bearing General French on instructions from Buller, escaped under fire to Pietermaritzburg and the Boers blew up the railway behind it. The investment of the British at Ladysmith was now complete.

8 General Joubert's Plan

"The whole siege of Ladysmith and the manner in which the besieged garrison was ineffectually pounded at with our big guns for several months,

seem to me an unfathomable mystery which, owing to Joubert's untimely death, will never be satisfactorily explained." (General Ben Viljoen, Assistant Commandant-General, Transvaal Burgher Forces, *Reminiscences of the Anglo-Boer War*, 1902)

Having decided to hold Ladysmith, White prepared to face a siege. Here, his headquarters in Poort Road shows one of the results of that decision—damage by Boer artillery.

Viljoen's comment on his Commandant-General's conduct of the Ladysmith campaign has a bitter note to it. Yet this was not entirely sour grapes. Coming after the shock of the carnage he had witnessed at Elandslaagte a few days before, transformed into elation at the news of the British débâcle at Nicholson's Nek, Viljoen's reception by General Joubert at the Boer headquarters outside Ladysmith must have been severely discouraging. "Why did you not obey my orders and stop this side of the Biggarsberg as the Council of War decided you should do?" Joubert asked.

This sharp rebuke was a measure of Joubert's stubborn commitment to principle and to discipline. Viljoen's only offence was an excess of zeal beyond the call of duty which had twice in a week landed him and his commando closer to the enemy than the war plans of the Boer high command envisaged. It was only with some reluctance that the irate Commandant-General agreed to Viljoen's further participation in the fight for Ladysmith—a reasonable afterthought, considering that Viljoen's manpower contribution was equal in strength to the total Boer casualties which Joubert could expect in any attempt to take the town.

For the British, it was difficult to assess Joubert's calibre as a foe, for Joubert presented no common image, even to his own people. Some speak of a large, powerful man, but he was, in fact, small of stature. Even his voice seems to be a matter of dispute. Ben Viljoen, describing his harrowing interview at the Pepworth Hill headquarters, wrote: "After much storming in his fine bass voice, he grew calmer, and in stentorian tones ordered me for the time being to join General Schalk Burger at Lombard's Kop." Writing more recently, however, Joubert's biographer, Johannes Meintjes, deprived of the personal contact which Viljoen enjoyed but having the advantage of objectivity, serious research and scholarship, says, "His high voice was out of keeping with his physique."

Joubert was a mystery to most people. Deep generosity and genuine kindness were often marred by an acutely hostile tongue. "Slim (wily) Piet" to some and "Oom (uncle) Piet" to others, the two were never far apart. But, whatever personal opinions existed—and there were many—there was no doubt of his place in the hearts and history of the Boer people. As Commandant-General in the first Boer War of 1880–1881, he had won the war for the Boers. Majuba became his personal battle honour, and a Trafalgar-type victory symbol for the people of whom he was so much a part.

For the next twenty years, however, Joubert's energies were absorbed by the primary objective of trying to win for his country the realities of full independence which the Pretoria Convention of 1881 had only partially provided. These long years must have taken their toll. By 1899, Joubert was simply tired, his energies eroded by half a century of conflict with men—both black and white—by the challenges of a nation in the making, and by the harsh geography of a pioneer country. There were those who, during the Ladysmith campaign, hinted at arteriosclerosis when they pointed to Joubert's apparent lack of purpose and his generally unresponsive attitude to the ideas of others in his conduct of military operations. "Doddering defensively in the hilly borderland of Natal" is how W. K. Hancock put it.

Whatever the authenticity of some of the remarks attributed to Joubert, and used in support of the image of a general in his dotage, there seems no doubt that he was inclined to pessimism. His alleged declaration at the War Council—"You will never see the fall of Ladysmith"—is dubious, but his telegram to the State Secretary in Pretoria—"Our case is serious. We are now even as Napoleon before Moscow"—is not. However, this telegram was dispatched on 27th October, three days before the British reverses at Lombard's Kop and Nicholson's Nek—the events which were to so dismay General White and earn the nickname of "Mournful Monday".

It seems clear that there was a certain duality of personality about Joubert, which Meintjes recognizes in his appearance as much as in his character:

"His eyes were both kindly and suspicious, his mouth both generous and selfish, and his beard was white when there was hardly a grey hair on his head. Although of hardened pioneering stock, he was sensitive, moody and as much a dreamer as he was an astute man of business."

The puritanical sense of propriety, so deeply ingrained by Joubert's Calvinistic upbringing and so deeply outraged by the looting of Dundee by his own men after the battle of Talana Hill, was matched by an old-world sense of chivalry. On 24th October 1899 Joubert wrote to General White, offering his condolences to Lady Symons, whose husband the Boers had just buried. But even this courtly gesture of goodwill, sincere though it was, carried a political message in which Joubert gave, in one sentence, his own analysis of the cause of the war:

"Must express my sympathy. Symons unfortunately badly wounded, died, buried yesterday. I trust great God will speedily bring to an end this unfortunate state of affairs, brought about by unscrupulous speculators and capitalists, who went to the Transvaal to obtain wealth, and, in order to further their own interests, misled others and brought about this shameful state of warfare all over South Africa, in which so many valuable lives have been, and are being sacrificed as, for instance, Symons and others. I express my sympathy to Lady Symons at the loss of her husband."

This was not the first time that Joubert had occasion to write to the widow of a deceased British general whom he had defeated in battle. Eighteen years before, he had done the same in an equally sincere message to Lady Colley after her husband had perished at the top of Majuba Hill. These courtesies were soon to be reciprocated for, within six months of Talana Hill, Field-Marshal Lord Roberts was to send a similar telegram to President Kruger on the occasion of Joubert's death.

There was a certain military wisdom on "Oom Piet's" lack of élan, however. Mr. Easton, the New York *Journal* correspondent with the Boers, no doubt reflected a more dashing American approach to warfare when he found Joubert's strategy as baffling as Commandant Viljoen. This was clear from one of his early dispatches from the Ladysmith front:

Hauling a "Long Tom" to Ladysmith. Joubert believed that a preliminary bombardment by his artillery would soon bring about a British surrender. (National Army Museum)

A picquet manning an outpost on the Ladysmith perimeter defences. The exposed position of the soldiers suggests that hostilities had not yet begun.

P.J. LEMMER   J.D.L. BOTHA   S.J. PRETORIUS

Three generations in the war. Initial success made the Boer commandos impatient to storm Ladysmith, but Joubert refused to accept the casualties that would be involved.

"*I distinctly remember my own impression after the battle of Modder Spruit (more usually known as Lombard's Kop) when General White's 13,000 troops rushed into Ladysmith in disorder. I expected that on the following morning General Joubert would assault the town. One had simply to see that day's fight and the complete demoralisation of the English troops to know that the same men who had driven them off the girdle of kopjes could easily take the unfortified city.*

When the next morning came and I saw the Boers quietly smoking their pipes, I thought they were overlooking the opportunity of the war."

In fact, Easton was grossly underestimating both the opposing generals. Two weeks before "Mournful Monday" White had already satisfied himself, after a detailed personal inspection, that everything possible had been done to strengthen the town's defences. And General Joubert knew this. He also knew that the British might not be all that easy to dislodge. "Believe me," he is reported to have said, "the Englishman is just like an ant-bear; where his feet touch the earth, he digs a hole and fills it up with food."

Joubert's commitment to the idea of saving men's lives—particularly, but not exclusively, those of his own men—may have been too deeply held to satisfy some of the more impulsive and aggressive spirits among his followers. But this was a piece of military philosophy not of his own making, and was entirely consistent with the Boer attitude to warfare. Joubert's commandos might indeed have been able to take Ladysmith, but it would certainly have been a great deal more costly in human life than Easton appeared to think. According to him, it took three weeks before it became clear what was going on in Joubert's mind. During that time, the impatience of the Boer reinforcements was obvious enough:

"New commandos of Boers arrived every few days, and these newcomers were eager for immediate assault, but General Joubert quietly persisted in carrying out his own plan.

Suddenly it was announced to the surprise of nine out of every ten Boers surrounding the city, that it was not his intention to make an assault, but to lay siege to the town. He then took 2,000 men as a flying column and proceeded to Colenso and then to Estcourt."

Easton's estimate of the interval between Joubert's arrival at Ladysmith and the dispatch of the flying column to Estcourt is, in fact, inaccurate. The encirclement of Ladysmith was not completed until 3rd November and by the 15th Louis Botha's column had made considerable progress. Colenso had been reconnoitred, forward patrols had penetrated as far as Estcourt 40 miles to the south—with enterprising scouts probing another 30 miles to within 40 miles of Pietermaritzburg—and Churchill had been captured in an ambush of an armoured train at Chieveley.

The argument advanced by some historians that Joubert was opposed to the investment of Ladysmith seems hard to believe. There is plenty of evidence that he was against the idea of assaulting the town, with its 14,000-strong British garrison, but none that he was thinking of by-passing the place. The plans he followed during the first two weeks of the war, added to his known experience and taste for sieges, support the view that, in the short term at least, things had turned out roughly as he had expected. The bulk of the British army in South Africa was immobilized in Ladysmith, major carnage had been avoided and the prospects for a British surrender must have seemed high. Not without significance were the developments on the other main war fronts, where British columns were also bottled up at Mafeking and Kimberley. Although Joubert was in personal command at Ladysmith, he was nevertheless Commandant-General of all the Boer forces, and so certainly had a hand, however remote, in those operations as well.

Constantly in Joubert's mind was the memory of the military defeat he had inflicted on the British at Majuba in 1881, and the political concessions to the Boers which had swiftly followed. He was certain that this course of events would be repeated. Encouraged by the victories of "Mournful Monday" and confident of his own dispositions along the line of the Tugela, Joubert was entitled to conclude that General White was as powerless to get out of Ladysmith as General Buller was going to be to get through to it. After a few more setbacks, the British would call the whole thing off.

But Joubert was wrong. The British did not surrender, and, far from being over, the battle for Ladysmith had scarcely begun.

9 The Outsiders

"The meat is admirable, worthy of the fine pasture land which carpets this country. The bread is made at Glencoe by a Frenchman, M. de Sainte Croix, in ovens taken from the English. There is also a distribution of tea, coffee, rice, potatoes and spices. In fact, the administration secures you nearly everything. . . ." (Colonel le Comte Georges de Villebois-Mareuil in *Liberté*, Paris, 1900)

Boers on commando. The ages vary, but the militancy is the same.

Life for the besieging Boers in their laagers outside Ladysmith does not seem to have been too bad, on the whole. In other respects as well, de Villebois-Mareuil was highly complimentary to the administrative skills he saw around him, and he found the Marabout tents, the field kitchens and the Irish stews all very reminiscent of camp life in Algeria, where he had served with the French Foreign Legion. He was, however, somewhat astonished by the unmilitary spirit of democracy which prevailed among the Boers:

"The tents of the general, the major, or the field-cornet serve as clubs for anyone who likes. The life of the chiefs is for me a mystery of physical and intellectual endurance in the midst of this continuous invasion. There seem to be no punishments, nor recompenses, no altercations nor coercive measures, everything being done freely . . ."

Commandant Ben Viljoen might not have agreed with him, nor would any of the burghers brought up for looting before the Commandant-General. But the personal access granted by the officers to the men and the consensus-style system of command practised by the Boers would certainly have been a matter of deep amazement to any European regular officer—not just to a graduate of St. Cyr and a typical member of the nineteenth century French officer class.

The French colonel—the only title the Boers ever used for this foreigner with such a long and unpronounceable name—also drew attention, perhaps a little imprudently, to the technological backwardness of the Boers, which had obliged them to enlist foreign advisers. He inevitably incurred Joubert's displeasure, and more seriously that of his wife, by harping on the skills of Leon and Grunberg, the two French gunnery experts from Creusot. According to de Villebois-Mareuil, without these two, the Boer heavy artillery would have been a great deal less effective throughout the war.

In contrast to his admiration for the atmosphere of the Boer laagers and the quality of Boer military administration in general, some of the French colonel's observations about the Commandant-General's personal encampment were less than flattering. He remarked upon the fact that Joubert's staff seemed to be composed almost entirely of relatives. It was indeed true that the general's entourage was known, disrespectfully, as "The Royal Family", although none of his sons were actually on his staff. They were serving as ordinary soldiers. But, for the Frenchman, there was something altogether bizarre and unmilitary about the complex of tents filled with African servants clearing up after both people and domestic animals, with the whole scene dominated by the formidable Madame Joubert, challenged only by her son-in-law for the role of Chief-of-Staff.

Despite his generous praise for the Boer commissariat, it seems unlikely that de Villebois-Mareuil did much dining with the rank-and-file. The Boer biscuit, which he described, rather unconvincingly for a Frenchman, as being "much superior to ours in the sense that you do not tire of it; it greatly resembles bread and is not hard to the teeth", was known throughout the Boer laagers by a less flattering name—*Maagbomme* (belly-bombs). The quality and variety of meat dishes was, on the whole, unpredictable, depending not only on the calibre of the cook but also on the local availability of livestock. The farms around Ladysmith were either "laid under tribute" by the legalistically-minded Boers, or simply plundered by the more unprincipled British, depending on which of the two happened to be tactically the better placed. The Boers' staple diet was biltong, consisting of strips of dried and salted meat made from whatever was available, though there were more exotic items on their bill of fare. Among them was a barbecued kebab, made out of spiced morsels of mutton, beef or game, interspersed with layers of animal fat.

In some laagers, such as that of Christian de Wet's Heilbron commando, a highly organized system of distribution was introduced, with a *Vleeskorporaal* (meat corporal) in charge of ensuring fair shares for all. This exacting assignment meant that the *Vleeskorporaal* had first to be a man of known impartiality and, if possible, of such physical stature that his decisions would be accepted without question. De Wet described how, "to avoid favouritism, this useful personage used to

turn his back on the burghers, and as the men came up in turn, he would pick up the piece of meat which lay nearest to hand, and without looking round, give it to the man who was waiting behind him to receive it . . ."

"This arrangement," says de Wet, "should have been satisfactory to all, but it sometimes happened that some burgher, whom fortune had not favoured, made no effort to conceal his discontent, and thus squabbles frequently occurred." At this point, explains de Wet with great restraint, "The *Vleeskorporaal*, fully convinced of his own uprightness, would let his tongue go, and the burgher who complained was a man to be pitied."

If eating was not the only activity of the Boer commandos surrounding Ladysmith, there was in the beginning nothing very warlike about the other activities of daily life, apart from sniping at careless British picquets. Deneys Reitz was lucky enough to be joined

A group of Boer burghers camped in February 1900. On all fronts, the staple diet of the Boers was biltong, strips of which are here hanging up to dry. (National Army Museum)

by his brother and tracked down at almost the same time by one of the family's African servants:

"Needless to say, he (the servant) was received with open arms, as we were once more able to turn over to him our duties of cooking, carrying water, horseguard etc. So my brother and I settled down to a life of ease.

Camp life was a pleasant existence. There were no drills or parades, and except for night picket and an occasional fatigue party to the railway depot to fetch supplies, there were no military duties."

People's hair began to grow and most of those old enough cultivated full beards. It was only three weeks since the commandos had mustered at Sandspruit—not long enough for their clothes to show signs of wear, but at least the younger burghers were happy that the newness had gone from their wide-brimmed slouch hats, leather

bandoliers and fawn riding breeches. Camp followers—each one, perhaps for the first time in history, a properly certified wife of the man she tended—were not far behind. Discipline slackened. Hundreds departed for home on self-granted leave, so that the Boer commanders never knew from day to day how many men they could muster.

Most of those who remained did so for reasons of patriotism, for the thrill of the chase, or because of men like Louis Botha. As the American Michael Davitt wrote, "Botha had already won confidence all round by the clearness of his views, and the intrepidity of his actions, and his promotion to the command in question became exceedingly popular, especially among the younger and more ardent Boers." Botha was thirty-seven and the "command in question" was Commandant of the south-eastern Transvaal forces, an appointment he had taken over from Lucas Meyer during Lombard's Kop.

Botha's large and majestic physical presence went with a character

A trio of Boer generals. From left to right, Lucas Meyer, Louis Botha and "Maroola" Erasmus pose for the camera.

to match—unassuming, but of unswerving self-confidence, and a quiet sense of purpose which seemed never to offend even those who did not share it. He was rarely seen to be angry in public, except once on the Ladysmith front. On that occasion he banished from his presence a member of the Volksraad who had challenged his patriotism at the critical council meeting which voted in favour of Kruger's ultimatum to Britain.

For Botha, the first few weeks of the war had been acutely frustrating. The Boer leadership was vested in the hands of old and ailing generals who seemed to be content to play a waiting game and, Botha sensed, were devoid of that thrust and purpose which alone could bring ultimate victory. Joubert was not the only culprit, for Lucas Meyer, under whom Botha had served at Talana Hill, was in such poor health that he should never have taken the field in the first place. Finally, exasperated by Joubert's sluggishness, Louis Botha contrived to secure a more active role in the Ladysmith campaign. He was given command of the Boer flying column dispatched to the south to harass the British around Estcourt, leaving to others the problems of boredom and declining standards of discipline among the burghers investing Ladysmith.

Quite alien to the military instincts of Botha were those of Mr. Krogh, the Transvaal Commissary-General on Joubert's staff at Ladysmith. He had definitely come to stay. A little to the south of the railway siding at Modder Spruit, Krogh set up the supply base for the whole of the Transvaal force. There, too, the vigorous, bustling Captain Paul Paff, in charge of signals, established his communications centre. Very soon he had arranged a complete field telegraph system, linking up all the laagers around Ladysmith.

For the first two or three days of November, the Boer commandos circled the town, finally settling down into more or less static frontal positions on the Ladysmith outer perimeter. Westwards from the railway and Krogh's base camp—from Pepworth to Surprise Hill—Joubert deployed General Erasmus and his men, an incompetent leader in command of a controversial force. They included the Pretoria commando, the pillagers of Dundee whose performance after the battle of Talana Hill was so vividly described by Deneys Reitz. Also under Erasmus' command were van Dam's police, who had taken part in the highly effective Boer action at Nicholson's Nek, and the Irish corps—mainly Irish-American, according to *The Times* correspondent reporting from the Boer side—and consisting of "some of the worst sweepings of Johannesburg, led by an American adventurer called 'Colonel' Blake. Their avowed object was loot and that is probably all they would be good for."

Ben Viljoen was there with his Johannesburg commando, fretting at the somewhat chilly reception accorded him by the Commandant-General. And it was not simply Viljoen's non-compliance with orders or the quality of the Irish contingent that was Joubert's only source of complaint. "As for those Germans and Hollanders with you," he told him, "they may go back to Johannesburg. I won't have them here any more." But Viljoen seems to have won him round and most of the foreigners stayed, making a total force of some 4,000 men.

It was not long, however, before Viljoen, loyal on this occasion to his motley force of *Uitlanders*, was forced to concede that Joubert might

General Schalk Burger. He combined the office of Vice President of the Transvaal with being Joubert's second-in-command in the field.

have had a point, as this irate and abusive telegram to Fordsburg about the quality of his latest recruits shows:

"About twenty persons have arrived here from your ward. Some of them are sick or disabled, others crippled, blind or cock-eyed. The majority possess medical certificates which have been ignored either by you (Field-Cornet de Vries) or the Acting Commandant. What the hell do you think I have here, a hospital or a reformatory or a war on my hands . . . ?"

Schalk Burger, Vice-President of the Transvaal and Joubert's second-in-command in the field, held the centre of the Transvaal

position, with 6,500 men from Bethel, Carolina and the Transvaal towns between Johannesburg and Swaziland. Commandos from Middelburg and Heidelberg were encamped behind Lombard's Kop, and, to the south of them, was Louis Botha with the 4,500 burghers he had taken over from Lucas Meyer. The Wakkerstroom, Krugersdorp and Standerton commandos waited behind Bulwana, and the ridges across the Klip river to the south of Ladysmith, facing Caesar's Camp, were held by commandos from Utrecht, Vryheid and some Germans from Pretoria. The Boer circle around Ladysmith was completed by a 7,500-strong contingent from the Free State.

To the west of Erasmus' Pretorians on Surprise Hill, the powerful

A Transvaal howitzer in action before Ladysmith. The gunners were the only true professionals in the Boer army.

Kroonstad commando held the feature known as Thornhill Kopje, and on across the Harrismith railway to Telegraph Ridge, Sandspruit and Star Hill to the south of it. Commandos from Bethlehem, Vrede and Heilbron held Rifleman's Ridge. To the south of them, the men of Harrismith occupied Lancer's Hill, covering the road to Colenso and Long Valley, with detachments across the valley on End Hill and Middle Hill. Beyond them, the last link in the chain, the burghers from Ventersdorp and Winburg joined up with the Vryheid commando and the Pretoria Germans on the Transvaal left. General Martinus Prinsloo, in command of the Free Staters, had his headquarters' camp at Smith's Crossing on the Harrismith railway.

The essence of Joubert's plan was simply to hold these positions and see what time—and the Boer artillery—might do. This was the reasoning behind his refusal to pursue the retreating British on 30th October, his indignation at Ben Viljoen's unsolicited military élan, and his near-banishment of the sizable foreign volunteer contingent, though his child-like religious faith that God would see the justice of the Boer cause may well have played its part. But there is at least some reason to suppose that, as an artilleryman by training, Joubert was inwardly convinced that a preliminary bombardment would soon have the British suing for terms, so making actual battle unnecessary.

There was no doubt that the Commandant-General had immense confidence in the prestige, military prowess and professional competence of his artillery. Spurred on by their faith in the properties of their big guns, the Boers demonstrated great ingenuity, under the direction of Colonel Trichardt, in dragging the various pieces of ordnance to positions on selected hill-tops. But the "Long Toms" did not reduce the British into submission and the tedium of life on the outside soon began to tell.

Ben Viljoen had a rough way with the men under his command who made it clear that they had had enough of the siege. He wrote:

"I gave each one of these a pass to proceed to Johannesburg, which read as follows:

'Permit . . . . to go to Johannesburg at Government expense on account of cowardice.'

They put the permit in their pockets without suspecting its contents and departed with their kit to the station to catch the first available train."

Viljoen does not say in what language he wrote the passes or what was the victims' mother tongue.

Some of the burghers resorted to the time-honoured device of discovering "trouble at home" which demanded their presence. A steady flow of telegrams from Boer generals in the field to the *Landdros* (magistrates) at home requested urgent investigation of familiar family problems. General Erasmus was particularly plagued by this:

24th November 1899
From: General Erasmus, H.Q. Ladysmith
To: Landdros, Pretoria
D. van Vuuren, domiciled near the European Hotel, Pretoria, has complained to General Joubert that his wife—despite numerous

Women, too, joined the Boers in the field. Combining smart riding dress with a rifle, Martha Catharina Krantz is photographed on commando. Her husband was Commandant Krantz of the German Corps.

complaints—is suffering from want. Please investigate the matter immediately and send me a report. Enquire the whereabouts from the proprietor of the hotel; he can show you the house. We are getting complaints from the burghers from dawn to dusk. Contact the government about the matter the situation is intolerable. ends.

29th November 1899
From Landdros, Pretoria
To: General Erasmus, H.Q. Ladysmith
D. van Vuuren's wife since 10 October has received 408 lb. of meal as well as fish, candles, sugar, matches, soap, rice, coffee and tea. I visited her myself and she is quite satisfied. So her husband's complaints are groundless. Letter follows. The next distribution of foodstuffs is on Monday. ends.

Others had sick wives, whom the local Landdros found to be in perfect health. Most serious of all, perhaps, was the demoralising effect of false, or at least partially false, rumours. These sometimes led to major misunderstandings between commanders in the field and senior officials at home. General Louis Botha's telegram to the Landdros of Vryheid on 15th November was extremely acrimonious, as was the reply:

15.11.1899. Confidential
From Assistant-General Botha, H.Q. Ladysmith
To Landdros, Vryheid, begins—
Disquieting reports have been received by me, as well as other burghers here, that properties are not suitably protected in your area. Since you are expected to protect everything there without exception, I am most annoyed to hear of this and also that, although evil-doers already accused of plundering have been sent to you for lawful punishment, not only has such not been done but, on the contrary, you have armed them. They don't come here I notice! Various houses of burghers at the front have been looted. So unless you mend your ways and provide better protection, I shall, in order to end such disquieting things and reports, be obliged to press for affairs at Vryheid to be placed under better supervision and protection. Our burghers here are sacrificing their blood and all for our independence while you, I understand, have said that General Meyer and I are responsible for the loss of cherished men at Dundee. This will naturally undermine morale. It is a pity that you considered the Buffels River too dangerous to ford today, else I could have discussed things with you in person—ends.

15.11.1899. Confidential
From Landdros, Vryheid
To Louis Botha, Assistant-General, H.Q. Ladysmith, begins—
Concerning your telegram of today, I refute with scorn all false reports and information brought to your notice. These are beneath me. All is quiet and peaceful in this town. No property has been damaged and no harm caused to anyone, no matter what their nationality. No raiding takes place, and no booty in this district has been brought to my notice except that found and confiscated at Dundee and even that has passed on to Piet Retief. It is obviously impossible for me to keep control at Dundee since a Resident Magistrate has been installed there. All evil-doers brought to me

by the Public Prosecutor for correction have been dealt with according to law. I am unaware that I have ever armed any delinquent. Those burghers recently conscripted are apparently delayed at Dundee.

I dare anyone to prove to me that I have spoken to your detriment or that of L. Meyer. I am also unaware that I considered the Buffels River crossing unsafe; else I should not have just escaped from falling into the hands of the Lancers. Persons spreading such rumours at your end should—I consider—be prosecuted. All indigent families have been provided for—ends.

Indiscipline among the rank-and-file was one thing, but the rejection of *Krygsraad* (War Council) plans by the officers charged with carrying them out was quite a different matter. A telegram from the State Attorney (Smuts) to the Secretary of State in Pretoria, dated 1st December 1899, complained of a refusal to carry out orders which, in the British or any other regular army, would have counted as mutiny:

"At the Krygsraad held on 30th November, it was decided that an assault upon the Platrand should be made early on 1st December. Reinforcements were held in readiness, and if only the assault had been carried out, Ladysmith would have been by now in the hands of the Boers. The Krygsraad had felt no doubts whatever as to the practicality of the attempt, but after they had arrived at their decision, the junior officers convened themselves to another meeting, at which they took it upon themselves to resolve that the plan was too dangerous to attempt—a resolution which only became known to their superiors on 1st December. Much anger is felt by the latter, who will, however, not venture to punish their juniors for this insubordinate act."

A similar complaint was received in Pretoria from General Erasmus on the same day. His telegram stated that:

"The officers, 15 in number, who had been detailed to lead the assault on the position this morning had in the meantime, i.e. between the time when the Krygsraad rose and the hour prescribed for the assault, resolved amongst themselves to disobey the resolution of the Krygsraad. When dawn broke the covering parties of Boers fired heavily upon the Platrand with the objective of assisting the assaulting column—whose leaders, however, had in the meantime determined not to assault at all."

But, if a touch of brigandage here and there by the burghers, and non-compliance with orders by the Veldt-Kornets, seemed to be wicked and scandalous characteristics of the Boer army, its members were soon to show their real mettle. In a gruelling campaign of four months, 22,000 of them contained General White's force of 14,000 inside Ladysmith and held at bay 28,000 of General Buller's army trying to get in. And, during that time, they were to inflict stunning reverses on the British at Colenso and Spion Kop. By the end of January 1900, when the London *Daily Mail* reported that "Boers anticipate that Kruger will be crowned at Westminster," the British public may have raised a brave laugh, but Whitehall and Windsor were not amused.

10 Last Train to Maritzburg

"They forgot that, though the sieges of ancient history lasted ten years, nowadays we really cannot afford the time. The Boers, we hope, have scarcely ten days, yet they loiter along as though eternity was theirs."
(H. W. Nevinson, *Daily Chronicle*, Ladysmith, 13th November 1900)

British troops man an outpost on the Ladysmith perimeter. One man appears to be keeping watch while the others sleep.

As the Boers closed the ring around Ladysmith, nobody seemed in much of a hurry, except for Louis Botha on the outside and those on the inside who were anxious to catch the last train to Pietermaritzburg, the south and relative safety. The reporter Donald Macdonald, correspondent for the Melbourne *Argus* watched the preparations for departure at Ladysmith station.

"The engagement of October 30 had, from the military point of view, one good effect on Ladysmith. It cleared the town of its human refuse—the mass of Hindoos and unattached Kaffirs who form such a very large share in the population of Natal, and will one day, I have no doubt, furnish it with its great social and political problem. The Asiatic was prominent in the railway rush. He carried with him as much of this world's goods as he could bundle together. He was wildly excited, and the more congested the crowd, the more he chattered and the faster he ran. There were three

trains—the carriages filled with white women and children, the open trucks packed thickly with Kaffirs and Hindoos. White men who wished to go, and in many cases were ordered to go, stood back in despair or shame from this shrieking horde, steaming in the hot, thunderous Natal night, for they felt their manhood would have been smirched by flight in such company. The native police rounded up the blacks like sheep, and packed them as sheep are rarely packed, prodding them on with their knobkerries, while the seething mass inside protested in vain."

But it was for the white refugees from Johannesburg and the gold-rich Eldorado of the Reef that Macdonald reserved most of his talent for verbal abuse.

British infantry and artillery in position on Wagon Hill, one of the key points of Ladysmith's defences. The picture is heavily posed.

"They forced themselves into the trucks set apart for women, trampled upon them, thought of nothing but the safety of their own miserable skins,

INFANTRY FIRING, WAGON HILL

and for such human garbage were brave men in British uniforms wasting their lives by the kloofs and kopjes of Natal. It was a novel sight, and yet a noble one, to see English officers giving drink from their own flasks to some of these miserable refugees at Ladysmith station."

But, in addition to those castigated by Macdonald, there were others who had no choice in the matter. Among the passengers on the last train to the south were General French and his aide, Major Douglas Haig. They went under orders from Buller.

The train steamed out to the south, successfully running the gauntlet of Boer sniper fire. A few hours later, the Boers blew up the railway line, and Colonel E. W. Ward, in charge of administration and supplies in Ladysmith, knew he could start counting heads. A census revealed 13,500 officers and men of the imperial army and Natal Volunteers, 5,500 white civilians and 2,500 Africans and Indians. This made a total of 21,500 mouths to feed on supplies which Ward estimated would last approximately 50 days for humans and 30 days for the horses. Those who stayed behind made their dispositions as best they could. At Vine Lodge in Murchison Street, Mrs. George Tatham, one of the wives who elected to stay with the men, had placed

A British artillery unit poses proudly with its weapons. Ladysmith's town hall is in the background.

an order with Sparks Bros., the provision merchants, for supplies for "a few weeks"—but her husband, a major in the Natal Carbineers, doubled it.

Not far away, in 16 Poort Road where General White had set up his headquarters, the main preoccupation was the deployment of the available troops around Ladysmith's fourteen-mile perimeter. This was divided into four sectors of unequal length, each with varying vulnerability to harassment from the Boer artillery and riflemen on the outer ring of heights.

In command of Section A was Colonel W. G. Knox, a tough disciplinarian known disrespectfully as "Nasty Knox" to distinguish him from the much more popular "Nice Knox"—a Colonel Charles Knox, serving at the time in Buller's army. The Knox front was relatively short, but highly exposed, covering the north-eastern arc of the perimeter from Helpmekaar Ridge to Junction Hill, at the point where the Free State railway meets the Newcastle line. He was allocated the 1st Devons, 1st (Kings) Liverpool, two companies of the 1st Gloucesters, half a company of Royal Dublin Fusiliers, as well as some artillery.

The northern salient, Section B of White's plan, was commanded by Major-General F. Howard. It extended from Gordon Hill on Knox's left flank northwards to Observation Hill and from there south-west to King's Post, Ration Post and across the Klip river to Rifleman's Post. Within this area were included the inner positions at Leicester Post and Cove Redoubt. Howard had six companies of infantry along this front, drawn from the 1st and 2nd King's Royal Rifles, the 2nd Rifle Brigade and the 1st Leicesters.

Colonel Ian Hamilton was in charge of Section C, the western and southern front. There—from Flagstaff Spruit southwards through Range Post to Wagon Hill and across to Caesar's Camp—were positioned the 1st Manchesters, four companies of the 2nd Gordon Highlanders and the two companies of the Royal Irish Fusiliers who had survived Nicholson's Nek.

To guard the eastern salient, White chose Colonel W. Royston, the commandant of the Natal Volunteers who had rendered such invaluable service during the latter stages of General Yule's march from Dundee. From Caesar's Camp in Hamilton's area across the plain to Cemetery Hill, where his front linked up with Knox's, Royston placed the Ladysmith Town Guard, assigning to his mounted troops the task of patrolling his sector perimeter, the line of the Klip river. There were detachments of the Natal Carbineers, the Natal Mounted Rifles and the Border Mounted Rifles.

White deployed his main artillery strength in the north, his two most powerful weapons being the Royal Navy's 4.7-inch guns on Junction Hill and Cove Redoubt. Dawkins' 13th Battery, Royal Artillery, was also placed in Knox's area on Helpmekaar Hill and Devonshire Post. Here, too, was Captain W. H. Christie and a handful of gunners, survivors from the unfortunate 10th Mountain Battery lost at Nicholson's Nek. To them were assigned two 6.3-inch howitzers, which White had ordered up from Port Elizabeth. Though obsolete, these were to prove effective deterrents to any Boer guns advancing to within their 3,000-yard range. Goulburn's 42nd Battery was deployed along the plateau at Caesar's Camp, but first an approach track had to

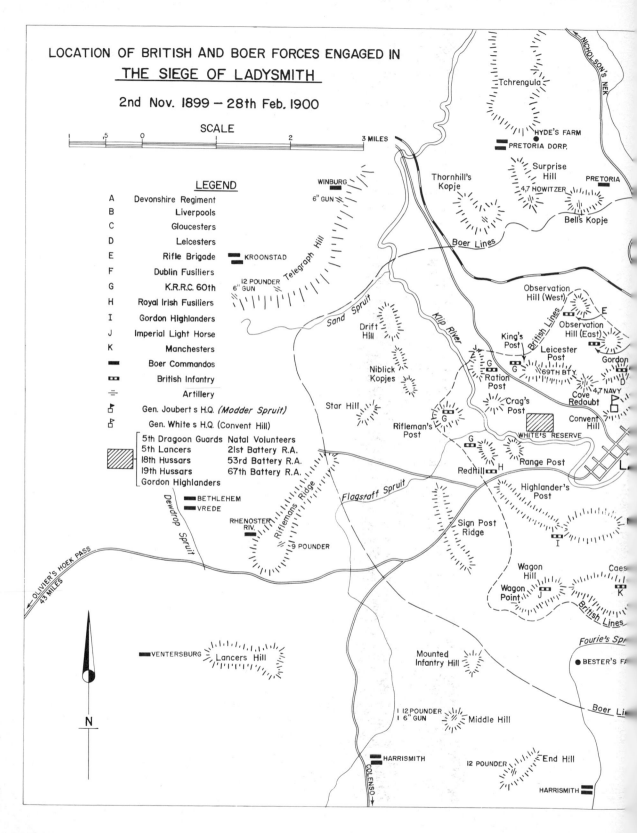

LOCATION OF BRITISH AND BOER FORCES ENGAGED IN
THE SIEGE OF LADYSMITH
2nd Nov. 1899 — 28th Feb. 1900

SCALE

|1| .5 | 0 | 1 | 2 | 3 MILES |

LEGEND

A Devonshire Regiment
B Liverpools
C Gloucesters
D Leicesters
E Rifle Brigade
F Dublin Fusiliers
G K.R.R.C. 60th
H Royal Irish Fusiliers
I Gordon Highlanders
J Imperial Light Horse
K Manchesters

▬ Boer Commandos
▭▭ British Infantry
= Artillery
⚑ Gen. Joubert's H.Q. *(Modder Spruit)*
⚑ Gen. White's H.Q. *(Convent Hill)*

5th Dragoon Guards Natal Volunteers
5th Lancers 21st Battery R.A.
18th Hussars 53rd Battery R.A.
19th Hussars 67th Battery R.A.
Gordon Highlanders

Map labels: NICHOLSON'S NEK, Tchrengula, HYDE'S FARM, PRETORIA DORP., Surprise Hill, PRETORIA, Thornhill's Kopje, 4,7 HOWITZER, Bell's Kopje, Boer Lines, Observation Hill (West), Observation Hill (East), King's Post, Leicester Post, Gordon, British Lines, 69TH BTY., 4,7 NAVY, Cove Redoubt, Convent Hill, WHITE'S RESERVE, Ration Post, Crag's Post, Rifleman's Post, Range Post, Redhill, Highlander's Post, Sign Post Ridge, Wagon Hill, Wagon Point, Caes., Fourie's Spr., BESTER'S FA., Mounted Infantry Hill, Middle Hill, End Hill, HARRISMITH, Boer Li., COLENSO, Drift Hill, Niblick Kopjes, Star Hill, Sand Spruit, Kilp River, WINBURG, 6" GUN, Telegraph Hill, KROONSTAD, 12 POUNDER, 6" GUN, Riflemans Ridge, Flagstaff Spruit, Dewdrop Spruit, BETHLEHEM, VREDE, RHENOSTER RIV., 9 POUNDER, OLIVIER'S HOEK PASS 43 MILES, VENTERSBURG, Lancers Hill, 1 12 POUNDER, 1 6" GUN, 12 POUNDER

N

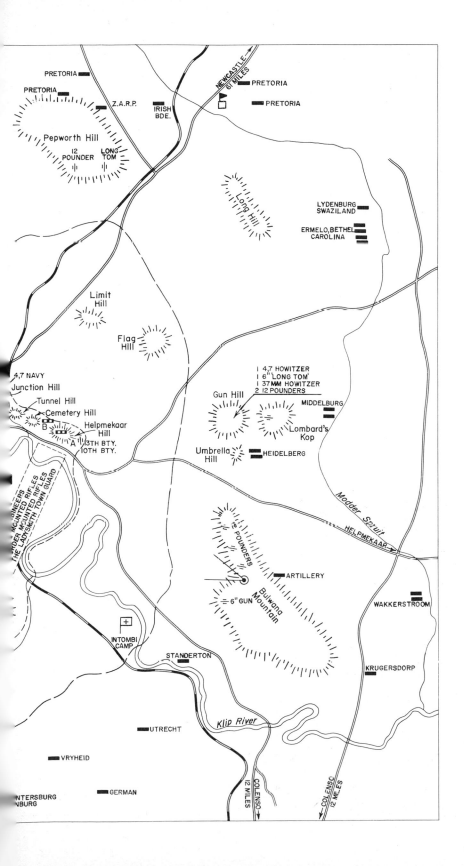

PRETORIA

PRETORIA

Z.A.R.P.

IRISH
BDE.

NEWCASTLE →
61 MILES

PRETORIA

PRETORIA

Pepworth Hill

12
POUNDER

LONG
TOM

Long Hill

LYDENBURG
SWAZILAND

ERMELO, BETHEL
CAROLINA

Limit
Hill

Flag
Hill

4,7 NAVY

Junction Hill

Tunnel Hill

Cemetery Hill

B

Helpmekaar
Hill

A   13TH BTY.
10TH BTY.

Gun Hill

1 4,7 HOWITZER
1 6" 'LONG TOM'
1 37MM HOWITZER
2 12 POUNDERS

MIDDELBURG

Lombard's
Kop

Umbrella
Hill

HEIDELBERG

BORDER MOUNTED RIFLES
THE LADYSMITH TOWN GUARD

NATAL MOUNTED RIFLES

Modder Spruit

HELPMEKAAR →

12
POUNDERS

ARTILLERY

Bulwana
Mountain

6" GUN

WAKKERSTROOM

INTOMBI
CAMP

STANDERTON

KRUGERSDORP

UTRECHT

Klip River

VRYHEID

GERMAN

NTERSBURG
NBURG

12 MILES

COLENSO

COLENSO
12 MILES

be carved out of the hillside. The 69th Battery settled near Leicester Post in support of Howard's section, but, over on the east, Royston had to make do with a dummy gun position. This deception served its purpose well, with no loss of life to the Volunteers but causing the Boers to waste a good deal of ammunition.

Major-General J. F. Brocklehurst, who succeeded French in command of the cavalry, was held with his mounted troops as a central reserve in the general area from White's headquarters on Convent Hill to the permanent garrison location, commonly known as "Tin Camp", to the west of it. In Brocklehurst's reserve were the 5th Dragoon Guards, 5th Lancers, 18th and 19th Hussars, and, in addition, the remaining Natal Volunteers not deployed under Royston. He also commanded three companies of Gordon Highlanders and, with them, the 21st, 53rd and 67th Batteries, Royal Artillery.

Behind these defences, everybody in Ladysmith settled down and waited. The Boers outside confidently expected the British to realize that their position was hopeless and settle for terms, while the British, with nothing much to do but sit tight, simply waited for Sir Redvers Buller to come and relieve them. In the meantime, both sides went through the motions of making war—the British by sending out occasional armed sorties to test Boer reactions and the Boers by starting a bombardment of the town. Though the Boers had no means of judging the military effect of this bombardment, in fact, the two 6-inch Creusot "Long Toms" hurling 96 lb. shells from Pepworth Hill and Bulwana, joined, after a day or two by other guns from Lombard's Kop, succeeded, not surprisingly, in unnerving the more timorous among the Ladysmith citizenry. Very soon, White had a morale problem on his hands.

For the first few days of the bombardment, according to H. Pearse of the *Daily News*, public anxiety hardly showed.

"Children were allowed to play about the streets, and women went shopping, according to the custom of their sex the world over. Kaffir girls stood in groups at street corners, swaying their bodies as they beat noiseless time with their bare feet to the monotonous drone of mouth-organs or Jew's harps which most of them carry strung about their necks."

But Donald Macdonald saw it differently.

"On the first day, when the shells were few in number, people laughed—a mechanical crackling laugh, like the rustle of dry straw, but still a laugh. On the second day, there was rather less laughter, and more smothered swearing. On the third day there was an impressive silence, people answering curtly when spoken to, everyone thinking a good deal. It was not a friendly act then to throw a bottle or a can amongst the rocks close to where a man stood. He was too proud to make any protests, but still his nerves betrayed him. On the fourth day men had a hunted look, and I never fully realized what a hunted look meant until the bombardment of Ladysmith. Most men were morose. It was not so much the Krupp shell that worried them, as the waiting for it. The most courteous man in the world became short-tempered then. On the sixth day he was savage, and asked people whether the British soldier had deteriorated, that he did not go out in the dark and take that cursed Krupp gun?"

Only after a shell landed on the clock-tower of the Town Hall, which had been turned into a makeshift hospital for the sick and wounded, did White ask for quarter. His plea for the casualties and non-combatants to be allowed to leave the town was promptly answered by Commandant-General Joubert.

"Respecting your request that the townspeople may be allowed to leave for the South, this I cannot possibly agree to. The wounded, with their Attendants and Doctors, may, as requested by you, be taken to a chosen place, and I shall agree that the people of the town shall also be removed there. The numbers of the civilians must be communicated to me and the removals of the wounded and civilians must be effected within twenty-four hours of the receipt of this, and the locality must be distinctly marked. I must further make it a condition that under the name of civilian there must not be sent out any who have taken up arms against the Republic."

White agreed to these terms and the move out to Intombi Spruit, four miles to the south-east of Ladysmith, took place on 5th November—a shell-free Sunday. Dr. H. H. Balfour from Johannesburg began to get ready early in the morning:

"The train left the station at four o'clock—a long, long train made up of trucks, carriages, etc. filled with patients and townsfolk, the sick and wounded lying on stretchers, in trucks, and in beds in the luggage van. We slowly steamed away, and in a short time reached our destination. A few tents were up and more were being put up. After much difficulty and trouble we got the beds right and the wounded fixed up in tents etc. It was late at night before this was finished and very dark."

Within a few days, things settled down as the army introduced a semblance of organization to this vast sea of tentage and makeshift shelter. One section was designated No. 12 Field Hospital and put under the command of Major Love, R.A.M.C. Another was called No. 1 Stationary Hospital of the Natal Field Force and a third was No. 1 Natal Volunteer Field Force Hospital, commanded by Captain Currie of the Natal Carbineers. Altogether, there were less than 30 qualified doctors—both civilian and military—120 trained medical personnel and 56 Indian bearers at any one time in Intombi camp. They had a total of 300 beds to start with. The whole area was put under the administrative command of Lieutenant-Colonel R. W. Mapleton, R.A.M.C., and authority for the adjoining civilian refugee camp was vested in Mr. Bennett, Resident Magistrate of Ladysmith.

But Balfour, Bruce, Currie and the other doctors were not alone in tending to the sick and wounded of Ladysmith. Leaving behind the polished floors and the silence of Convent Hill to the rough British soldiery and Boer bombardment, Mother Marie des Anges took her small community of nuns out to Intombi. After the initial shock at the crudities of tent life, where six of them shared three mattresses—sometimes with nightly visitations from scorpions, snakes and frogs—the nuns joined in with the nursing until, one by one, they too fell sick.

Young children also played their part; Mrs. Bamber, for instance, recalled how her small boys became hospital visitors, adopting this or that dying soldier, whose fevered brow they fanned patiently with

handkerchieves. And when the doctors themselves succumbed to dysentery and enteric fever, the housewives of Ladysmith took over. At Vine Lodge, the Tathams set up a nurses' home and casualty clearing station for wounded and fever victims awaiting the daily train to Intombi.

None were more worthy of mention on the medical scene than the Indian dhoolie bearers, whom Watkins-Pitchford remembers struggling back from the battlefields under their heavy burdens:

"Excellent little fellows these bearers are, some of them with four or five ribbons upon the breasts of their dirty khaki blouses. They trot out complacently under the heaviest fire and seem to know no fear. They have won the greatest admiration and respect from our Natal men."

Not content with what he evidently considered to be too passive a role, one peppery physician, Dr. James Kay from Plymouth, was so incensed by the army's failure to take effective action against "Long Tom" on Pepworth Hill that he wrote to White offering to do the job himself, asking only for a guide and some dynamite. The reply, a

touching example of honour and obligation to a contract with the enemy, came the following day—8th November 1899.

"*Sir,*
I have been directed by Lieutenant-General Sir George White to acknowledge your letter received today and to thank you for your offer to perform so dangerous a service, but apart from any considerations of your personal safety Sir George White could not consent, as the terms under which the Military Hospital has been established at Intombi Spruit preclude any persons who use that camp engaging in any hostilities against our present enemy.
(Signed) B. Duff,
Colonel, Assistant Military Secretary."

Not everybody in Ladysmith was scared by the shelling. Miss Isabella Craw was thirty-two when she started her Siege Diary. "Today has been a disappointing day," she wrote on Monday, 6th November. "It seems a dreadful thing to be disappointed because there has been no shelling." Three days—and a thousand shells—

Officers and NCOs of the 19th Hussars at Ladysmith. Their well-fed look places this picture at the beginning of the siege. Within three months their horses were to become the staple diet of the people of the town.

later, returning from the family bolt-hole, where it became customary for civilians to spend the daylight hours, Bella and her cousins decided to embark on a sight-seeing tour and pay calls on a few friends. It seemed that nobody was at home, although there were plenty of signs of life, for many of the deserted houses had become officers' messes.

"After we got home this afternoon, what a relief to get out and away from the warren and have a bath and clean up. Wilfred, Bert and I went to town to see the damage done. Illing Bros. store had a shell through one door and wall; not much damage done. Then we walked round to the late government school. Shells had burst all round there. The ammunition is stored there, but not much damage. A chimney gone and a few holes through the corrugated iron fence. Next door, at Dr. Rouillard's stable, one wall was completely levelled. From there we passed the General's house (General White's headquarters). What a change from when Mrs. Adams lived there; tents pitched all round and everything looking lively, horses and soldiers standing about. Where we should cross a little bridge below Mrs. Christopher's gate, we noticed it all barricaded and heaped up with bales of forage. We crossed through the dip below and saw it was meant for a burrow for someone. Mrs. Christopher's place looked all serene. I picked some mignonette and roses and geraniums. We went into the house and her old kitchen boy greeted us. He had everything looking nice and clean, and all the plants were watered. The table was laid for six—it has been commandeered like most unoccupied houses by some officers. I put some of the flowers in vases on the table and took the rest home . . ."

Less surprising, perhaps, was Ian Hamilton's own indifference to personal danger, but he might perhaps have worded a letter he wrote to his wife a week later slightly more considerately:

"I fear, darling mine, that you must have been anxious. As a matter of fact this shelling is unpleasant but not really formidable. Of course it is possible that one may be hit but certainly even a small infantry fight like we had on Caesar's Camp at my defences on the 9th inst. is much more deadly. This house which I have taken over from Valentine (his Brigade-Major) has been most unlucky. We got one enormous 6 inch shell on to the lawn, and then, 14th inst. another 97 lb. shell from a 6 inch Creusot gun hit the end of the dining room on the ground floor at 8 o'clock precisely; just in fact as we should have been sitting down to breakfast. You would laugh if you saw the room. The flooring is simply ripped up and jammed through the ceiling. Of the long table nothing is left at all, and of the chair I sit in nothing certainly as big as a match. The doors are torn off their hinges and all glass, pictures, crockery etc. simply ground into powder. Ava is on my staff and Frankie Rhodes lives with us. He is great fun and runs about all along the defence line collecting and retailing news. Dick-Cunyngham is recovering fast from his wound and is in very good spirits and general health. Riddell of the 60th is also on the mend although he was shot bang through the body."

It is highly unlikely that Hamilton's wife found this letter at all reassuring! And it was just as well that she was probably unaware of the theory widely held in Ladysmith at the time that Colonel Frank Rhodes was a marked man for the Boer artillery. Many believed that Boer informants, of whom there were doubtless plenty in Ladysmith at the time, were daily reporting on the whereabouts, movements and routine of Dr. Leander Starr Jameson, Frank Rhodes, Sir John Willoughby and others of the Johannesburg Reform Committee and participants in the Jameson Raid. As far as the Boers were concerned, these were the real villains of the piece—not General White, nor Colonel Royston, nor any other of the English and colonial gentlemen obliged by honour and duty to take up arms against them. The Royal Hotel, as the known lunch-time meeting place for the Johannesburg–Jameson set, was soon shown to be an unhealthy place to drink in. It cost Dr. Stark his life. And to have shared a house with Frank Rhodes was asking for trouble.

Of all the varying reactions to life in the first days of the siege of Ladysmith, ranging from the vicarious anxiety of Mayor Farquhar, the demure fortitude and resolution of Bella Craw to the professional disregard for personal safety of Ian Hamilton, among the most appropriate for the occasion must surely be counted the philosophic attitude of Lieutenant the Hon. R. L. Pomeroy of the 5th Dragoon Guards. He, too, kept a diary during the siege and the entry for 12th November reads:

"Had the whole of my tent turned out and a general clean-up. Finished second volume of Gibbon's Decline and Fall *today."*

Assuming Pomeroy was reading the 1872 edition, annotated by Dr. W. Smith, he had six volumes to go—and, though he could not know it, nearly four months to do it.

11 Buller Goes To War

"The Boers'll cop it now, Farver's gone to South Africa an' he's tooken 'is strap." (*Punch* cartoon, October 1899)

Victorian military heroes have long since been out of fashion. If any general memory of General Sir Redvers Buller survives, it is of a John Bull-type effigy on a mock patriotic tea caddy. In the imperial high noon of Victorian England, however, Buller was anything but a figure of fun. To the vast crowds who cheered his departure from Waterloo, lined the route of his special train to Southampton and watched him board the *Dunottar Castle* on 11th October 1899 en route for South Africa, he was the apotheosis of British might. One of his fellow passengers, J. B. Atkins, recorded the dockside scene:

Crowds throng the quayside to cheer a departing troop ship on its way. Filled with patriotic pride and confidence in Sir Redvers Buller, the chosen Commander-in-Chief, the British public was confident of speedy victory. (National Army Museum)

"At last we were off, and then a cry of farewell crackled below the ship and spread; along the lines it went—such a shout as the oldest captain had never heard at Southampton before. And then we on the Dunottar Castle *glided away till the screen of faces was watered down into the vague solidity of the quay walls. One excursion steamer ran alongside us for a few moments; her passengers swarmed at her side to snatch a last glimpse of Sir Redvers Buller."*

Besides Buller and his headquarter's staff, the ship's sole passengers were journalists, for the one army corps available at the time was not yet ready to sail. Father's strap was not to hand. So Buller travelled out with nothing much more than strategic plans, inadequate maps, his immense personal prestige and Winston Churchill. On top of characteristic governmental parsimony in matters of Defence, there were also those in Whitehall who argued that Buller probably had all he needed—10,000 men already in South Africa, a redoubtable reputation as a soldier, and another 5,000 reinforcements on their way from India.

This complacency, both contagious and reassuring, was reflected in the shipboard mood of Buller's staff, whose main anxiety seemed to be the fear that all would be over before they reached Capetown. "Absolute tranquillity lapped the peaceful ship," wrote Churchill, "and Buller trod the deck each day with sphinx-like calm." For days the now familiar game of journalists stalking generals in the hope of obtaining a picture and an interview was played up and down the decks and companionways of *Dunottar Castle*. Some of the journalists may have recalled with trepidation the Ashanti War story of the reporter trounced by Buller for rummaging in his mess tent in search of a scoop. But he had mellowed now and came to an accommodation with his fellow travellers. "Catch me if you can, but I will not pose for you," he said to the wielder of a primitive ciné camera.

Buller's last port of call before his ship began the long haul down the African coast was Madeira, where the *Dunottar Castle* anchored on 17th October. There, Buller received his first telegrams from the war zone. Such snippets of news as these contained, however, did nothing to shake his confidence. Then came the meeting with S.S. *Australasian*, three days out of Capetown. "Men and women who would not stop in Regent Street if a hansom fell to pieces before them," wrote Atkins, "will spend hours watching a speck on the horizon when they are in mid-ocean." The message hung on a blackboard from the ratlines of the northbound steamer was clear enough, first to those steadying their powerful binoculars and then to the naked eye. "BOERS DEFEATED. THREE BATTLES. PENN SYMONS KILLED."

In a few minutes the *Australasian* was hull down on the skyline and nobody seemed disposed to break the silence, for Buller had read the message himself and made no comment.

"It looks as if it will be all over, sir," ventured one of Buller's staff officers after a while. "I dare say there will be enough left to give us a fight outside Pretoria," replied the general.

What were the characteristics of the man in whose hands now lay the fate of British hegemony in South Africa? A contemporary admirer wrote:

"There is no stronger commander in the British army than this remote, almost grimly resolute, completely independent, utterly fearless, steadfast, and always vigorous man. Big-boned, square-jawed, strong-minded, strong-headed . . . Smartness . . . Sagacity . . . Administrative capacity . . . He was born to be a soldier of the very best English type, needless to say, the best type of all."

This larger-than-life eulogy was soon to be tarnished as far as some of the military virtues it listed were concerned, and was already somewhat inaccurate on details of physical appearance. Champagne, a taste for good living, and advancing years had rounded out the original squareness of the jaw and rendered the size of the bones a matter of pure guesswork.

But Buller had not always been fat and sixty. His reputation for gallantry dated back to the Zulu War of 1879. There were none who had ever served under him who did not know the details of how he won the Victoria Cross in that campaign, in which Buller, the commander of the Frontier Light Horse, showed the utmost courage in personally rescuing his comrades in the face of the Zulu hordes at Hlobane.

Redvers Buller's first distinction in life was to have been admitted to

Eton, having been asked to leave Harrow, thus establishing himself as one of the few Englishmen to have been educated at both schools. Whilst still at Eton, he suffered a traumatic shock, which may well help to explain his later reputation for great sympathy and human compassion. Returning for the Christmas holidays to the family estates in Devon, the young Buller was met by his mother at Exeter station. She collapsed on the platform and died in his arms two days later, still on the station from which it had been deemed too dangerous to move her.

Two years later, by now a mature and muscular figure, Buller was commissioned into the 60th Rifles and, by the age of twenty-one, he had seen his first action during the Chinese expedition of 1860. Though he survived the fighting, violence and danger soon entered his life. On one occasion he was nearly drowned and, for a minute or two, given up for dead after being dragged from the water. A kick in the face from a horse removed some of his front teeth, making his speech slightly indistinct for the rest of his life.

Soon after this, Buller met the first great military influence in his life, when he was posted to Canada to serve under Robert Beaufoy Hawley, the commander of the 4th Battalion of the 60th Rifles and acknowledged in his day as one of the finest regimental commanders in the British army. Buller was to stay with Hawley for seven years, during which time the older man became almost a father figure to the younger one. In fact, Buller never ceased to look upon Hawley as a kind of military godfather long after he had surpassed the latter in rank. As Adjutant-General of the army in the 1890s, Buller was still writing letters to his former commanding officer with an engaging touch of deference, and always addressing him as "My dear Colonel", at a time when the retired veteran was, in fact, a general.

The next major military influence on Buller's life and career was even more eminent and even more decisive. In 1870 he came to the attention of Garnet Joseph Wolseley, a knight at thirty-eight, Major General at forty, and finally Viscount and Commander-in-Chief of the British army. He enlisted Buller in his famous "ring"—a group of officers chosen either as radical military theorists or distinguished by their success and bravery on the battlefield—who were to follow their chief in his "private thirty-year war . . . against the British military system, the bow-and-arrow Generals and the draconian Commander-in-Chief, the Duke of Cambridge." Buller was one of the latter. He had impressed Wolseley in Canada and in several battles in the Ashanti War as an exceptionally enterprising and courageous officer, and as a good leader of men.

The two men were to serve together again in a third campaign—in the Sudan from 1884 to 1885—where Buller once more demonstrated both unusual bravery and his ability as a commander. By now, however, Buller was forty-five and there were signs of the hedonistic tendencies that were to be heavily criticized in later years. Some jealous-minded officer, not in Wolseley's "Ring", counted forty camels in Buller's personal baggage train.

This was Buller's last appearance on the field of battle before Colenso, and the formation he led consisted of only a brigade. And this lack of command experience was used as an argument by Buller himself against his appointment as Commander-in-Chief in South

Africa. In response to Lansdowne's initial soundings, made as early as June, he noted:

"I said that I had never actually held an independent command, that a war in South Africa, if one occurred, would be a big thing, and that I could only say with regard to the command of it (that) I thought (that) Lord Wolseley as Commander-in-Chief and myself as Chief of Staff, was the best I could recommend for the war in South Africa. I said that I always considered that I was better as second in a complex military affair than as the officer in chief command."

Such was the background of the Commander-in-Chief who finally disembarked at Capetown on 31st October 1899. Fifteen years of comfort in Cork, Whitehall and Aldershot, following a quarter century suffering the rigours and hazards of campaigning on three continents, was probably enough to turn any man's thoughts to the good things of life. For among Buller's personal equipment unloaded on to the dockside was a hip-bath, a full-sized bed and prodigious quantities of champagne.

The Commander-in-Chief certainly needed some form of comfort, for the news he received on arrival in Capetown was far too grave to be assuaged by the cheering crowds and a triumphal drive up Adderley Street in Milner's coach. Details of the disasters at Nicholson's Nek and Lombard's Kop the day before were still incomplete, but the main facts were clear. The Royal Irish Fusiliers, the Gloucestershire Regiment and the 10th Mountain Battery had been lost and Ladysmith almost totally encircled. In Cape Colony itself, Kimberley and Mafeking were under siege. Small wonder that half-way up Adderley Street Buller relaxed his confident military smile and turned to Milner. "So now I am expected to conquer all South Africa—not just two small Boer republics," he said.

This was not at all what Buller had been bargaining for, as he and his staff had pored over maps on *Dunottar Castle* during the previous two weeks. Nor indeed was it in line with the situation the War Office had believed would exist in South Africa at the time of Buller's arrival, and upon which British strategic plans had been based. London had envisaged a direct thrust through Bloemfontein to Pretoria launched from the Cape midlands, taking advantage of the promise of neutrality given by President Steyn of the Orange Free State. This strategy, based on an advance through the Free State, had a twofold advantage over the very much shorter Durban–Pretoria route. The British could utilize three separate supply bases at the ports of Capetown, Port Elizabeth and East London, each with road and rail routes northwards to the target area. It also avoided passage through northern Natal, with its unhappy memories of British defeats at Majuba, Laing's Nek and Schuinshoogte in 1881.

Throughout November, Buller and Milner saw a great deal of each other. The two men had little in common but their patriotism and, sometimes, their recognition of each other's special difficulties. The one had by far the greater part of his army locked up in Ladysmith and the other his source of wealth—and Cecil Rhodes—in Kimberley. For both, the entry of the Free State into the war on 1st November and the threat of a Boer uprising in the Cape itself only added to their anxieties.

Milner must have been as dissatisfied with the communications received from Kimberley as Buller was with the news coming out of Ladysmith.

From the Ladysmith front, Buller heard a rather fuller account of the "three battles" announced so cryptically from the steamship *Australasian* and was finding it hard to square the facts of Talana Hill, Elandslaagte and Rietfontein with the simple notion of "Boers defeated", "Boers engaged" might have been a more apt description. General White's telegram from Ladysmith on 28th October was also far from reassuring:

"Have a very strong force in front of me with many guns. Natal Colony requires earliest reinforcements possible. Troops here very heavy work, especially cavalry. I will do all my means admit of to conquer enemy. Hunter indispensable."

To describe Hunter, actually assigned by the War Office as Buller's Chief-of-Staff, as indispensable, must have sounded strange, coming from a war zone where the situation was visibly deteriorating and the chances of Hunter suffering the same fate as Penn Symons reasonably good. Buller must have been sorely tempted to think that he was not only being cheated out of his senior staff officer and effective deputy, but also that White perhaps lacked the qualities of leadership needed in a rapidly deteriorating situation. The news of "Mournful Monday" did nothing to increase Buller's confidence in White; neither did the exchange of telegrams during the next few days.

From these telegrams Buller finally understood—perhaps later than he should have—that White's Ladysmith garrison could not be counted on to defend Durban and Natal, apart from defending themselves and so pinning down a sizable Boer force in the process. Buller's final request to White for a contribution of one infantry battalion and a cavalry regiment was not complied with. But, as a token gesture, White did send General French out of Ladysmith at the eleventh hour, and Buller left it at that. He had other worries to contend with.

Emboldened by the Transvaalers' successes on the Natal front and spurred on by Pretoria's appeals for Boer solidarity, President Steyn revoked his pledge of non-intervention, and, on 1st November, his commandos crossed the Orange river. Rayne Kruger described the scene:

"The invaders advanced into village after village, where they were received with cheers, flowers and recruits. They hoisted the Republican flag, made fiery speeches, and rode on. Local parsons fanned the embers of revolt with exhortations from the pulpit. A theological seminary closed down because the students rushed to join the commandos."

With the Natal Field Force trapped at Ladysmith, Buller was short of troops—his army corps being still on the high seas—and the Free State commandos were now depriving him of territory. Their line of march was towards Naauwpoort, Stormberg and de Aar—each one a vital railway junction for the ports of Cape Province. So much for the War Office plan and the march on Pretoria.

But worse was to come—from Kimberley, where the imperious Cecil Rhodes found himself trapped by the Boers he so despised. Together with the other directors of the mighty de Beers Consolidated Company, he composed a telegram which was dispatched directly to the High Commissioner. It read:

"We hope with arrival of General Buller measures will be taken for the relief of this place. Our information which is reliable, gives not more than 2,000 to 3,000 Boers between this place and Orange River, and in our opinion we could already have been relieved without risk by the present force in Cape Colony. We have a very limited supply of coal, and when it is done we must close down the works, which will cause serious trouble among our 10,000 savages in our compounds, who are now kept quiet by being kept at work. If we discharge them, and send them home, they are sure to be driven back to the town by the Boers, which must lead to heavy loss of life. As to the question of food supply, though well-provided with some things, we have only nine days' tinned meat in case cattle are taken by the Boers, which, of course, is probable. We do not know the reasons which have delayed our relief, but we think Your Excellency ought to weigh the risks caused by delay to this place with its 30,000 inhabitants, 10,000 of whom are raw savages. Now the General has arrived we respectfully request to be informed as to the policy to be adopted regarding our relief, so as to enable us to take our own steps in case relief is refused. We are sending this by special messenger to Orange River, and will await your reply."

Milner and Buller were both far from amused by this communication, which they not unreasonably construed as a thinly-veiled threat that the authors reserved the right to negotiate their own terms with the Queen's enemies if their demands were not satisfied. In addition, Milner and Buller were irked by the fact that neither the Kimberley civil authorities nor Colonel R. G. Kekewich, the commander of the small garrison, seemed to have been consulted. But the pressure from Kimberley continued unabated. Other telegrams poured in—from the Legislative Assembly, from the Mayor and from Rhodes himself. All pointed to the desperate plight of the town; some hinted darkly at surrender; and each assessed differently from the next the size of the Boer force outside. Only Kekewich was resolute and confident.

Buller realized that the bluster, the touch of fantasy and the fear in these first messages from Kimberley would soon become reality unless something was done to meet Rhodes' demands. The question was what, and, in making the decision, the magic of Rhodes' name left Buller little choice. Neither Windsor, Whitehall, nor, in fairness, his own military judgement would allow him to let the towns fall. Their relief would proceed as speedily as possible and so would that of Mafeking, where the beleaguered Colonel Baden-Powell made no complaint and demanded nothing.

This plan, however, depended on one factor outside Buller's control—the Boers. Would they wait until his army corps arrived? Happily for Britain and for Buller, they were in no hurry to press home their advantage. While Joubert camped grandly and comfortably around Ladysmith, Barry Hertzog and the Free State commandos were ranging across a vast front south of the Orange River from which

Reinforcements leaving for the front. The defeats suffered by the British before his arrival, combined with the lack of troops in the country, meant that Buller had soon to reshape his strategic plans. (National Army Museum)

they could have thrust deep down into the Western Cape. But they chose not to do so, and de la Rey, directing operations against Kimberley, made no move either. In the meantime, the ocean ferry service from Britain had got under way.

The troopship *Kildonan Castle* was one of the first to cast off from Southampton docks, carrying the 1st Battalion of the Black Watch, the 2nd Battalion of the Northumberland Fusiliers, some sappers and two Companies of the Welch Regiment. By 23rd October, 21,000 men

had been embarked in a dozen ships, and those on board *Kildonan Castle* were already being decimated by sea-sickness in the Bay of Biscay. To their sufferings was added yet another, described by Colonel Rees Banfield of the Welch Regiment:

"The medical officer pinches up a great piece of loose flesh in your side, drives in a hypodermic syringe, and injects about a teaspoonful of nasty yellow-looking liquid, having first boiled the syringe in oil to kill any possible

Horses, too, had to be sent from Britain to the Cape. A cavalry shortage soon hampered the efforts of the British army in the field. (National Army Museum)

germ that might obtain entrance to your body through the syringe. What follows is different in different men. Some are knocked over within ten minutes, turn green and blue, collapse and go to bed. Others feel more or less seedy, but stick it out."

Many of the superstitious Aberdonians from the Black Watch would sooner have contracted typhoid than be protected against it by this new-fangled treatment. On most ships it became a worse breach of etiquette to brush against a man's left side than to tread on his toes.

On some ships, enterprising officers arranged target practice using bottles and empty boxes thrown overboard, bobbing elusively and always retreating in the ship's wake. On *Orient*, there were musical concerts with choral performances twice a day. Many ships were inevitably subject to complaints, both real and fanciful, about the quality of the food, and such was the resultant abstinence on board *Armenian* that one of the men predicted that any Boers who came too close would be transfixed by the bones protruding from the soldiers' bodies. There were no complaints from *Malta* and those on board *Diaki* also ate well. *Dilwara*'s organized line-crossing games, complete with the unaccustomed pleasure of playful persecution of the officers, were particularly well-reported on.

Of all the ships, only one came to grief on the long voyage. This was the *Ismore*, which failed to live up to the expectations of a singularly auspicious send-off at Birkenhead, where three dukes, two earls, their attendant wives, and the military attaches of Italy, France and Germany turned up to wave good-bye. She foundered in Table Bay and, though none of the men perished, the guns and 500 terrified horses went down with the ship.

Roslin Castle was the first to arrive in Capetown on 9th November, with Major-General Hildyard and his staff on board. By the end of the month, 50,000 men had arrived in South Africa, and the first-comers had already been committed to action.

The situation as it existed in South Africa was compelling Buller to split up his force as it arrived. He had already abandoned the original unitary plan. Now each arriving unit was assigned to one or other of his individual force commanders. A division was formed under General Lord Methuen and was sent off towards Orange River Station with instructions to relieve Kimberley, and so relieve Milner from the persistent clamouring of Rhodes, which he found so upsetting. "If Kimberley falls, everything goes," had been the clarion call from that quarter for some time. A mounted column, commanded by General French, was dispatched northwards as a "flying column" to intercept and disperse any Free State commandos penetrating into Cape Colony itself. General Gatacre, sent on by sea to East London, was to assist in this defensive role. His instructions were to proceed with what was left of his division—two brigades having been sent by Buller to Natal—in the general direction of the north-eastern Cape beyond Queenstown, where the Free State commandos were already stirring up rebellion and enlisting recruits from among the local population. General Hildyard was dispatched with his brigade across country to Port Elizabeth and thence by sea to Durban. From there, he was ordered northwards through Pietermaritzburg to the Natal front. He was followed by Generals Clery, Hart, Barton and Lyttelton, with such remnants of their original brigades that had not been diverted elsewhere.

This, then, was the general situation on 21st November. It may have been clear to Buller, because he communicated it to London, but very few in South Africa seemed to know exactly what was going on. The following day, Buller himself left for Natal, without warning some say, but having clearly concluded that the relief of Ladysmith had first call on his energies as Commander-in-Chief. He had obviously calculated that Methuen would now take care of Kimberley, that French and Gatacre would look after the Cape and that, soon, they would all join up in a grand advance on Pretoria, by which time Mafeking would have liberated itself.

Historians still dispute whether or not Buller told enough of the right people what was going on in his mind, but there is no doubt that his three weeks in Capetown were well spent. He arrived to find his Chief-of-Staff virtually confiscated by White, all his intelligence officers with South African experience locked up in Ladysmith, and a total railway staff of Colonel Girouard, one batman and a groom. There was a chronic shortage of horses and mules and, in addition, the constant irritant of Milner breathing down his neck about the danger of uprisings amongst the sizable Boer "fifth column" in Cape Colony.

The most acute problem of all, according to Buller himself, was the shortage of time. "Ever since I have been here," he told General Walker before leaving for Natal, "I have been like a man who, with a long day's work before him, overslept himself and so was late for everything all day." Yet, during this period, he and his depleted staff organized the reception, equipping, briefing and dispatch of 50,000 men—together with their arms and their supplies—to four separate war fronts, dispersed over an area as large as central Europe. By any standard, this was a brilliant feat of organization, particularly as the four sea-port supply bases were spread over a thousand miles of coast and each of them was 300 miles distant along single-track railway from its target railhead in the hinterland.

Although Milner was reported to have been taken aback by Buller's sudden departure from Capetown, he probably was quite glad to see him go. And so probably, but for less personal reasons, were the staff officers he left behind—Colonel A. S. Wynne doing General Hunter's job as Chief-of-Staff, Colonel à Court in charge of recruiting local volunteers and Major Byng in command of the South African Light Horse. Most of the other staff officers were quite junior, the senior ones having been packed off to command various formations at the front. General Elliot Wood (Commander, Royal Engineers) went to take over at Orange River, General Miles to de Aar, and Colonel Douglas to join Lord Methuen.

Buller arrived in Pietermaritzburg on 25th November and stayed there for ten days organizing the main part of his Ladysmith Relief Force, while the forward troops stayed under the command of General Clery at Frere. On 2nd December, he sent a dispatch to the War Office declaring his intention of moving up to Frere shortly and giving details of the force assembling there. By 7th December 1899, Buller estimated, he would be ready to go forth and relieve Ladysmith, just 25 miles away. He calculated that it should take him two weeks; it took him nearly three months.

12 The Chieveley Incident

"It had been my intention to get into Ladysmith where I knew Ian Hamilton would look after me and give me a good show." (Winston S. Churchill, *My Early Life,* **London 1930)**

Winston Churchill (seated second from left) returning as a war correspondent from South Africa. His Boer War exploits laid the foundations of his national reputation. (National Army Museum)

While Lieutenant Pomeroy of the 5th Dragoon Guards was passing the time in besieged Ladysmith with Gibbon's *Decline and Fall of the Roman Empire,* another cavalryman, Winston Churchill, late of the 4th Hussars, was becoming bored with life at the British forward position at Estcourt. Profoundly well connected and, at the age of twenty-five, already a skilful practitioner in the art of manipulating influential

contacts, Churchill had secured terms as a war correspondent which were probably the most lucrative that any journalist had received up to that date. On 18th September 1899, when Alfred Harmsworth, the proprietor of the London *Daily Mail*, offered Churchill the post of South African correspondent for his paper, Churchill immediately sent a telegram to Oliver Borthwick of the *Morning Post*. The same day he was able to tell his mother, Lady Randolph Churchill, that, after only a few hours of negotiation, he had accepted the *Morning Post*'s offer of £250 a month, plus all expenses. A month's pay for Sir Redvers Buller, the 60-year-old British Commander-in-Chief designate, was about £200.

With a prodigious appetite for "fixing things" and an extensive range of well-placed friends of the family to help him, albeit reluctantly at times, Churchill set about the task of earning both his keep and, if possible, a reputation as well, with immense energy. He persuaded Joseph Chamberlain, the Colonial Secretary, to provide letters of introduction to Alfred Milner and other members of the British establishment in South Africa, looked into the question of investing money in a biograph machine—the precursor of the modern ciné camera—and contrived to obtain a passage on the *Dunottar Castle*, the same ship that carried Buller and his staff to South Africa.

Nor did Churchill neglect the creature comforts of life. The order placed with Randolph Payne and Sons, a distinguished firm of London wine merchants, a week before the sailing date might well seem generous for a young man whose tour of duty was only expected to last four months.

	6 October, 1899	61 St. James's St. S.W. (per dozen)	£	s	d
6 bottles 1889 Vin d'Ay sec		110/-	2	15	0
18 bottles St. Emilion		24/-	1	16	0
6 bottles light Port		42/-	1	1	0
6 bottles French Vermouth		36/-		18	0
18 bottles Scotch Whiskey (10 years old)		48/-	3	12	0
6 bottles Very Old Eau de Vie landed 1866		160/-	4	0	0
6 × 1 dozen cases for same, packing, marking etc				10	0
Cartage, dock charges and Insce.				13	0
			£16	0	0

Sent by *SS Dunottar Castle*
to South Africa

Within a month, Pomeroy and his fellow officers in beleaguered Ladysmith were to be paying nearly as much for a tin of sardines as Payne's prices to Churchill for a single bottle of vintage whisky, and by 21st February 1900 Mr. Dyson, the Ladysmith auctioneer, was quoting £195 for a case of Scotch which, if challenged, he almost certainly could not have produced.

But it was not for the good things of life that Churchill had come to South Africa. Possessed by a sense of urgency of which he detected no trace in General Buller, Churchill conspired with J. B. Atkins of the *Manchester Guardian* to hurry across to Natal, leaving Cape Town and the General Staff to politics and planning. The journey was both hazardous by rail to East London, with Free State commandos poised to over-run the line in several places, and utterly sickening by sea from East London to Durban. Atkins was composed enough to record his impressions of the voyage on the 150-ton coaster *Umzimvubu*:

"At the first wave the little Umzimvubu *tilted up her nose, and skipped across it with scarcely a quiver, but the next she took with a gasp and a heave, burying her nose in the third, which in its turn picked her high up and threw her on the fourth; and the fourth accepted her with a shout, and cast her out into the bay on her side . . . She would climb slowly up one wave on her side, flop somehow over the top, and slide down the decline on her other side. She would also shoot downhill with a circular stabbing motion of her bows as though not quite certain where to strike in the trough of the seas, and her masts would pencil the most fantastic figures on the sky. When she did dive her nose into the sea, the water burst over the bows, and her bows coming up with a jerk, seemed to throw it back on to the bridge as an elephant spurts water behind it."*

But for Churchill, prostrated for twenty-four hours in an agony of sea-sickness, the experience was both horrifying and unforgettable. Thirty years later, he described it as

"a recollection which, in the jingle of the Bab Ballads,
'I shall carry to the catacombs of age,
Photographically lined
On the tablets of my mind
When a yesterday has faded from its page.'"

However, Churchill did finally arrive safely at Estcourt, a day by train from Durban. There he found several old friends, notably Leo Amery, the correspondent for *The Times*, who was later to produce the monumental *Times History of the War in South Africa*. But, as yet, there was little military activity and Churchill, according to his own account, was pining for action. This wish was soon to be satisfied through a chance meeting with Captain (later General Sir Aylmer) Haldane. An acquaintance of Churchill's from the Tirah campaign, Haldane was now nursing a foot wound received at the battle of Elandslaagte and waiting until the tiny force he was part of at Estcourt became a big army—big enough to march on Ladysmith.

It was the 14th November and Louis Botha, under the watchful tutelage of his Commandant-General, was not far away. The Boers had crossed the Tugela that morning at Colenso and when one of

Botha's patrols was sighted near Estcourt, the garrison was nearly stampeded back to Pietermaritzburg. "That evening, walking in the single street of the town," wrote Churchill, "whom should I meet but Captain Haldane." Their separate records of this encounter were written many years later and are slightly at variance on the question of Churchill's reaction to Haldane's proposition. This was that the young journalist should accompany Haldane's troops on the next day's reconnaissance by armoured train to the north. As Churchill put it:

"Haldane told me on the night of the 14th November of the task which had been set for him and on which he was to start at dawn. He did not conceal his misgivings on the imprudence of the exercise, but he was of course, like anyone else at the beginning of a war, very keen upon adventure and a brush with the enemy . . . Out of comradeship and because I thought it was my duty to gather as much information as I could for the Morning Post, *also because I was eager for trouble, I accepted the invitation without demur."*

Haldane remembered it slightly differently:

"As I came out of the office (of Colonel Long, in temporary command at Estcourt) feeling rather lugubrious I noticed Churchill who, as well as some other correspondents, was hanging about to pick up such crumbs of information for his newspaper as might be available. I told him what I had been ordered to do and, aware that he had been out in the train before and knew something of the country through which it was wont to travel, suggested that he might care to accompany me the next day. Although he was not at all keen he consented to do so, and arranged to be at the station in time for the start."

In fact it was almost certainly Churchill's first trip on the train and at 4.30 in the morning of Wednesday 15th November, he woke up Atkins with whom he was sharing a tent and told him he was going. Atkins, who had watched the entraining performance the previous day, had more sense and went back to bed. His account of the daily diversion of watching the train's departure explains why:

"It was not really an armoured train at all; it was not an armoured train, that is to say, with trap doors and proper outlets for the muzzles of Maxim guns. It was made up of an ordinary engine and ordinary iron trucks belonging to the Natal government railway protected by boiler plates; and through the boiler plates were cut loopholes for the rifles. The trucks had no roofs. To get in or out of the trucks one had to climb over the walls. It was fun to see a small and clumsy climber pushed up from the inside by his comrades, then squirm preposterously on his stomach over the wall and drop or scramble down the seven feet on the outside. I used to imagine the men under heavy fire performing their slow and painful acrobatic feat to get out of their cage.
The train, in short, was a death trap."

It is highly unlikely that Atkins, or anybody else in Estcourt, got much more sleep that night. The rumble of artillery was heard from the north shortly after seven o'clock and Atkins, accompanied by Leo

Amery, set off on foot along the railway line in the direction of the firing:

"About two miles from Estcourt we heard the shrill whistle of the armoured train among the hills, and not long afterwards it appeared out of a gully close to us—but, behold, an armoured train no longer; only the armoured engine and a tender, and these crowded with clinging men! Men stood on the footplate of the engine, sat on the cowcatcher in front, and hung on to the sides of the tender; and when we ran to the track they waved their arms and pointed backwards and threw up their arms again, like men who would signalize something horrible. They were nearly all plate-layers."

The story of what had happened is well documented. The armoured train was ambushed in the way which Haldane, among others, had thought was inevitable. "Before I went to sleep that night," he wrote, "I lay for some time thinking what I would do should the Boers ambush the train and cause it to leave the rails."

The train which left Estcourt in drizzle and mist at five o'clock that November morning consisted of three armoured trucks, one before and two after the engine and tender, preceded by an ordinary truck containing a nine-pounder muzzle-loading naval gun and a detachment of sailors from HMS *Tartar*. Coupled on at the rear was a breakdown truck, manned by a party of platelayers. As many as possible of the Dublin Fusiliers assigned to Haldane climbed into the leading armoured truck and the remainder joined the Durban Light Infantry in the two trucks behind the engine. Churchill, eager to secure the best possible observation position, joined Haldane in the leading truck. In all, 164 men were on board as the train steamed slowly out of the station.

It took an hour to reach Frere, ten miles away, and, after a short platform consultation with some Natal Mounted Police who reported the presence of Boers at Chieveley, the train was ordered to move in that direction. There, the first signs of Boer activity were seen and a hasty telegraph was dispatched to Colonel Long, back in Estcourt. Long replied "Remain at Frere in observation guarding your safe retreat. Remember that Chieveley station was last night occupied by the enemy. Do not put faith in information obtained from native sources."

With this disquieting news, Haldane began to wish that he had never proceeded further. But, though he blamed only himself in his autobiography, he noted that had it not been for the ardour of his "impetuous young friend", he might have thought twice about throwing himself "into the lion's jaws by going almost to the Tugela".

Haldane ordered an immediate retreat and the train rapidly puffed its way back down the line towards Frere. Then, as it climbed a ridge about two miles short of its destination, the first Boer shells burst over it. Churchill got a quick glimpse of the Boer artillery before the driver put on full steam downhill, as bullets from the rifles of Louis Botha's Wakkerstroom and Krugersdorp commandos splattered on the steel sides of the armoured trucks.

It seemed for a moment as though the prey was going to escape its hunters. But, in fact, the driver's increase in speed played straight into Boer hands, for, three-quarters of a mile from Frere at the foot of the gradient, the line had been blocked by a huge stone. When the train hit it at forty miles an hour, the leading truck with the platelayers was overturned and the two armoured cars carrying the Durban Light Infantry were completely derailed, one of them coming to rest athwart the line.

Churchill was in action at last, scarcely a month after he had left home. For the British were not "long left in the comparative peace and safety of a railway accident." While Haldane endeavoured to provide covering fire, Churchill took charge of the track-clearing operations. The Navy's 9-pounder was soon out of action and Churchill had trouble with the breakdown crew, who, not surprisingly, were reluctant to buckle down to the task of clearing the line. After an hour, by a process of butting and pulling, the locomotive was forced past the obstructing truck, which then fell back across the line.

This was not Churchill's first experience of warfare by any means, but here was a composite scene of horror, farce and indignity, heightened by danger and challenge, all rather different from the simple, heady exhilaration of the cavalry charge he had taken part in at Omdurman. He was struck by the hideous sight of a soldier's arm shattered to pulp by a shell with the untouched, perfect hand still hanging at the end. Later, somebody stood on Haldane's fingers while he was hanging precariously to the train, causing him to fall sprawling to the ground, his untied puttees entangling his feet. But Churchill found the sheer desperation and danger of it all sublimely exciting:

"Nothing was so thrilling as this; to wait and struggle among those clanging, rending iron boxes, with the repeated explosions of the shells and the artillery, the noise of the projectiles striking the ears, the hiss as they passed in the air, the grunting and pulling of the engine—poor tortured thing—hammered by at least a dozen shells, any one of which, by penetrating the boiler, might have made an end to all—the expectation of destruction, the realization of powerlessness and the alternations of hope and despair—all this for seventy minutes by the clock with only four inches of twisted ironwork to make the difference between danger, captivity and shame on the one hand—safety, freedom and triumph on the other."

The engine and tender were sent off to safety with the wounded and Haldane rallied his surviving soldiers to make a dash for some houses a few hundred yards away. But there was no cover and the troops were soon dispersed and surrounded by the Boers, to whom Haldane, Lieutenant Frankland of the Royal Dublin Fusiliers and 50 men surrendered. Churchill had ridden off on the engine but, realizing after a few hundred yards that he might be missing something, got off and returned to the fray:

"Suddenly on the other side of the railway, separated from me by the rails and two uncut wire fences, I saw a horseman galloping furiously, a tall dark figure, holding his rifle in his right hand. He pulled up his horse almost in its own length and shaking the rifle at me shouted a loud command. We were forty yards apart. That morning I had taken with me, correspondent-status notwithstanding, my Mauser pistol. I thought I could kill this man, and after the treatment I had received I earnestly desired to do so. I put my hand to my belt, the pistol was not there. When engaged in

clearing the line, getting in and out of the engine, etc., I had taken it off. It came safely home on the engine. I have it now. But at this moment I was quite unarmed. Meanwhile I suppose in about the time this takes to tell, the Boer horseman, still seated on his horse, had covered me with his rifle. The animal stood stock still, so did he, and so did I. I looked towards the river, I looked towards the platelayer's hut. The Boer continued to look along his sights. I thought there was absolutely no chance of escape. If he fired he would surely hit me, so I held up my hands and surrendered myself a prisoner of war."

At this point, however, mythology begins. There were none competent to comment—from Haldane in command of the troops to Walden the family retainer—who did not testify to Churchill's immense sense of purpose and outstanding gallantry on that miserable morning. There was even talk of his being recommended for the Victoria Cross. And yet Churchill's own record of the event ends with a fairy tale.

"Don't you recognize me?" asked General Botha three years after the war, when he and Churchill met in London, "I was that man. It was I who took you prisoner. I myself."

This at least was the exchange as reported by Churchill. The euphoria of the occasion, a good lunch during a goodwill mission with former enemies now at peace, as well as the mood of reconciliation which possessed these two great statesmen in the making could account for the misunderstanding. So also could the language problem, for Botha's English was shaky at that time and Churchill's Afrikaans was non-existent. But misunderstanding or calculated self-deception was certainly what it was.

One historian of repute, Dr. J. H. Breytenbach, favours the cause of Chris van Veijeren of the Krugersdorp commando as Churchill's

captor and, indeed, van Veijeren's sworn statement testifying to this is held in the Pretoria State Archives. But a great deal more convincing is the evidence of Captain Danie Theron, in charge of dispatch riders at Colenso at the time of the Chieveley incident. He reported on 28th November in a telegram to Pretoria that representations from the captive Churchill to the Transvaal government demanding recognition as an unarmed non-combatant should be disregarded. "These are all lies," said Theron, having described quite accurately the part played by Churchill in the armoured train affair. "He also refused to stand still when Field-Cornet Oosthuizen warned him to give himself up. Only when the Field-Cornet levelled his rifle at him did he surrender."

The exact identity of the "tall, dark horseman" to whom Churchill surrendered might now seem a matter of little consequence. It was almost certainly Oosthuizen, the "Red Bull of Krugersdorp" who was killed later in the war, and even more surely it was not Louis Botha. But it is a touching reflection of the deep mutual respect and life-long friendship that developed between the two men that for twenty years until he died as the Prime Minister of the Union of South Africa, Botha "went along" with the myth of this first meeting, while Churchill carried it to the grave as a much-cherished illusion.

All this was in the future, as Churchill, Haldane and the other British prisoners were marched off by their Boer captors. However, Churchill did not stay long in captivity. Within two months he had escaped from prison, reached safety and got back to Natal again to embark on another attempt at relieving Ladysmith. In the meantime Buller, almost as though waiting for him, had not advanced far, while Joubert offered less cash reward for his recapture than General White's officers were paying for a bottle of Scotch. "He is just 'n Klein Koerant-skrywertjie", said Joubert, but nobody told Churchill what it meant. "A little bit of a newspaperman" would be a rough translation.

A Boer laager. The wagon on the right suggests they may be the Fordsburg commando.

13 December Sorties

"The news of your deed is now ringing through the Empire."
(General Sir George White, 8th December 1899)

Melton Prior. Ladysmith Dec -99

An Old Boer saves Capt Paleys life, who lies wounded on the ground—

November had been a sombre month in Ladysmith. For the troops it was a question of maintaining vigilance in conditions of monotony, broken only by the rumble of the Boer guns. As Lieutenant-Colonel C. W. Park, commanding the Devons, wrote:

"We just sit here day after day and week after week, doing nothing except eat our hearts out, and wondering how much longer it is to go on. Now that the building work in the posts is pretty well finished, there is not much to do at night beyond small repairs and improvements, and I am generally in bed

A war artist's impression of the action at Surprise Hill. The old Boer (left) is saving the life of a British officer.

by nine. Up every morning at 3.30, and as soon as day dawns I start round all the posts and see if everything is all right and what they want, and then stay up watching for Boers till about 6.30, and then down to breakfast—tough beef, bread and jam (of which there is lots). Then any little work there may be about the camp; more watching for Boers and more boredom until tiffin at 12.45. After that I generally try to find a sheltered corner and snooze for a bit, but am mostly routed up by people with chits or staff officers wanting things done. Then at 4.30 tea, followed by another round of the posts to settle work to be done after dusk; dinner at seven—soup, more tough beef, bread and cheese—and bed."

Others were more philosophical, and for Bella Craw it was a positive thrill when "a real live lord" came to Vine Lodge for Sunday afternoon tennis. "He is very tall and wears an eyeglass and his name is Lord Creighton." She also explained how realists like Colonel Royston and some of the other officers came to be in possession of tennis racquets in the middle of a siege—"commandeered I am afraid from some of the deserted houses, to say nothing of the shoes." Indeed, sport seemed to be the order of the day. The Gordon Highlanders seized the opportunity provided by the smoke of a Boer shell on their football pitch to score a sneak goal against the Imperial Light Horse. The Natal Carbineers relied mainly on cricket as a diversion, while the cavalry managed the occasional game of polo for as long as their ponies still had the strength to carry them. In the 5th Dragoon Guards, Lieutenant Pomeroy and his fellow officers discovered a new gambling game called "Clock", which made an enjoyable alternative to baccarat. And all this time General White worried about Boer spies, who, he was coming to think, were aware of all his plans before he could implement them.

There were rumblings of discontent as well. Mr. G. W. Willis, no longer Mayor of Ladysmith but still self-appointed spokesman for the town's civilians whenever there were disputes with the military, came close to being locked up at times. He was particularly outspoken about the requisitioning of private stocks of food, drink and other provisions. Despite a massive build-up of army supplies in Ladysmith before the outbreak of war, Colonels Ward and Stoneman—in an act of great foresight—impounded the large privately-owned stocks of grain and livestock some time before hoarding was recognized as a wise personal precaution and rationing became a public necessity.

This was not Willis' only complaint. He claimed to have exerted pressure on White to take action against the Boer siege guns positioned around Ladysmith. His advocacy, combined with the effect of an anonymous and fiercely-worded poster, was, Willis believed, the factor which finally roused the army from its state of torpor. But, in fact, General Hunter's ride across Ladysmith during the afternoon of Thursday 7th December 1899, to discuss with Colonel Royston plans for a raid that night, is unlikely to have had anything to do with Willis. The initiative probably came from Hunter himself, encouraged by Colonels Ian Hamilton and Henry Rawlinson.

Preparations for the raid were made with great secrecy, although Bella Craw guessed that there was something in the wind when "Uncle George" (Major G. Tatham, one of the chosen guides) failed to come in and say goodnight. At 10.15 pm 500 men of the Natal Carbineers,

Border Mounted Rifles and Natal Police under Colonel Royston assembled quietly near Devonshire Post. They were joined by 100 men of the Imperial Light Horse, under Colonel A. H. Edwards, and Major D. Henderson with a few of the Corps of Guides, as well as a detachment of Royal Engineers under Captain G. H. Fowke. Here, they reported to Hunter, who was in overall command. The Devons had already been sent out half a mile to take up a covering position to the north of Helpmekaar ridge.

The column proceeded eastwards along the Helpmekaar road for about a mile and then were led across open scrub country for another mile by Major Henderson. Finally, they halted at the foot of Gun Hill—the flat-topped feature they were soon to attack. It was not men they were after that night, but guns—the 6-inch Creusot and a 4.7-inch howitzer—both of which had been exceedingly troublesome over the previous few weeks. A measure of Hunter's control, Henderson's navigational precision and the discipline of all ranks was the undetected arrival of 650 men at the right place at 2 am in pitch darkness within 300 yards of their target.

Then the ascent began, a 250-foot scramble up the boulder-strewn slope with Hunter, the I.L.H. and the sappers in the middle of the line, and the Natal Volunteers on the flanks. A startled, piercing cry of "Wie daar?" was followed by a volley from the summit and battle was

Officers of the Imperial Light Horse (I.L.H.) under the command of Colonel A. H. Edwards (centre). They played a major part in the British success at Gun Hill.

joined. It did not last long. "Fix bayonets!" shouted Colonel Edwards and the order was taken up by Major Karri Davies on the left. It was an effective ruse, for, in fact, none of the I.L.H. were carrying bayonets with them. The Boers were taking no chances, however, and beat a hasty retreat. The raiders reached the deserted summit with no further resistance.

Once more, it was up to Edwards. He and the guides groped their way across the plateau, closely followed by Captain Fowke, Lieutenant Turner and the sappers, with the explosive charges draped about their necks. The 6-inch "Long Tom" and the 4.7-inch howitzer were 150 yards apart, each behind a mountain of sandbags. Sledge hammers were used on the breech screws and gun-cotton charges placed down the muzzles and up the breeches of the two guns. Two loud explosions followed and, after a swift assessment of the damage by the light of a lantern, the job was over. It remained only to carry back the trophies—an automatic Maxim gun and the sights and 80 lb. breech block of the Creusot. By 7 am the raiders were back in Ladysmith, a few of them wounded, including Major Henderson, and one dead.

Less rewarding, but equally stimulating to the defenders' morale, were the simultaneous raids made by others to the north and northeast. Colonel Knox, with three companies of Liverpools and a squadron of the 19th Hussars, occupied Limit Hill and advanced up the Newcastle road almost as far as Pepworth. The Hussars pushed on further still and reached the point where the road and railway almost touch. Meeting no resistance, they could think of nothing better to do than cut the telegraph lines from Lombard's Kop to Joubert's headquarters and set fire to a few huts.

But Colonel Knox, reluctant to return empty-handed, had far more ambitious thoughts. At 3 am he sent a message back to Ladysmith appealing for the immediate dispatch of the cavalry brigade to launch a lightning raid on Joubert's camp at Modder Spruit. The idea appealed to White, but, by the time the 5th Lancers, 18th Hussars, 5th Dragoon Guards and 53rd Battery Royal Artillery moved off, dawn had broken and the element of surprise had been lost. The opportunity was lost and so were three men; 25 others were wounded in the canter back to Ladysmith.

The Leicesters, however, had a disappointing time. A march in the dark to Hyde's Farm, halfway to Nicholson's Nek, revealed no sign of the enemy and they returned without a shot being fired.

The Boer reaction was swift and indignant, each of the commanders on the spot looking for a scapegoat to blame for the loss of the artillery on Gun Hill. Not surprisingly, the first to break the news to Commandant-General Joubert, at that moment sick in Volksrust, was the director of communications at the Boer headquarters. Less than an hour later, at 9.30 in the morning of 8th December, General Erasmus went one further and sent a telegram to the State President in Pretoria, reminding him that the incident took place in General Schalk Burger's sector and that the mounted force in his own—the uneventful dawn sortie by the British cavalry—had been successfully repulsed. By midday in a further telegram—this time to Joubert—Erasmus had identified a major of his own name and a Commandant Weilbach as the guilty parties—both of them, Erasmus was happy to add, serving under acting Commandant-General Burger's direct command. By

3.30 pm, the unfortunate Major P. E. Erasmus was himself telegraphing to Pretoria:

"From: Major Erasmus, H.Q. Ladysmith
To: The President, Pretoria
To my great sorrow I have to inform Your Honour that at 1.30 am a raid was carried out by the English. They completely destroyed one of the 15½ cm cannons and a 12 cm howitzer with dynamite. Be assured, however, that the Artillery, both officers and men, have acquitted themselves magnificently, but confronted without any warning or the least help, by an overwhelming superiority of 500 men, the twenty artillerymen under my command were forced to retire. We hope to do our duty further, but with better support from the burghers. The affair will surely be investigated by a court of enquiry."

For two days the telegraph wires between Pretoria, Volksrust and

A Boer "Long Tom".
This is almost certainly the gun damaged by the British raiding party on 7th December 1899. The gun was later repaired by the Boers and is seen here on its way to Mafeking.

Modder Spruit hummed with accusations of negligence, counter charges and further recriminations. Major Erasmus, Commandant Weilbach and two other officers were suspended from duty pending a court of inquiry to be conducted by the Transvaal State Attorney, Jan Christian Smuts. General Burger was himself reprimanded by Joubert for his injudicious use of the word "unexpected" in his description of the British attack. "I fully concur with the Government," he told Burger, "that the word 'unexpected' does not or should not exist in a state of war."

But these exchanges were rudely interrupted, for, on the night of 10th December, the British did it again.

While Dr. O. J. Currie of the Natal Carbineers, Colonel Green, Major Addison and some others were enjoying Sunday afternoon tea—complete with strawberries and cream—at Vine Lodge, Lieutenant-Colonel C. T. Metcalfe, commanding the 2nd Rifle Brigade, was closeted with Brigadier-General F. Howard up at Convent Hill. The 4.7-inch howitzer on Surprise Hill was their target. Hamilton and Rawlinson had already played their part in the operation by an exchange of partially coded signals designed to divert Boer attention to Bulwana, and, to further the deception, Major A. J. Murray went out after dark with a few guides and fired a volley or two in Bulwana's direction.

At 10 pm that night, 500 officers and men of the second battalion of the Rifle Brigade, accompanied by Lieutenant Digby-Jones of the Royal Engineers and a dozen sappers, set off northwards from Observation Hill, as quietly as their hob-nailed boots, rifle straps and steel-tipped bayonet scabbards would permit. Soon there was a halt at the railway, where the tension of compulsory silence was heightened by the noise of the officers attacking the barbed wire fence beside the track with their heavy-duty wire cutters.

Lieutenant Byrne and half of E company were left at the railway in reserve, with the other half company in a nearby donga. The guides, Thornhill and Ashby, now pointed out to Metcalfe the configuration of Surprise Hill, flanked by Bell's Kopje to the east and Thornhill's Kopje to the west. But there was still an hour to go before the moon set, so Metcalfe halted the column once again. The silence of the night was complete, save for an occasional rifle shot from an over-vigilant picquet, and soon there was total darkness, except for the intruding beam of the Boer searchlight on Telegraph Hill "dancing along the fringe of the town's defences, peering fixedly at every suspected exit."

Just after midnight the soldiers moved silently out of their dongas. Captain Gough's company deployed to the right of the line and Major Thesiger to the left, with Captains Paley and Stevens in support. For a second time in a week, the Boers were not on the alert and 500 infantrymen stumbled uphill in the darkness—the clang of iron-heeled boots on loose stones and the metallic jangling of equipment apparently undetected. When the Boer picquet eventually challenged the advancing British and opened fire, the leading riflemen had scarcely ten yards to go. It was too late to stop them, and, after a sergeant had led a bayonet charge which dispatched the howitzer crew, Digby-Jones was soon at work with his gun-cotton. The first fuse, however, was defective, and, after some minutes, the sappers scrambled back to do the job again. This delay was soon to cost lives.

By the time the retreating infantry heard the massive double explosion signifying Digby-Jones' successful destruction of a 4.7-inch howitzer and an ammunition dump, the Boers were fully alerted. The Transvaalers from Bell's Kopje and the Free Staters from Thornhill's began a furious enfilading fire from both flanks, while a band of gallant Pretorians took up position to cut off the British withdrawal. In the darkness confusion was inevitable—Boers firing at Boers, and British soldiers addressing enemies as friends. In addition, the Boer command of the English language, with beckoning calls of "Rifle Brigade this way", lured some men to their deaths. But resolute control by Metcalfe, the unfaltering sense of direction of the guides, notably Major Wing, in rounding up stragglers, and some determined use of the bayonet triumphed. Reforming at the railway crossing, the column came back in unbroken formation, bringing with them most of their fifty wounded. Fifteen men, however, were never to return.

More telegrams from Generals Erasmus and Schalk Burger sought to reassure President Kruger that nothing less than "black treason" could possibly account for two such setbacks occurring in such quick succession. Principal culprit for the Surprise Hill affair was named as Corporal of the Guard Tossell, and, with him, four others—Cooper, MacArthur, Walker and Miller—whose only demonstrable crime was their British names. But Pretoria would have none of this and they were all eventually released.

While Boer leaders exchanged telegrams about the "guilty men" of the two sorties and General White was publicly congratulating the attackers on their achievement, some among their number—notably the Imperial Light Horse contingent from Wagon Hill—were entertaining thoughts of an altogether different night escapade. For days, they had looked down on Bester's Farm, less than a mile to the south, and observed a Red Cross flag on a thorn bush, together with the nocturnal visits of the Boer commandos to collect eggs, chickens and a weaner or two. The I.L.H. argued that the Geneva convention applied to all combatants alike, and, on the night of 9th December, they struck a blow for imperial solidarity. No citation came forth from Natal Field Force headquarters for the success of their expedition, but they earned the undying gratitude of the nearby Manchesters and Gordons, grateful beneficiaries of an unheralded foraging party. The pigs, turkeys and other poultry that the I.L.H. carried off would not last till Christmas, but, after forty days of siege, there was not much chance of that anyway.

On the 14th December, yet another raiding force was assembled in Ladysmith, this time under General White's personal command. It consisted of four regiments of cavalry, two brigades of infantry, five field batteries, Natal Volunteers, engineers and other support units—in fact, well over half the garrison. For three days they waited for Buller's signal to break out to the south and join up with the relief army coming from the Tugela river. At last it came:

"*No 88 Cipher. 16 December 1899*
I tried Colenso yesterday, but failed."

The next day, White disbanded his column and sent the men back to their locations. The largest and most spectacular December sortie of all never took place—and the siege was to continue.

14 Colenso

"Never had there been such an extraordinary sight—an enemy so conspicuous on the one side against an invisible foe on the other." (J. B. Atkins, *Manchester Guardian*, December 1899)

As December 1899 opened, the British army in South Africa was ready to take the full offensive. The three commanders—Buller, Gatacre and Methuen—were each advancing to the attack, but, for Buller himself, the question to be answered was which way to go?

The obvious route was via Colenso, but Buller was unfavourably impressed when he first saw the position. "After careful reconnaissance by telescope," he wrote from Frere in a letter to Lord Lansdowne, the Secretary of State for War, on 12th December, "I came to the conclusion that a direct assault upon the enemy's position at Colenso and the north of it would be too costly. The approach to the drift (across the Tugela) this side, is a dead flat without any cover, and the enemy have a very strong position which they have systematically

The Imperial Yeomanry, lined up ready for action on the veldt, as depicted by Lucy Kemp-Welch in her "Sons of England". At Colenso, however, the cavalry awaited a breakthrough that never came. (National Army Museum)

fortified just the other side of the drift."

Buller's telescope was probably the best visual aid to planning available to him, for the maps his staff had assembled at Pietermaritzburg were totally inadequate—a one-inch Military Survey of Northern Natal which only extended as far south as Ladysmith, a five-inch to the mile Education Department school map, and a few farm surveys, devoid of military detail or dependable contour markings. His visual observations, supplemented by the local knowledge of Mr. Lang, the chosen guide for Buller's force, produced a composite picture which was far from advantageous from the British point of view. The panorama consisted of a gentle, downward, cover-free slope reaching to a river of indeterminate depth and serpentine configuration, backed by a wall of hills concealing an unknown number of Boers and their artillery. Perhaps there were a few picquets—perhaps thousands of watchful, motionless riflemen. In the centre of this stage was the village of Colenso itself, a single street with a cluster of corrugated iron roofs covering one-storey houses, and two iron bridges over the Tugela, one—demolished by the Boers—for the railway and one for the road.

Buller, therefore had all this very much in mind when he drew up his plan for the Ladysmith relief army, now some 18,000 strong. This first plan was not unreasonable. Dispatching Major-General Barton's 6th Brigade of four Fusilier battalions from the base at Frere northwards to a position in front of Colenso to distract the Boers, Buller would meanwhile march the remainder of his force westwards by night, force the passage of Potgieter's Drift, about eighteen miles upstream from Colenso, and then, having successfully turned the Boer positions, advance through the seventeen miles of open country to Ladysmith. Accordingly, he signalled to White:

"I have definitely decided to advance by Potgieter's Drift. Expect to start on 12th December and take five days."

On the evening of the 12th, Buller's army started to move, but, suddenly, a halt was called. At this point, some time during the daylight hours of 13th December, Buller changed his mind—a decision which subsequently attracted so much attention, provoked endless speculation among military historians and marked the downward turn in a hitherto shining military career. Certainly the disastrous news from the other fronts—the defeat and death of General Wauchope at Maggersfontein as well as General Gatacre's reverse at Stormberg two days previously, had something to do with it. Whatever the reasons, an instinctive reluctance to face a twenty-mile deviation from his railway supply lines—railways having an almost umbilical significance for some British generals of the day—or simply an overall and overwhelming feeling of inadequacy for the occasion, Buller's decision was swift enough. Less than twenty-four hours after announcing his flanking movement plan, he heliographed to White:

"Have been forced to change my plans; am coming through via Colenso and Onderbroek Spruit."

He also signalled the War Office:

"This operation (the original plan) involved the complete abandonment of my communications, and, in the event of success, the risk that I might share the fate of Sir George White and be cut off from Natal. I had considered that with the enemy dispirited by the failure of their plans in the west, the risk was justifiable, but I cannot think I ought now to take such a risk. From my point of view, it will be better to lose Ladysmith altogether than to throw open Natal to the enemy."

Louis Botha (seated) and members of his War Council a few days before the battle at Colenso. His commandos, only 4,500 strong, successfully held off the might of Buller's relieving army.

The frontal assault, so recently rejected as impossible, was now to be tried, but the message to White did not even say when. A perfectly understandable enquiry from White, poised to co-ordinate a break-out from Ladysmith with Buller's attack, produced the laconic answer "Probably 17th December."

Even this date was incorrect, for, in fact, it was during the early hours of 14th December that the Ladysmith relief column moved out of Frere and went forth, for the first time as a composite force, to discharge their noble task of Empire—the recovery of Ladysmith and Natal for Britain. "In a strange mixture of smoke and dust and mist," they marched out beyond Chieveley to the dry plains sloping down to the Tugela and there took up new positions. In all, there were sixteen battalions of infantry, a mounted brigade and five batteries of artillery. Before them the lyddite shells from the naval guns landed from HMS *Tartar* and *Terrible* blasted huge cascades of red dust out of the Boer positions on the hills beyond the river, though, unbeknown to the British, they were achieving little else. Louis Botha had his men firmly under control and nobody moved from their trenches. There were about 4,500 of them to defend the Boer positions.

Unluckily for Buller, Botha had anticipated the British move; indeed, so firmly convinced had he been that Buller would order a frontal attack that he had planned all the Boer defences to meet it. It is therefore tempting to speculate what would have happened had Buller stuck to his original plan. But, though Buller was doing exactly what he expected, the Boer general still had his own difficulties to contend with. Already seen by many of his fellow Boers as heir-apparent to Commandant-General Joubert, Botha inevitably attracted jealous glances from his paternalistic elders who were now junior to him on the battlefield, and it needed all his considerable personal magnetism and charm to gain acceptance of his orders. At thirty-seven, his youthful appearance and military bearing singled him out from some of his comrades. As Johannes Meintjes noted in his biography: "Where other Boer generals were inclined to look like church elders or businessmen in their everyday suits, Botha was in riding breeches and a pouched tunic and looked like a soldier."

In deploying his commandos, the biggest problem Botha had to face was to find volunteers to take up position on Hlangwane. This was the hill on the Boer left, which, though Botha declined to emphasize the point during a two-hour War Council, was actually on the British side of the Tugela. Eventually, after a telegraphic intervention from President Kruger, lots were drawn to decide on whom the task should fall, and Botha was much relieved that it fell to a brave and proven warrior, Joshua Joubert, and the Wakkerstroom commando to swim the Tugela and occupy the position. On Fort Wylie, in the centre of the Boer position, Botha placed the Krugersdorp commando under Veldt-Kornet van Wyk, and with them the Vryheid commando under his own brother-in-law, Cheere Emmett. To the west of them was the Heidelberg commando with Commandant Oosthuizen, and it was from near this position that Botha chose to direct operations. Further still to the west he placed the men of Ermelo and Middelburg. He had some 15-pounder Creusot guns and two quick-firing Krupps.

Botha's plan was simple enough. No movement or fire until the British had crossed the Tugela, preferably by the road-bridge (suitably mined) in Colenso village—a course they would be encouraged to adopt on discovering the barbed wire entanglements strategically placed in the river itself—and then let them have it.

On the British side, Buller called his generals together on the night of 14th December to outline the plan of attack, though the orders actually issued to all units at 10.00 pm were signed by General Clery, still nominally in command of the relief force. A bizarre officer who dyed his side-whiskers blue, Clery had at one time been Professor of Tactics at Sandhurst. But now at 61—a year older than Buller—he allowed himself the comfort of flared trousers and soft boots to accommodate his varicose veins, the normal tight-fitting cavalry breeches being quite unsuitable leg-wear for such a painful condition.

The night before the battle was cold. An hour before midnight the carts came round the British camp issuing each man extra rounds of ammunition—bringing up the allocation to 170 cartridges per man—and a ration of biscuits and bully beef. The same carts took away their overcoats, so, while some men slept, others shivered in the dark until reveille at 2.30 in the morning. Then breakfast and bustle, the filling of water-bottles, checking of weapons, dousing of fires and feelings of

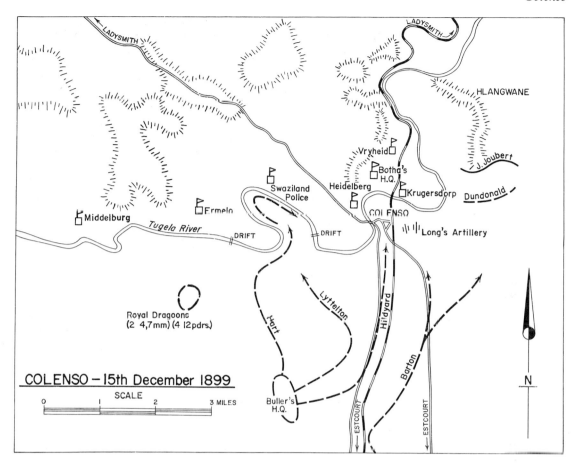

COLENSO – 15th December 1899

SCALE

0   1   2   3 MILES

expectation as the order was passed down the lines: "We attack at daybreak!"

But already things had started to go wrong for the British. By the time Clery's army order reached the brigade commanders it was too late for them to reconnoitre the positions they were to attack at dawn. So it was hardly surprising that Major-General Hart's 5th Brigade— the Irish Brigade—was in serious trouble soon after it marched out of camp at 4.30 in the morning of 15th December.

Directed out to the left flank, Hart's Irishmen, consisting of the Royal Dublin Fusiliers, Connaught Rangers, Inniskillings and Borderers, were to cross the "bridle drift immediately to the west of the junction of the Doornkop spruit and the Tugela" and then wheel right along the northern bank "towards the kopjes north of the iron bridge" to join up with Major-General Hildyard's 2nd Brigade attacking the central position frontally. But instead of one drift, Hart found two, one at each end of a totally unexpected loop in the river describing a deep horseshoe enclave into the Boer salient. Undaunted by these new factors, which the terrified and speechless African guide did nothing to explain, Hart marched his men straight into the trap, ignoring a warning from the Royal Dragoons covering his left that there were Boers in the hills surrounding the loop. To make matters worse, Arthur Fitzroy Hart, a caricature of an Aldershot general with a

waxed moustache that defied the laws of gravity, drove his men on in tight columns of four as if on the parade ground, completely ignoring the drill-book recommendation that "troops advancing across open ground in face of the enemy should be extended in open order." Private Dwyer of the 1st Connaught Rangers knew that this was wrong and said so in a letter to his father. So did Corporal Grace of the Inniskillings.

"Fancy us marching straight up to the front of the position in quarter column, or en masse, until we were within 1,200 yards. We were soon woke up by two shells from the Boers, the first going over the Dublin Fusiliers, and killing about seven men of the Connaughts. The next fell shorter and took seventeen of the Dublins clean out of one company. We were following the Connaughts, and the last words I heard from our Colonel was 'Deploy to the left', and away we went as well as we could."

Hart's brigade was caught on three sides by a withering fusillade of artillery and small arms fire, but still his men surged forward. Some of the Dublins eventually succeeded in crossing the river, though others were drowned in the attempt, weighed down by a hundred pounds of kit and ammunition.

Buller was horrified at the spectacle of Hart's brigade being mauled in a location he was obviously surprised to find them occupying. With the words "Hart has got himself into a devil of a mess down there—get him out", he ordered Lyttelton and his 4th Brigade to assist in extracting the Irish from the loop. By early afternoon they came stumbling back in the heat and the dust and the blood, 400 of them no longer on their feet, the jokers among them scribbling the name of the man in front on his back. No Irishman wants an unknown warrior's cross on his grave.

Over on the British right flank was Douglas MacKinnon Baillie

British troops watching their comrades in action at Colenso. It was one of the chief criticisms of Buller that he never satisfactorily involved his entire force in the battle. (National Army Museum)

Hamilton, 12th Earl of Dundonald, a Guardsman by background but with some pretensions to being an inventor. Dundonald's colourful personality and handsome appearance, with curly black hair, trim side-whiskers and pointed moustache, gave him more the air of an Albany dandy than that of a Victorian army general. But there was nothing very spectacular or colourful about the role given to Dundonald's Mounted Brigade that day.

Their task was based on Buller's appreciation of Hlangwane's importance to the operation—and this was most obscure. In his revised plan for a frontal attack at Colenso, Buller described the occupation of Hlangwane as a tempting move, but one which he rejected on the grounds that "its possession did not in any way assist the crossing." Yet he obviously could not simply ignore the feature. In these circumstances, it is hardly surprising that Dundonald's orders were somewhat imprecise. He was not told actually to <u>take</u> Hlangwane but to "cover the right flank of the general movement and endeavour to take up a position <u>on</u> Hlangwane"—which was not quite the same thing.

In the event, Dundonald's thousand men from the 13th Hussars, Thorneycroft's Mounted Infantry, Bethune's Mounted Infantry, Natal Carbineers, Natal Police and Imperial Light Horse soon came under heavy fire from Joshua Joubert's 800-strong Wakkerstroom commando. With his whole force committed in an attempt to envelope the feature, Dundonald, not unreasonably, appealed for help to Major General Barton's 6th Infantry Brigade, assigned specifically to give support to the centre and right flank. Barton, however, declined to act without reference to higher authority. Accounts differ as to what then took place. Buller's biographer states that the three generals then met to discuss the matter and reached a consensus view, but Dundonald's recollection in his autobiography was different.

"I do not criticise the decision arrived at by General Barton not to give the infantry support I asked for; he may have received orders during the battle of which I knew nothing. This sort of thing often occurred during the Natal campaign, ie. changes made in the orders previously issued without notification being sent to all concerned."

But it was in the central sector that the main drama of Colenso unfolded—a drama which in the end was to lead to Buller's defeat and eventual downfall. Here, the plan provided for Major-General Hildyard's 2nd Infantry Brigade to advance on the village of Colenso, take it, cross the river and attack the Boer positions on the other side. In the meantime, the target would have been softened up by Colonel Charles Long's eighteen guns of the 14th and 66th Batteries of the Royal Artillery and the Naval contingent of 12-pounders. W. Baring Pemberton's vision of the scene as Long began his advance at 6 am on 15th December, a dawn without wind or cloud and every prospect of a torrid midday, is most illuminating:

"An aerial reconnaissance would have shown the following picture. Ground scouts well ahead of the guns were approaching the Tugela, making their way through the trees and scrub which covered the south bank for a depth of 1,000 yards or so. Behind them and a little way to the east of

the railway line and roughly 1,250 yards from the Tugela, Long with Hunt, his second in command, and Lieutenant Ogilvy in charge of the naval guns, were riding side by side. Further away at some 200 yards and 650 yards respectively, the two field batteries and the naval guns were on the march approaching a large donga. A mile behind them Barton's brigade was making its leisurely progress."

Soon Long reached the spot from which he decided to discharge Buller's orders to "prepare the crossing for the 2nd (Hildyard's) Brigade." The only trouble was the spot that Long had chosen.

The subsequent testimony of Long, Buller's evidence before the Royal Commission and the researches of latter-day military historians have all failed to establish satisfactorily whether the position chosen by Long to unlimber his batteries was wrong due to errors of geography or errors of judgement. It is known that the final position was only a thousand yards from the river bank, that Buller was horrified when he observed how close they were, and that Long himself made no secret of his personal commitment to the idea of close-range bombardment. He explained his theories to Atkins on the journey out to South Africa—"the only way to smash the beggars is to rush in at 'em." One of the soldiers, Gunner Platt, observed: "Colonel Long was so confident he could sweep the Boers off the face of the earth that he took the guns right into the Boer camp."

Whether it was the deceptive light in the early morning mist, or the over-confidence of the artilleryman who had decimated the dervishes at Omdurman the year before will never now be known. Certainly, Long was much too close to the Boer lines for Buller's peace of mind— or Botha's.

J. D. Kestell, later Dutch Reform Church chaplain to General Christian de Wet, was present at Botha's field headquarters, and recorded the urgent appeals made by the Boer officers to be allowed to open fire on the spectacular and fearsome panorama of British soldiery, nearly 20,000 strong, advancing proudly over the plains. But Botha stood firm. Not a shot was to be fired until he was ready.

Suddenly, on the British left, a Boer commando, unable to resist the target offered by Hart's brigade, opened fire. Immediately, from the Boer centre, the Krugersdorp commando directed a ferocious fusillade towards Long's artillery, sounding to one recipient like "an anchor chain rattling through the hawser hole." Contrary to some accounts, however, the initial casualties were not heavy. The evidence of Bombardier Stevens of the 66th Battery, for instance, suggests anything but the instant devastation recorded by others.

"In an instant we were amongst one of the deadliest fires yet known. We kept on advancing, and reached the point where we had to commence firing. We halted and unlimbered the guns, and the drivers turned about with the horses and limbers and got in rear of the guns. The range was 1,200 yards and our gunners and officers worked at those guns as if on parade."

A gunner from Birmingham recorded a similar impression of disciplined control. "Everything was done as cool as if it was on a drill field instead of a battlefield."

It was probably a shortage of ammunition, and not of men, which silenced the British guns at Colenso, although few Boer commentators have accepted this appreciation of what happened. At all events, by 7 am they had fired a thousand rounds, Long had been shot through the liver, and the wounded and unemployed led to the shelter of a nearby donga by Major Bailward, there to keep still and await supplies. The guns stood silent and unattended.

At this point, the real tragedy of Colenso began to unfold. According to Buller, the two officers sent back by Long to call for more ammunition now arrived and announced, quite unaccountably, that the gun crews had been annihilated. Buller confirmed this report to his own satisfaction by a visual observation, which revealed twelve unattended guns but no sign of the gunners concealed in the nearby trench. Buller's consternation was probably increased by another factor. A few minutes before, a shell had exploded near him, killing his personal surgeon and badly bruising both his ribs and his composure. In fact, it might be a kindness to argue that following this physical blow, the sight of the deserted guns and the spectacle of Hart being thrashed on the left, Buller was temporarily in a state of shock. The explanation arrived at by the German General Staff in a subsequent appreciation was simply that he was "now no longer the leader, but merely a fellow combatant."

For the second time in forty-eight hours Buller made a rapid and far-reaching decision. For the second time it was wrong. The situation was as follows. The leading battalions of Hildyard's 2nd Brigade were already deployed in a highly professional manner towards Colenso, where they took up position as a protective screen for the guns. Atkins watched them manoeuvring.

"I shall never forget the advance of the Devons and the Queens and the Scots Fusiliers (who had bored across the plain diagonally from Barton's brigade) on the right of the railway to the river. Line after line rose up and ran forward; some reached a shelter trench and dropped into it, others passed on beyond . . . Here and there you could clearly see a man drop, and the line rolled on without him, and the next straight as a ruler, like the one before it and the one behind it."

Dundonald's Mounted Brigade was intact, as was Barton's 6th Infantry Brigade and Lyttelton's 4th Brigade. The Naval guns were still pounding away and Louis Botha's plan for the surprise and destruction of the Ladysmith relief force on the north side of the Tugela was obviously in tatters. Yet, not much after 10 am, those nearest to Buller learned that the attack was called off.

Buller had only one more thought for the day—to fetch in the guns—immediately. "Now my lads, this is your last chance to save the guns," he said. "Will any of you volunteer to fetch them in?"

Captain Congreve of the Rifle Brigade stepped forward, followed by Lieutenant Freddie Roberts, son of Lord Roberts, the military hero of the Victorian public. Some gunners shuffled to their feet—Corporal Nurse and Driver Williams of the 66th Battery, followed by Young, Petts, Rockall, Lucas and Taylor. Captain Schofield, Buller's ADC, was denied some of the honour and glory of volunteering. Buller told him to go.

A dramatic artist's impression of Long's guns in action at Colenso. (National Army Museum)

They rode off as four teams, Roberts laughing and looking over his shoulder at Schofield and twirling his cane like a point-to-point jockey. Soon they were in the midst of it. Congreve's tunic was torn to shreds but, for a time, his body was untouched. Bullets ripped their way through Nurse's pack as he struggled with Roberts to limber up the left-hand gun. Men and mangled horses fell all around, but Schofield miraculously came through without a scratch. Meanwhile, Captain Reed and two teams of the 7th Battery also joined the rescue operation. Altogether two guns were recovered, and Congreve, with a bullet through his thigh, struggled to the shelter trench with Roberts on his back.

"From the hill above I saw how the matter went," wrote Kestell on the Boer side, "and I do not think that a more heroic deed was done in the whole war than the rush of the English to save those guns."

Drawing some comfort from the thought that "there are plenty of guns at the Cape to replace these," Buller abandoned the ten in front of Colenso and took the names of those who had tried so valiantly to save them. The Victoria Cross was later awarded to Congreve, Reed, Nurse and also to Roberts—posthumously. Eighteen months later, the *London Gazette* announced that Schofield's case for a VC had also been approved by the new king, Edward VII.

At 11 am, unnerved by the adverse developments on the left and centre, Buller ordered Dundonald to disengage from the right and return to camp. The Mounted Brigade's casualties had been slight, and its commander saw no reason for breaking off the action. But his personal disappointment was not yet complete. All day he had looked forward to a bottle of vintage port which he planned to broach if he

survived the battle. He did, but the port did not. On arrival at his mess-tent Dundonald discovered the empty bottle quite close to a red-faced veteran colonel of the Crimea, and with him his own ex-coachman, sheltering from the sun under a nearby wagon. "I told the colonel," wrote Dundonald in his autobiography, "that before the next battle I would send him down to Durban—which I did."

Dundonald's retreat was almost the last inglorious act in a miserable day. By 4 pm the British withdrawal was complete and an hour later the Boers crossed the Tugela and carried off the abandoned guns, together with nine ammunition wagons that had also been left behind. Botha telegraphed the news to Kruger.

In the British camp, Buller, shattered by the day's events, compounded his errors by two disastrous signals. No amount of post-war explanation by Buller himself, advocacy by his biographer or subsequent annotation of the original texts has ever been able to expunge the literal interpretation of his messages. To White he helio-graphed:

"I tried Colenso yesterday but failed; the enemy is too strong for my force, except with siege operations, and these will take one full month to prepare. Can you last so long? If not, how many days can you give me in which to take up defensive positions? After which I suggest you firing away as much ammunition as you can and making the best terms you can . . ."

Then, a further message:

"Also add to end of message: Whatever happens, recollect to burn your cipher, and decipher and code books, and any deciphered messages."

The actual place where Long's action was fought. Bones of horses can be seen in the foreground of this view, taken after the battle. (National Army Museum)

To Lansdowne, he telegraphed:

"My failure today raises a serious question. I do not think I am now strong enough to relieve White . . . My view is that I ought to let Ladysmith go, and occupy good positions for the defence of south Natal and let time help us . . ."

The reaction from both Ladysmith and London was immediate and predictable and Buller never lived it down. But, for the rank-and-file of the British army, Buller's prestige and reputation remained untarnished. They only knew what Trooper Billing of Buller's personal bodyguard saw that day:

"All the time we were going along at a walk, with General Buller in front; he did not seem to care a bit for all the bullets and shells, and I saw them

*bursting all round him ; he never even turned his head, but walked on as if
nothing had happened.*

*I think General Buller is about the bravest man I have ever seen and he
is also a very nice man to speak to."*

Personal bravery, however, was not viewed in Whitehall as being an
adequate substitute for competence in command, particularly after the
other two shattering defeats of Black Week. As Lyttelton commented,
Colenso was "one of the most unfortunate battles in which a British
army has ever been engaged and in none has there been a more
deplorable tactical display."

Clearly, a change was needed and the British government was swift
to act. On 18th December, Buller was informed that he had been
relieved of supreme command in South Africa by Lord Roberts,
whose son at that moment lay dying in the British camp.

*The victor of Colenso
reads Buller's dispatches,
the day after the battle.*

15 A View From Overseas

"The English War with the Transvaal"—a Russian view. This anti-British propaganda depicts the rout of White's forces at Nicholson's Nek.

"The South African War will end with a complete defeat of the English." (Count von Bülow, German Foreign Minister, 1897–1900)

It is often argued that nothing is more certain to galvanize the British into effective action than abuse from political rivals and military setbacks on the field of battle. And both of these they suffered in good measure during the early months of the Boer War.

When Queen Victoria declared after Colenso "We are not interested in the possibilities of defeat"—a pronouncement at once characteristically imperious and supremely confident—she was not only expressing her own feelings but also faithfully reflecting the views of the vast majority of her subjects. Even the Liberal leader, Sir Henry Campbell Bannerman—a committed protagonist of the notion that wars "should

Joseph Chamberlain, as seen by the cartoonist Phil May. To some, he was the villain of the Boer War— to others, its hero. (National Portrait Gallery, London)

be muddled through rather than provided for"—proclaimed in Parliament with solemn optimism: "There is no ground for despondency . . . our moral and material success is certain." And besides, Black Week, as the week of Maggersfontein, Stormberg and Colenso came to be known, only served to reinforce the feeling that total victory must and would be won—at whatever cost.

Support for the war was, however, by no means unanimous among the people's elected representatives. In Parliament, the Liberal opposition, legatees of Gladstone's distaste for Britain's imperial role, were divided amongst themselves. The so-called Liberal Imperialists, led by Lord Rosebery, Asquith and Haldane (the last two the rising stars of the party), accepted with some uneasiness the inevitability of war before it came, and the inescapable duty of supporting it once it had happened. On the other hand, the radical wing of the party was bitterly opposed to what they termed "Chamberlain's War". David Lloyd George proclaimed his uncompromising opposition to war in a telegram from Canada: "If I have the courage I shall protest with all the vehemence at my command against this outrage which is perpetuated in the name of human freedom." But for the moment Lloyd George's trenchant message was unwelcome and the general public paid it no heed.

The moral doubts and hesitations of those who viewed with misgivings the gathering confrontation between their own mighty Empire and the two tiny Boer republics vanished in a flurry of patriotism on the day of Kruger's October ultimatum. That the British army was invincible they had no doubt, but even so, the nation convinced itself, there was a clear and solemn duty to support the cause. In an atmosphere almost of a crusade, crowds followed reservists to their mobilization points, employers offered half-pay to the families of breadwinners called to the colours, and army deserters came trickling back voluntarily from as far away as the United States, prepared to face the music in order to have a crack at the Boers. Workers gave their shillings and the rich their guineas to hastily-organized charities. Rudyard Kipling's patriotic verse stirred up the nation's emotions and the Princess of Wales, known affectionately as the "Princess of Pity", took charge of the Red Cross, where she set about with immense dedication the task of equipping hospitals and providing other medical aid for the troops.

All this enthusiasm for the war was reflected in Britain's associated territories overseas, both in dependent colonies and those of Dominion status. They, too, shared the view that the Boers would not prove to be a formidable adversary for the British army. But, for reasons of their own—broadly speaking, a belief in imperial solidarity and also a substantial and legitimate self-interest—they were keen to join in. There was an eagerness, as Leo Amery put it, "to try the mettle of their sons in action and to show England and the world that in them the quality of British blood had not suffered dilution."

The Australians were the first in the field. On 11th July 1899—three months before the war broke out—the government of Queensland made London an offer of help. The following day, Lord Brassey, Governor of Victoria, announced that volunteers were already enrolling in Melbourne and, almost as if to "up the ante", Earl Beauchamp telegraphed a week later from Sydney, informing

Chamberlain that 1,860 men from New South Wales were ready to sail.

Scarcely had the news of General White's defeat at Nicholson's Nek appeared in the Australian newspapers than the first contingents were ready to set off. On 6th November 1899, Reuter reported the embarkation of 11 officers and 193 men from New South Wales, lurching their way through a back-slapping, bawling and singing crowd on the water-front at Sydney. The same day, a contingent of West Australians sailed from Perth on the SS *Medic* and Sir George Turner, Prime Minister of Victoria, announced that 250 men would be leaving Melbourne that week.

Mindful of the importance of the Cape route for Australia's trade with Europe, the Australians had a special interest in South Africa. In addition, they were better informed of the situation there than other colonial and dominion territories, having a substantial number of their countrymen working as miners on the Reef. It was small wonder that they were somewhat offended when the imperial government declined the offer of a joint Australian force of 2,500 men, drawn from each of the separate States, including Tasmania. Instead, the home government decided to accept representative colonial contingents of only up to 125 men, and these were to be mustered into the imperial army on arrival at Cape Town. But, after Colenso and Black Week, this principle was quickly abandoned and ruffled Australian feathers were soon smoothed over when Chamberlain made it clear he would be glad of all the help he could get—"mounted men preferred".

By the time Ladysmith was relieved, 5,000 Australian officers and men had arrived in the Cape and, by the end of the war, nearly 17,000 of them had served the Empire in South Africa. Not least among their number was Major Karri Davies, one of the leading lights in the beleaguered Ladysmith garrison throughout the siege.

New Zealand, relatively tiny in size and even further from the theatre of war than Australia, was no less ardent in its response. On 28th September 1899, the New Zealand House of Representatives not only voted its rapturous approval of an offer of men—albeit only two companies of mounted infantry—but also the money to pay for them. In less than a month, Colonel Penton, Commandant of the army, and Mr. A. Douglas, Under-Secretary for Defence, had made the plans for embarkation. The first New Zealanders to arrive in South Africa under the command of Major Robin were in time to participate in all of General French's operations in the northern Cape.

The news of Colenso was like an electric shock to New Zealand, particularly since, as parliament was in recess at the time, its members got the news by personal telegram. The message from the Prime Minister proposed the dispatch of a second contingent to South Africa and almost all the replies were couched in terms which eloquently revealed the sentiments of imperial solidarity between Wellington and London, sentiments which were to survive unchallenged for half a century. "Send contingent at whatever cost," wrote one MP. "Wish I were a few years younger," cabled another somewhat wistfully. In a language less direct and prosaic, but totally to the point, came the reply of yet a third. "Our duty to the mother country, the unity of the Empire, and the immense importance and unbounded benefit to New Zealand of the maintenance of British rule in South Africa, demand that a second contingent be sent, and that quickly."

Out of a total of 120 MPs there were no dissenters. The second New Zealand contingent set sail on 20th January 1900, to be followed by a third, a fourth and a fifth, until 6,500 New Zealanders altogether had fought in Britain's war against the Boers.

In Canada there were many whose view of South Africa was blurred by inherited attitudes unknown in either Australia or New Zealand. Here was a nation which, like South Africa, consisted of two white communities—in this case, the one having gained the ascendancy by armed conquest of the other. Furthermore, it was the French section, and not the English, which predominated in the ruling Liberal party of the day. But still the Canadian parliament, led by Prime Minister Sir Wilfred Laurier, expressed its unqualified support for Britain in a resolution passed without a division on 29th July 1899.

Throughout the following weeks, Canadians in the USA—mainly cattlemen from the prairies, trekked back home to volunteer for military service. General Hutton, commanding the Canadian Militia, and Colonel Sam Hughes worked hard to muster and equip a Canadian force from the 5,000 volunteers already enrolled. However, difficulties soon broke out with government ministers, who, confronted by the political anxieties of precedent and military involvement overseas, began dragging their feet. But not for long, for the pressure of press and public opinion was too great. The Montreal *Star* published telegrams from the mayors of 300 cities and townships throughout Canada urging the government to delay the dispatch of troops to South Africa no further. And the Toronto *Globe* joined in the gathering mood of imperial togetherness. "It must not be said," wrote the editor, "that Canada is a fair weather friend of Great Britain."

On 30th October—the day of "Mournful Monday"—Lieutenant-Colonel W. D. Otter embarked in Quebec with 1,000 men, only seventeen days after the Canadian government had finally made up its mind to send them. They were followed by others—the Canadian Mounted Rifles, recruited from the North-West Mounted Police, and a brigade of artillery under Colonel Drury. None were more spectacular than Strathcona's Horse, a hardy band of roughriders from Manitoba and the north-west, equipped and paid for by a quarter of a million pounds from Lord Strathcona's private funds.

Volunteers also came from Rhodesia under Colonel Plumer and from Ceylon came a contingent of white tea planters mobilized into a unit of mounted infantry. But offers of armed contingents from non-Europeans in India, New Zealand and Trinidad were turned down by London with as much tact as a government could reasonably be expected to show in an age before racial equality became the norm. However, Chamberlain accepted their money—$72,000 from the *Straits Times* in Singapore, including $10,000 from a single Chinese donor, and a day's pay contributed by the 3rd Bengal Cavalry Brigade.

Outside Britain and its empire, however, the mood was different. In Europe, anti-British feeling ran high. "Without the circle of the British Empire, as well as within it," wrote Amery, "the tidings of the Boer victories sent a thrill of emotion, as unique historically, and politically as significant, as any that has shaken the civilized world in the last generation."

Some of the anti-British reaction in Europe was of a wholly

Some of the German Corps near Ladysmith. Volunteers on the Boer side, however, were far outnumbered by their counterparts from the British Empire.

sentimental nature, the feelings provoked by the spectacle of a battle between David and Goliath. In Holland inevitably the ties of blood turned that country against Britain, and this factor, too, was an element in the pro-Boer sympathies generated in France and Germany. In these countries the press unleashed a virulent campaign of abuse directed against Britain, Queen Victoria, the army, and, above all, Joseph Chamberlain. Even though Ladysmith was still holding out, its fall was presented as an accomplished fact, a symbol of defeat for British imperialism. Scientists and poets joined in to add scholarship and literacy to what was often a flood of coarse and even obscene invective.

But foreign resentment of Britain was not entirely a matter of emotions, for there were deep political frictions which the war served to reveal and give expression to. Envious eyes in St Petersburg were trained on India and contemplated once more the traditional Russian "warm water" policy, now that the British army was committed elsewhere. In Germany, the Kaiser's love-hate relationship with England had already combined with the Prussian brand of *realpolitik* to produce support for the Boers, such as the incident of the celebrated Kruger telegram, even before the outbreak of war. In France, memories of Napoleon's humiliation, accusations of cross-channel complicity in the Dreyfus case and what had been seen as British arrogance in the Fashoda incident all served to inflame passions against *perfide Albion*. And everywhere in Europe people were angered by the general "one-upmanship" of the British, their commercial prosperity, their military power, their naval supremacy, their haughtiness. It was time they were taken down a peg, and the Boers were not doing badly.

Feelings were not so strongly raised on the other side of the Atlantic. In the USA, people were more relaxed and the government less interested. Anti-colonialism was strong, but so, too, was the prestige of Rudyard Kipling. There were some, chiefly Irish, who pressed unsuccessfully for intervention on the Boer side, but President McKinley would have none of it. It was left to the adventurer "Colonel" Blake to bring over an Irish contingent to fight the British. But there were many more Irish in General Hart's 5th Brigade at Colenso, or manning the ramparts in Ladysmith.

Certainly not everybody was against Britain and some of the less powerful nations of the day, notably Japan, Italy, Portugal and Greece, were solidly behind her. And when the ranting and raving died down, there were in all only 2,500 volunteers from continental Europe and the USA fighting on the Boer side—less than one third of the number which came from tiny, faraway New Zealand to join the British.

But nowhere outside of South Africa did the war have more impact than in Britain itself, and the reaction there to "Black Week" was greater in London than Ladysmith. For the garrison town, the battle of Colenso was a non-event, the prelude to a relief which did not happen. It was seen as something quite different in England. The main reason was the telegraph. Introduced into public service within living memory, this new medium was able to bring immediate news of distant events to the attention of an increasingly literate population. And the telegraph was used to great advantage by a highly competitive popular press, already conscious of "circulation" and the selling-power of instant drama.

For the moment there was plenty to be emotional about. Three lost battles and 3,000 casualties made immense, if only temporary, inroads into the people's self-confidence and sense of national invincibility. Soon, however, they rallied as "a universal impulse of patriotism swept the nation." Portraits of national heroes became almost an essential item in every shop-window display, small boys sported cheap cameos depicting their favourite generals, and, while the merchant princes of London formed an Imperial Yeomanry Committee, the landed gentry mustered their own private armies. In London, the City Imperial Volunteers (C.I.V.) raised 2,000 keen riflemen from the shooting clubs around the town, while, out in the country, Earl Dunraven recruited his famous Sharpshooters and Lord Latham the Roughriders. At the same time, up in the Scottish Highlands, groups of eagle-eyed ghillies and gamekeepers came in from the glens to join Lord Lovat in what was to become one of the most distinguished of the family regiments—the Lovat Scouts. Lord Donoughmore's squadron, in an act of impressive patriotism, not only paid for the passage and equipment of the regiment, given the name of the Duke of Cambridge's Own, but even donated their pay to charity.

No response to the turn of events in South Africa in December 1899 was more effective than that of the British government itself. Even before the news of Colenso reached London, Lord Lansdowne, the Secretary of State for War, had already become uneasy about Buller's performance and stayed in the capital, even though other ministers, including the Prime Minister, Lord Salisbury, had either gone away for the week-end or slipped away to their country retreats for Christmas. Thus, on receipt of Buller's "let Ladysmith go" telegram, Lansdowne was able to act promptly. It was Saturday 16th December, and Arthur Balfour, Lord Salisbury's nephew and *de facto* deputy premier was also in town. Between the two of them they concocted a holding telegram to Buller, instructing him to sit tight, and at once made plans for his immediate dismissal from the post of Commander-in-Chief, South Africa. The Prime Minister was recalled to London and a meeting of ministers was held that night. An obvious candidate was Field-Marshal Lord Roberts, a highly prestigious Victorian military hero. The redoubtable and relatively youthful Kitchener of Khartoum was to be his Chief-of-Staff, a fact which helped overcome Salisbury's uneasiness about Roberts' age. Lord Wolseley, the Commander-in-Chief, was simply not consulted.

A telegram was immediately sent to Roberts in Ireland offering him the command in South Africa. On the Sunday morning he appeared before the cabinet in Downing Street to make formal acceptance. In the afternoon, Lansdowne brought him the news of his only son's death at Colenso. "I said how much I felt for him," wrote Queen Victoria in her personal record of Roberts' call to take his leave of her. "He could only answer, 'I cannot speak of that, but I can of anything else.'"

"Bobs" and "K" were soon to change British fortunes in South Africa. But not before further reverses, mainly the continued blunders of the unfortunate Buller, were to test still further the fortitude of the Ladysmith garrison and the morale of the British people.

16 Christmas Cannonade

"They kept me in on every side, they kept me in, I say, on every side; but in the Name of the Lord, I will destroy them." (Ps. 118 v. XI. Psalm for the day, Christmas Eve)

The Boer bombardment of Ladysmith began in earnest nine days before Christmas—on Dingaan's Day, 16th December. The first of "Long Tom's" victims were two British artillerymen, mangled on the main street of Ladysmith as they exercised their horses at dawn, and a young officer's horse, decapitated as if by a butcher's cleaver. Only General White and a few of his senior officers knew that the Boers had more to celebrate than the memory of Andries Pretorius' victory over the Zulus in 1838 and the hoisting of the Boer republican flag at Heidelberg in 1880. News of Buller's defeat at Colenso was still a closely-guarded military secret, but its release could not be long delayed. Accordingly, the next day, with a noon temperature of around 104°F., White—discomforted both by the intense heat and the chilling news from Buller—issued an exceptionally short special order.

"The General Officer Commanding the Natal Field Force regrets to have to announce that General Sir Redvers Buller failed to make good his first attack on Colenso; reinforcements will therefore not arrive here as early as was expected. Sir George White is confident that the defence of Ladysmith will be continued by the garrison in the same spirited manner as it has hitherto been conducted, until the General Officer Commanding in Chief South Africa does relieve it."

There was little else that White could do for the present. He signalled to Buller that he had enough food to last for six weeks but that enteric fever and dysentry were spreading rapidly. Some 850 men were now on the sick list and White himself was quiet and bad-tempered, perhaps because he, too, had now got a touch of the dreaded fever.

More carnage was to come on Monday 18th December, when a salvo landed in the lines of the Natal Carbineers, killing a handful of troopers and a dozen horses. Up on Caesar's Camp, two unwary men of the Manchesters perished, and down at the other end of the town some Africans were killed while digging trenches. Twenty-two casualties in one day was the highest score so far in the Boer bombardment. And so it continued; on 21st December, a shell landed on White's house in Poort Road, narrowly missing the general and forcing him to move his headquarters to the house of the Christopher family on Convent Hill. The following day, another shell found its mark on the camp of the Gloucesters, killing five men.

A Christmas tree at General White's party for the Ladysmith children.

But while the anxieties of some—the bereaved, the timorous and the eye witnesses of horror—were chiefly concerned with how to avoid becoming cannon-fodder, food was already a major preoccupation of people uncertain of the prospects of festivities and Christmas fare.

Despite the great skill and energy of Colonel Ward, the Army Service Corps and the Indian Commissariat in husbanding and fairly distributing the meagre food reserves, luxuries and money were beginning to count. While Major C. W. Park, in command of the Devons, fretted mainly about promotion, he also worried about the diminishing stocks of whisky. "We are the only regiment that has any," he wrote on 17th December, "and ours will be finished within a week." He went on philosophically ". . . and after that we shall have to take to Commissariat rum and lime juice every other day," At the same time, Bella Craw noted that whisky was still available at £5 a bottle, but it seems, from his account, that Lieutenant Pomeroy and the officers of the 5th Dragoon Guards could not find any for their Christmas dinner and settled for sherry instead. A month later, Colonel Knox produced a carefully-hoarded case of whisky and raised £150 for it in aid of charity.

With the pre-Christmas price of eggs around twelve shillings a dozen, potatoes at 3d each and chickens £1, it was small wonder that housewives began to show signs of stress. Mrs. Hayden, trying to cater for a household of sixteen—mainly newspaper correspondents—had an unusually anxious time producing "varied and appetising dishes to set before these kings." Good foragers soon made a name for themselves. Not least among their number was Sergeant Cowl of the Devons, whose West Country skills and instincts served his officers well. By Christmas Eve, he had amassed one small pig, a cock, four hens and the ingredients for plum duff and mince pies. Pomeroy's manservant seems to have been equally competent in foraging for provender, while up at Captain Lambton's Naval headquarters, some enterprising wardroom steward had collected together two turkeys, a sucking pig and enough plum pudding for fourteen officers.

On the Sunday—Christmas Eve—the shelling abated. A special ration of Christmas delicacies was distributed to all units, while, in the town, supplies of fruit, butter, eggs, poultry and other luxuries had been released for public auction. As the regimental cooks and housewives of Ladysmith took stock of their larders and families returned from church, some misguided musician with a borrowed harmonium worked up a few tears here and there by playing sentimental reminders of Christmas at peace. But the Natal Carbineers struck more of the popular mood with their burlesque of a cavalry band. A pair of empty oil drums slung across the withers of a dressed-up horse and a set of cymbals fashioned from kerosene tins made a credible enough sound, backed up by real tin whistles. The tinsel and gauze uniforms of the Volunteers and the Drum Major's baton, surmounted by a child's tin spinning top, made a bizarre, but colourful, spectacle—and many who listened to the actual music were impressed with that as well.

In the centre of the camp the Gordons played their bagpipes—which kept the Boers on their toes—and Major Park rejoiced at the news of his promotion to Lieutenant-Colonel. And the biblical scholars of Ladysmith drew comfort from the Psalm for the day—

"They kept me in on every side, they kept me in, I say, on every side, but in the Name of the Lord I will destroy them."

Both the garrison and civilians hoped that the Boers would continue to respect the spirit of Christmas, but, when the great day came, it started with a bang, as salvoes of Boer shells fell on the embattled town. However, the first two to land—in the camps of the Natal Carbineers and the Imperial Light Horse—were found not to be filled with high explosive, but with Christmas puddings. On the casings, the Boer gunners had inscribed "With the Compliments of the Season."

Soon the shelling subsided, and everybody made the most of it, exercising their developing skills at cannon-spotting as they made their way to Holy Communion or to call on friends with Christmas greetings. "I feel quite festive already," wrote the newly-promoted Colonel Park, having had two eggs for breakfast, ". . . some sports in the afternoon, a sing-song at night, and the men have an issue of rum, tobacco and their plum puddings, so they will not do badly."

Captain Lambton, General Brocklehurst and a few of the Natal Volunteers called at Vine Lodge for a drink with the Tathams, while Dr. Kay came up from Intombi to dine with the Navy. Some enterprising journalists sponsored a mule gymkhana for their neighbours, the Rifle Brigade, using the brigade's pack animals as mounts, while the Imperial Light Horse worked off the best meal of a month or two by taking on the Gordon Highlanders in a tug-of-war. And the children of Ladysmith were not forgotten.

Colonel J. G. Dartnell, assisted by Major Karri Davies, had been conspiring for days with the Tatham family and the mothers of Ladysmith to assemble a vast quantity of toys and a few Christmas trees in the Walton and Tatham hall. A gum tree was found to represent Australia, an acacia thorn for South Africa, a fir for Great Britain and another one for Canada. Not only Dartnell and Davies but also Colonel Frank Rhodes and Major Doveton acted as "uncles", standing by their national trees laden with presents, while the burly R.S.M. Bill Perrin of the I.L.H. appeared as Santa Claus. In due time, 200 over-excited and exhausted children were taken home, the trees removed and an older age group took over, among them a few off-duty army subalterns. Dancing lasted until well past midnight.

None were more festive than the officers of the 1st Battalion, Devon Regiment, whose Colonel was celebrating more than Christmas:

"We had a great dinner last night, with table-clothes and real wine glasses, and the menu included hors d'oeuvres, soup, beef, olives, roast chicken and pork, anchovies, plum pudding, and figs. We drank the Queen, my health on promotion (with much cheering), sweethearts and wives and absent friends. Then we moved on to the sing-song, which was a very good one, and when that was over we came back to the Mess with a mob of other fellows, and had hot rum punch, and very good it was; and about eleven we toddled to bed. I expected to be very ill this morning . . ."

The festive season in Ladysmith was short, however. The war started again in earnest on Boxing Day, when shelling was resumed. Several of the carousing officers of the Devons were killed at breakfast on 27th December—and a week later three more of them were to die at the battle of Wagon Hill.

17 Wagon Hill

"What enchantment lay over that hill! From the first moment that we had come south of Ladysmith, it had been the talk of everyone that the hill should be taken." (J. D. Kestel, chaplain to President Steyn, *Through Shot and Flame*, 1903)

Platrand, a two-and-a-half-mile ridge, 600 feet high, boulder-strewn and barren, except for a few flowering thorns, runs east–west to the south of Ladysmith. Since the beginning of the siege it had been held by the British, and many among the Boer besiegers were quite content that it should remain so. But other Boers—more adventurous and with a greater sense of strategy—looked up covetously at this feature, held by the Manchester Regiment at the eastern end (which the British called Caesar's Camp), and by the Imperial Light Horse to the west, on Wagon Hill. For Platrand was the key to Ladysmith. From there, the town itself was but 3,000 yards away—downhill. And, once captured, there would be no British position on the entire perimeter which would not be vulnerable to artillery attack, and even long-range rifle fire, from both flanks and rear.

No Boer leader was more committed to the notion of capturing Platrand than Commandant C. J. de Villiers, in charge of the

A British outpost, probably garrisoned by the Manchesters, under fire at Caesar's Camp on the Ladysmith perimeter defences.

Harrismith commando. Since 9th November, when Commandant-General Joubert had vetoed his plans for a full-scale frontal assault, de Villiers had been planning another attack, for which he had the full support of General Prinsloo. This time the operation was to be a joint action, carried out by a combined Transvaal/Free State force of 900 men, and the date was set for the night of 29th/30th November. However, by midnight on the 29th most of the assault parties had dispersed, leaving their leaders to convince de Villiers that the whole operation would have cost the Boers too dearly.

Things were decidedly more promising on the afternoon of 5th January 1900. Three days earlier, a general War Council had finally voted in favour of a full-scale attack, and plans were formulated accordingly. A thousand men from the Transvaal commandos under General Schalk Burger were to attack in the east at Caesar's Camp, while 400 Free Staters from Harrismith, Heilbron and Kroonstad were to storm Wagon Point and the south-western end of Wagon Hill. In between would be 600 men of the Vryheid and German commandos on the right centre, with the men of Winburg on the left centre. Six-inch Creusots on Bulwana and Telegraph Hill were to bombard the British flanks, while a mounted force would lurk in Flagstaff Spruit, nor far from Mounted Infantry Hill, ready to launch an Elandslaagte-type charge on the British retreating from Wagon Hill.

Not all the Boers committed to attack Platrand on the night of 5th/6th January were as anxious to take part as the leader of the Harrismith commando. Though the Boers of Krugersdorp were quite prepared to face the British, they could not bring themselves to cross the Klip river, now in spate, and went back to their camp. So did half the Pretoria commando on the other side of Ladysmith. In the centre of the Boer front, some of the Vryheiders and the Germans found Fourie's Spruit an attractive place to regroup and generally linger. But no such lack of fortitude was tolerated on the western front, where the Free Staters, with de Villiers in the van, marched straight to the starting place and prepared for the assault. "At about ten o'clock," wrote Pastor Kestell, "we, the Harrismith burghers, left the laager in order to climb the hill at half past two . . . we halted a while, and those who could, slept till one o'clock on Saturday morning, 6th January, 1900."

It was probably as well for de Villiers that the commandos clambering up through the scrub, grass and stones were almost certainly unaware of the true state of the British defences at the top, imperfect though these were soon shown to be. Since the early days of the siege, when White had only been able to spare 600 men of the Manchesters and Imperial Light Horse to defend a 4,000-yard front, the British had been active. Three companies of the 60th Rifles now held the central sector of the line. In addition, substantial earthworks, with walls seven feet high and twelve feet thick, had been constructed at the top of the reverse slope, interspersed with gun emplacements for Goulburn's 42nd Battery R.F.A., as well as a protective screen of picquets on the forward edge of the plateau. But the failure to remove the grass on the flat land in between—200 yards wide in some places and 800 yards in others—cost many British lives on the day of the battle.

There was very little sleeping that night on Wagon Hill. While the expectation of the battle to come kept the Harrismith commando awake, as its members rested among the boulders on their side of the hill, it was the noise and the clatter of fatigue parties which deprived the Imperial Light Horse of sleep. Lieutenant R. Digby-Jones, the man who had destroyed the Boer howitzer on Surprise Hill three weeks before, was now about to install two British guns at Wagon Point. He and his party of sappers arrived shortly after dark and began preparing the gun pits. Soon after that, a fatigue party came over from the Manchesters and, finally, fifteen officers and ratings from the Naval Brigade struggled up the hill, driving a team of oxen hauling the 4.7-inch naval gun from Junction. Two companies of Gordon Highlanders came to act as guards.

All was quiet until, at about 2.45 in the morning, Corporal Dunn, in charge of the I.L.H. forward picquets, challenged the advancing Boers in what Kestell described as "a beautiful voice ringing out in the morning air." Immediately, battle was joined.

Captain Mathias of the I.L.H. got in a few shots with the Hotchkiss, Digby-Jones kicked over the lanterns at the 4.7-inch gun emplacement and, while sailors joined sappers in a scramble for rifles, the Gordons poured up the hill to lend a hand. Some of the Boers retired to safety, joining those of their comrades who had failed to advance at all, but many held their ground. Veldt-Kornets Lyon and Zacharias de Jager urged their men on with great dash and determination, bounding from boulder to boulder upwards in the direction of the British gunfire. For two hours, the clashes in the dark continued, as first one side and then the other fought to capture or hold individual positions. But there were no sides, just groups, and here and there a lone rifleman, everyone firing at flashes directed towards them. Both Boer and Briton found it difficult to distinguish between each other in the dark, and, of those who died on Wagon Hill that night, some never knew if it was friend or foe who killed them.

The sound of firing sparked off feverish activity in the British command. Colonel Ian Hamilton, blasted out of his town house in Ladysmith on New Year's Day, had moved himself and his 7th Brigade headquarters out to Caesar's Camp in a position near the Manchesters. Woken by the firing, Hamilton took immediate action. He contacted General White through his newly-installed field telephone to ask for reinforcements and then, ordering Major Miller-Wallnut to follow him with two companies of Gordons, he set out in the direction of trouble. He very soon found it.

Arriving at the foot of Wagon Hill at 5 am, Hamilton learned that a good part of its crest was firmly in Boer hands. He was much relieved to welcome a few minutes later Colonel Edwards, who, with three squadrons of I.L.H., had galloped out from Ladysmith, while, not far behind, were four more companies of Gordon Highlanders. These were the first of the reinforcements ordered into action by White, but, already, tragedy had struck the Gordons. Their commander, Colonel Dick-Cunyngham, had been killed by a stray bullet as they marched out of Ladysmith, so, without him, the Gordons were sent off to Caesar's Camp to reinforce the Manchesters, while the Light Horse were immediately committed to the task of driving the Boers off Wagon Hill.

In the gathering light of day, wave after wave of British troops poured up the slopes of Wagon Hill, only to be bloodily repulsed by the tenacious Boer marksmen. The Earl of Dufferin's only son, Lieutenant Lord Ava, was shot through the forehead as he confidently rose up from behind a rock to inspect the field. Within an hour such redoubtable warriors as Colonel Edwards, Major Karri Davies and Captain Codrington were all out of action. Even the arrival of the 60th Rifles could do nothing to dislodge the Boers.

The main moment of drama was yet to come, however. At midday, both de Villiers and Hamilton hit on the same idea of turning their opponent's flank at Wagon Point. De Villiers' men got there first, and drove the defenders downhill in disorder. Hamilton, fortunately, was on the scene and, rallying the retreating troops, led his men in a mad race with the Boers for the 4.7-inch gun pit. His fitness and sprinting ability got him there just ahead of the field, though the effort of doing so showed up in his shooting, for he missed the leading Boer at point-blank range. Then Jacob de Villiers (not the Commandant) shot Major Miller-Wallnut dead and was himself immediately killed by Trooper Albrecht of the I.L.H. De Jager of Harrismith shot Albrecht and Lieutenant Digby-Jones shot de Jager. The British gun was saved and the flank remained unturned.

Meanwhile, the Manchesters at Caesar's Camp had also been in the thick of the action. Only minutes after Hamilton had set off for Wagon Hill, the Boer commandos reached the crest of the hill between the left-hand picquet of the Manchesters and the right flank of the Natal Volunteers. Turning to their left, the Boers set upon the Manchester picquet and, having overwhelmed it, moved on to the next. For an hour the Manchesters held grimly to their rifle-pits and sangars, whilst, with equal bravery and resolution, the Boers pressed on.

With the Boers in possession of the eastern slopes of the hill, outflanking the Manchesters and harassing them from the front as well, the situation at daybreak was clearly unsatisfactory. No one was better placed to observe it than Colonel W. Royston, commanding the Natal Volunteers. He at once dispatched a squadron under his namesake, Captain "Galloping Jack" Royston, to the rescue. The leading troopers were soon in trouble—four of them being shot down when they were tricked into revealing themselves by a group of Heidelbergers claiming to be members of the Ladysmith Town Guard. But the Heidelbergers were swiftly dispersed when Royston met up with a company of Gordon Highlanders, whose commander, Captain the Hon. R. Carnegie, led a highly-effective bayonet charge. Before long the Scotsmen were in possession of the rifle-pits so recently tenanted by the now-dead men of the Manchesters, and, for the moment, the British position was stabilized, if not restored.

While the infantrymen of both sides found what cover and comfort they could, watching each other for signs of movement and feeling the ever more blistering rays of the sun, the gunners took over. Goulburn's 42nd Battery on Caesar's Camp pinned down the Boer reinforcements south of Platrand and he, in turn, became the main target for the "Long Tom" on Bulwana. Then, Major A. J. Abdy's 53rd Battery came into action, effectively dispersing the Boers on the eastern crest of Caesar's Camp.

Abdy's performance had an august spectator, for Commandant-

General Joubert, together with his wife, was on Bulwana watching the battle. It was this gaunt, determined, little old lady who is reputed to have been the first to notice the damage being done by Abdy's guns and to have ordered the gun-crew of "Long Tom" to change target and open fire against them. Luckily, Abdy was well-concealed and casualties among his battery were slight, with the exception of Sergeant Boseley, who was carried off the field minus an arm and a leg, but still shouting encouragement to his men. It is unlikely that Mevrou Joubert stayed long, for Lieutenant Halsey's 4.7-inch naval gun on Cove Redoubt quickly sent over a few well-placed shells in the direction of "Long Tom" of Bulwana.

Meanwhile, back in Ladysmith, White was becoming progressively more anxious about the position. He heliographed Buller, asking him to launch a relieving demonstration from Chieveley, but little was done. By four o'clock that afternoon, he had committed Major W. Blewitt's 21st Battery R.F.A., two companies of the 60th Rifles, 5th Dragoon Guards, and 18th Hussars—the cavalry dismounted—as reinforcements to Wagon Hill. The 5th Lancers, 19th Hussars and six companies of the Rifle Brigade were to fill the gaps between the Manchesters, Gordon Highlanders and Natal Volunteers at the Caesar's Camp end. But still de Villiers held his ground.

Then, a thunderstorm broke. Ian Hamilton described it as "Terrific rain—never—before or since—have I seen anything like it", while Donald Macdonald wrote:

"Hail fell in blinding flakes as large as a shilling. It was as though an offended heaven were visiting upon men her punishment for the carnage there. Everything was blotted out. At fifty yards, figures of men were seen as faint shadows through a fog. The sixty guns were silenced in a moment in the face of heaven's more vivid and deafening artillery."

In the midst of the storm, White decided on his last throw. Having sent his entire reserves of cavalry and infantry to the battle in the south, he now ordered the Devons to retire from their position on the defence perimeter on the opposite side of Ladysmith, and make a forced march to Wagon Hill. The Boers must, at all costs, be driven from their positions before dusk. At about 5 pm, five officers and 184 men under Colonel Park arrived, soaked to the skin, at the foot of the hill and Park reported to Hamilton for orders. He recorded the conversation thus in his diary.

"Well, Park, there are about fifty Boers holding a small ridge of rocks right in front of the line we are holding here, and only a hundred yards off; they have been there all day and are picked shots, and we cannot get them out . . . We have men almost on three sides of them, but they are all under cover of the rocks and pick off our men, if they show even their heads . . . The only way is to rush them with the bayonet; can you do it?"

With parched lips, despite the rain, shuffling feet and hands fidgeting with ammunition belts, the Devons waited anxiously for the inevitable order. "Fix bayonets" said Park, and turned to the bugler. The metallic clatter of cold steel on muzzle clips stopped and the first company, under Lieutenant Field, moved off, followed by the second wave under Captain Lafone and then a third under Lieutenant Masterson. There was no one more competent to tell the story of the charge than Colonel Park himself.

"When all was ready Colonel Hamilton said, 'Go on, and God bless you', and away we went, the men cheering and shouting for all they were worth. The first few yards we were under cover, but when we reached the top of the crest we were met by the most awful storm of bullets. I have never heard such a hot fire in my life, and can only compare it to the crackling of a dry gorse branch when thrown into a fire. We saw then for the first time what we had to do. The little ridge of rocks which the Boers held was right in front of us, and between us was 130 yards of open flat grass without the smallest cover or shelter of any kind. The men behaved most splendidly; every man went as straight and hard as he could for the enemy's ridge, and there was not the slightest sign of checking or wavering, though, as I ran, I could see men falling like ninepins on both sides of me; and then at last, to my intense relief, when we were within about fifteen yards of them, I saw the Boers suddenly jump up, turn tail, and fly down the hill for their lives, and the position was ours."

Unfortunately for the Devons, there were still some Boers on their flanks. Under a hail of bullets, about six of which found their mark, Masterson ran two hundred yards to the I.L.H. to direct their fire before collapsing. Over on the other flank, half a company of Manchesters under Captain Menzies extended the line of the Devons, and, between them all, they drove the Boers from the hill. But not without resistance. The tenacity and courage of Commandant de Villiers and the Free Staters who had survived the sixteen hours of battle was at no time more resolute than now. Determined not to be pursued headlong downhill into the dongas in flood, they stuck it out

in the gathering dusk—saturated, hungry, exhausted and many of them wounded.

While de Villiers was parrying questions about missing men whom he knew to be dead, Colonel Park did the round of the bodies behind him. He had seen Lafone sink quietly to his knees with a bullet hole behind his ear. Then he found Field and Walker, attached from the Somersets, and about thirty of his men. At 7.30 pm he was given soup by the 60th Rifles; at the same time de Villiers went back to his camp. Platrand and victory was left to the British. Ladysmith had been saved.

One hundred and fifty British and Natal officers and men died that day, and many more were wounded. Five were awarded the VC.

> Lieutenant R. Digby-Jones, R.E. (posthumous)
> Lieutenant J. Masterson, 1st Bn. Devon Regiment
> Private J. Pitts, 1st Bn. Manchester Regiment
> Private R. Scott, 1st Bn. Manchester Regiment
> Trooper H. Albrecht, Imperial Light Horse (posthumous)

The Boers had no similar system for counting their casualties or honouring their heroes, but their losses that day were probably as high as the British and their level of bravery was certainly no less. If awards for gallantry had been issued, the following would undoubtedly have received them.

> Commandant C. J. de Villiers
> Veldt-Kornet Jan Lyon
> Veldt-Kornet Jacob de Villiers
> Veldt-Kornet Jan van Wyk
> Veldt-Kornet Zacharias de Jager

All, except C. J. de Villiers, posthumously.

A Boer commando, somewhere near Spion Kop, scene of one of the most bloody battles of the war.

18 Spion Kop

"There cannot have been many battlefields where there was such an accumulation of horrors within so small a compass." (Deneys Reitz, *Commando*, London 1929)

Three days after Wagon Hill, *Dunottar Castle* came back to South Africa, this time bearing the famous old soldier Field-Marshal Lord Roberts to replace Buller as Commander-in-Chief, and the almost equally celebrated young soldier, Lieutenant-General Horatio Herbert Kitchener, as his Chief-of-Staff. On the same day Lieutenant-General Sir Charles Warren's 5th Division was sloshing its way into rain-sodden Frere, where the forward units had arrived the afternoon before, hot-foot from Durban and England.

The 5th Division was a timely reinforcement for Buller, but there was bad news, too, for the luckless commander of the Natal Field Force. Winston Churchill, with the enhanced glamour of an escaped captive, was back at the front and a sardonic comment in the *Morning Leader* announced his arrival. "We have received no confirmation of the statement that Lord Lansdowne (the British War Minister) has, pending the arrival of Lord Roberts, appointed Mr. Churchill to

British dead at Spion Kop, with a Boer wearing a velvet waistcoat lying among them. Note the missing boots in this picture, which was probably taken two or three days after the battle.

command the troops in South Africa, with General Sir Redvers Buller, V.C., as his Chief-of-Staff."

The recuperative effect of four weeks' contemplation and preparation since the traumatic experience at Colenso and the steady inflow of reinforcements had emboldened Buller to think positively once more, and the scene was set for another attempt to relieve Ladysmith. Buller, replaced now by Roberts as Commander-in-Chief, but still left in command on the Natal front, reverted to his original idea of a flanking movement westwards to Potgieter's Drift. On 10th January 1900 he was ready to start.

Leaving Barton's 6th Brigade to pass the time at Chieveley, not far from the position from which they had been given so little to do at the battle of Colenso, Buller set off in rain, mud and mist with an army of nearly 25,000 men. Atkins, the *Manchester Guardian* correspondent who watched the army depart on the sixteen-mile journey to Springfield, Buller's chosen spot for the new base, thought the column looked like a rope being dragged across country.

"It seemed endless, this rope made of all the strands that hold an army together—infantry, guns, gunners, ammunition, horsemen, waggons with forage, rations and tents, waggons hung all over like a gypsy van with clattering utensils, kaffirs plying whips like fishing rods, bakers, cooks, farriers, telegraphists, type-writers, paymasters and paymasters' clerks, telegraph wires and poles, sappers, chaplains, doctors, ambulance waggons, bearers, 'body-snatchers', signallers with flags and heliographs, sailors, naval guns, headquarters' staff, cobblers, balloons, and aeronauts, limelight flashlights, traction engines with heavy lists to port or starboard, pontoons, etc . . . etc . . . etc . . ."

The "rope" which Atkins watched in the strengthening light of mid-morning, squirming its way through the mud and slurry at an average speed of one mile per hour, was, in fact, Lieutenant-General Sir Cornelius Clery, wearing his celebrated loose-fitting trousers, and the 2nd Division. There were men from Surrey, Devon and Yorkshire in General Hildyard's 2nd Brigade, the Irishmen of General Hart's 5th Brigade and the daring Lord Dundonald leading the Mounted Brigade. And, if Atkins had returned the following day, he would have seen the newcomer to South Africa, Lieutenant-General Warren, take the field. Two brigades of Warren's 5th Division—the 10th under Major-General Coke and the 11th under Major-General Woodgate— were equally inexperienced in South African conditions, as they had arrived from England on the same day as their divisional commander. However, the 4th Brigade, under Major-General Lyttelton, were not newcomers. But the real mud-churners of the expedition were the eight batteries of Royal Artillery, the Navy with their two 4.7-inch guns and their eight 12-pounders, and the corps troops, the supply columns, the engineers and the ambulances.

While the lumbering, struggling soldiery battled their way to Springfield with 650 wagons—the wheels frequently buried to the axle-trees—the Boers kept pace on a parallel course across the Tugela. Winston Churchill, for one, was not surprised:

"The vast amount of baggage this army takes with it on the march hampers

its movements and utterly precludes all possibility of surprising the enemy . . . the consequence is that roads are crowded, drifts are blocked, marching troops are delayed, and all rapidity of movement is out of the question. Meanwhile, the enemy completes the fortification of his positions, and the cost of capturing them rises."

The enterprising Dundonald soon became irked by the rate of progress, however, and obtained permission to press on with the Mounted Brigade in advance of the main force. Having reached Springfield and secured the bridge there, he carried on to Spearman's Farm. By nightfall he had consolidated his position and the Mounted Brigade was in command of Spearman's, Mount Alice and Potgieter's Drift below it. Buller's first objective had been achieved.

Nor did Dundonald stop here. The following morning, the use of the crossing point was denied to the Boers in a gallant and enterprising act by a volunteer detachment of the South African Light Horse. Under heavy rifle fire, Captain Carlisle and his men swam the eighty turbulent yards of the Tugela in full spate and brought back the pontoon from the northern Boer-held bank. Finally, Dundonald heliographed a confident message to Ladysmith.

Dundonald was straining at the leash by now, but Buller was in no hurry and was quite content to wait nearly a week for the provisioning of the Springfield camp, having issued to his assembled army a stirring declaration of intent:

*"Springfield, 12 January, 1900
The Field Force is now advancing to the relief of Ladysmith, where, surrounded by superior forces, our comrades have gallantly defended themselves for the last ten weeks. The General Commanding knows that everyone in the Force feels as he does; we must be successful . . ."*

Adopting his customary posture of a game-spotting deer stalker reclining against a convenient rock with telescope propped upon bent knees, Buller now took stock of the situation. The view was too much like Colenso for his liking—the same gentle downward decline, the same swollen, serpentine Tugela river, and Boers on the range of hills beyond. They, for their part, were busy preparing for attack.

But there was one dramatic difference. From Potgieter's Drift, a thousand feet below him, Buller traced a road winding gently uphill to his right between the features of Brakfontein and Vaal Krantz and on into the plain, beyond which, sixteen miles away, he could actually see Ladysmith. Scanning the horizon from east to west, Buller noted with some concern the furious activity of the Boers on the opposing ridge, and over to his left the massive buttress of Spion Kop with the craggy, serrated face of Thabanyama beyond.

Perhaps his observations left doubts in Buller's mind, for two days went by without orders or action. The officers stopped taking bets on the date for the Ladysmith march-in, while the ordinary soldiers furtively began to chant the traditional song "Oh, why are we waiting?" Still Buller remained silent, though Captain C. E. Radclyffe of the 1st Bn. Rifle Brigade expressed his general's thoughts quite well in his diary. "Charging hills is an absolutely irresistible temptation to Generals out here."

So matters rested until the 16th of January. On that afternoon, Winston Churchill, now serving as an unpaid Lieutenant in the South African Light Horse as well as a highly paid war correspondent, saw signs of movement.

"We noticed a change in the appearance of the infantry camps on the reverse slopes of Spearman's Hill. There was a busy bustling of men; the tents began to look baggy, then they subsided together; the white disappeared, and the camping grounds became simply brown patches of moving soldiery. Lyttelton's brigade had received orders to march at once. Whither?"

Buller's plan had been finalized and the relief force was once more on the move. Lyttelton's 4th Brigade, supported by Coke's 10th Brigade, Bethune's Mounted Infantry, the ten naval guns and some additional artillery were to demonstrate noisily and frontally across Potgieter's Drift against the Boers on Brakfontein. At the same time, Warren, with the main force of twelve battalions of infantry, thirty-six guns and 1,600 cavalrymen, was to proceed quietly by a night march to Trichardt's Drift, five miles to the east. From there, Dundonald's mounted force was to be dispatched round to the extreme right of the Boer position on Thabanyama. "The Boer covering army was to be swept back on Ladysmith," wrote Churchill in vivid, though somewhat anatomical imagery, "by a powerful left arm, the pivoting shoulder of which was at Potgieter's, the elbow at Trichardt's Drift, and the enveloping hand—the cavalry under Lord Dundonald—stretching out towards Acton Homes."

The one thing that was not clear was the role that Buller had chosen for himself. In paragraph five of his orders to Warren he stated:

"5. At Potgieter's there will be the 4th Brigade, part of the 10th Brigade, one battery Royal Field Artillery, one howitzer battery, two 4.7 inch naval guns. With them I shall threaten both the positions in front of us, and also attempt a crossing at Skiet's Drift, so as to hold the enemy off you as much as possible."

In fact, Buller turned over control of the main operation to Warren and retired with his telescope to his camp at Spearman's Farm. He had relegated himself to a role more appropriate to that of an umpire at an Aldershot exercise than that of General Officer Commanding the Natal Field Force.

The fact that Warren and Buller did not like each other made a most unpromising basis for a successful campaign on the Tugela. Though both were life-long soldiers, their careers had little in common, apart from a few battles against primitive tribesmen. War and the War Office were all that Buller knew, but Warren had made sorties into both politics and the police force in a career noted for its turbulence.

Warren had won high marks as a student at both Sandhurst and Woolwich and his first job on leaving the "shop" was to conduct a trigonometrical survey of Gibraltar. More surveys followed in South Africa, a battle or two in the Kaffir Wars and an exercise in re-imposing Pax Britannica in Bechuanaland (Botswana) after a Boer-provoked rebellion. A determined effort to win a parliamentary seat as an Independent Liberal led inevitably to disciplinary clashes with the War Office and, for a time, Warren was content to serve again as a soldier—this time in Egypt.

In 1886 Warren, still only forty-six, became Commissioner of the Metropolitan Police. Though he survived the inconclusive investigations of the "Jack the Ripper" murders, sharp criticism of his militant dispersal of Socialist meetings in London eventually forced his resignation. Back in the army again, Warren served for five years in Singapore, and then returned to England, with, it seemed, little to look forward to but semi-retirement. However, the outbreak of war changed his fortunes; on 7th November 1899 he was given command of the 5th Division and orders to sail to South Africa.

For good or ill, Buller had made his decision. But, unfortunately, Warren showed no more sign of haste after the operation was launched than Buller had in planning it. Two full days after Warren's forward units had arrived at Trichardt's Drift his rear echelons were still crossing the Tugela—a spectacle which provoked a Boer presidential command cancelling Louis Botha's leave and removed all vestige of surprise from Buller's original plan. Even an eminently restrained appeal from the newly-arrived Lord Roberts—"It is, I am sure, needless for me to urge the importance of there being no delay upon the road. Rapidity of movement is everything against an enemy so skilful in strengthening defensive positions"—seems to have been disregarded. The whole concept of a flanking movement from the left, with Lyttelton "refusing" from the right, was nonsense. The British army was seen to be poised for a frontal assault all along the line from Brakfontein to Thabanyama.

The one senior British officer still keen to apply the plan for turning the Boer right flank seems to have been Dundonald—and his attempts to do so led only to an eventual rebuke by Warren. Pushing on westwards on 18th January across Venter's Spruit, where he left 300 men of Thorneycroft's mounted infantry—and had another 500 of the 1st Royal Dragoons "confiscated" by Warren to guard his cattle kraals—Dundonald had advanced almost as far as Acton Homes by early afternoon. At about 2.30 pm his vanguard, under Major Graham, intercepted some Boer reinforcements, inflicted heavy casualties, brought back twenty-four prisoners, and the Boer leader—dead.

Encouraged by the spectacle of Acton Homes with the easy road to Ladysmith beyond and by his quick success in the first direct encounter with the Boers since Colenso, Dundonald appealed for immediate support for a drive onwards to execute the relief. But Warren was obdurate and reinforcements were denied. "Our objective is not Ladysmith," he said, "our objective is to effect a junction with General Sir R. Buller's force and then await orders from him." Not content with this, Warren summoned Dundonald to appear before him. Dundonald found him personally directing the passage of his baggage wagons across the Tugela. Between bellowed orders, Warren delivered a pedantic lecture on the role of cavalry, ending up with the injunction "I want your cavalry close to me".

Dundonald was rightly furious, for Warren's obduracy may well have cost the British the chance of a quick and spectacular victory. Nor was Buller himself best pleased with Warren's fiddling about in the

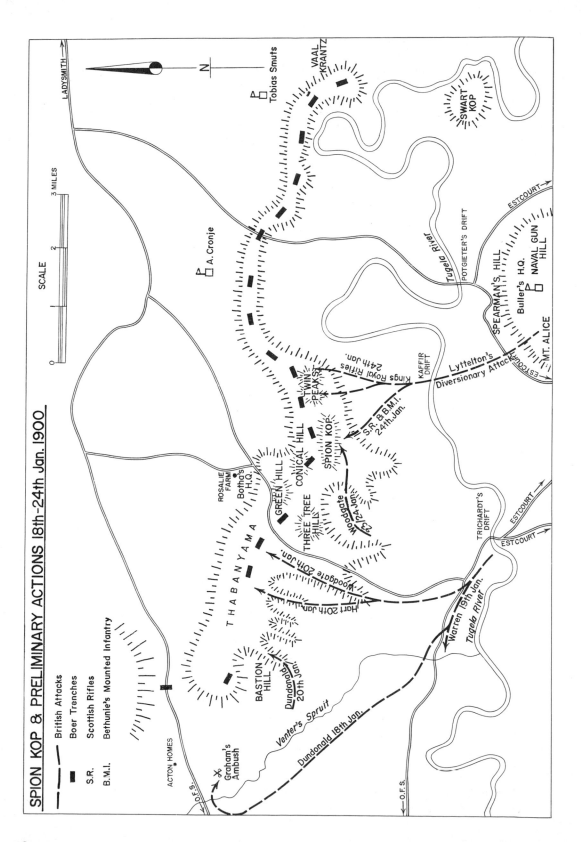

SPION KOP & PRELIMINARY ACTIONS 18th-24th Jan. 1900

SCALE

0   2   3 MILES

- — — — British Attacks
- ▬ Boer Trenches
- S.R. Scottish Rifles
- B.M.I. Bethunie's Mounted Infantry

LADYSMITH

N

Tobias Smuts

VAAL KRANTZ

SWART KOP

A. Cronje

Tugela River

POTGIETER'S DRIFT

ESTCOURT

SPEARMAN'S HILL

Buller's H.Q.

NAVAL GUN HILL

MT. ALICE

ESTCOURT

Kings Royal Rifles 24th Jan.

KAFFIR DRIFT

Lyttelton's Diversionary Attack

TWIN PEAKS

S.R. & B.M.I. 24th Jan.

GREEN HILL

CONICAL HILL

SPION KOP

THREE TREE HILL

Woodgate 23/24 Jan.

ROSALIE FARM

Botha's H.Q.

THABANYAMA

Thabanyama Woodgate 20th Jan.

Hart 20th Jan.

TRICHARDT'S DRIFT

ESTCOURT

Warren 19th Jan.

Tugela River

ESTCOURT

BASTION HILL

Dundonald 20th Jan.

Venter's Spruit

ACTON HOMES

O.F.S.

Graham's Ambush

Dundonald 18th Jan.

O.F.S.

area of Trichardt's Drift, conducting "dress rehearsals", while the Boers entrenched on Thabanyama.

Eventually, goaded on by Buller's occasional sorties from semi-retirement on Mount Alice, Warren began his attack. Choosing to disregard completely the left-flank concept proposed by Buller, seconded by Dundonald, and accepted by nearly everybody else who had thought about the matter, he preferred to cut the corner and opted for the track past Fairview and Rosalie Farms as his line of march.

At first things went well enough. An assault on Thabanyama during the afternoon on 20th January led by Woodgate's brigade on the right, followed by Hart's brigade in the centre and the dashing Dundonald on the left was not unsuccessful, except that the positions the British carried turned out to be a false crest. The main Boer entrenchments were a thousand yards further uphill. Only Dundonald achieved undisputed possession of his target, the summit of Bastion Hill. Two more days of artillery pounding failed to dislodge the Boers, or satisfy Buller's growing appetite for results, and once again the commander of the Ladysmith relief force rode over to see Warren.

"I told him," wrote Buller afterwards, "that unless he could attack, he must withdraw". At the end of a heated exchange, with Warren's dismissal a real possibility, Warren proposed and Buller agreed—reluctantly as he claimed—an attack on Spion Kop. Neither general went as far as to express any precise view about why the feature should be taken or what should be done thereafter by the attacking force. "It has got to stay there," was Buller's tart and unenlightening reply to Colonel à Court's question on this point. Woodgate's brigade was chosen for the task, while the rest of the mighty army looked on.

Topographically, the assignment was no sinecure, for only on the northern side, held by Schalk Burger's commandos, was the approach to the summit an easy one. From the level of the Tugela river there was 1,500 feet to climb, but not much else was known to Warren about what happened at the top, for the only reliable source—the proprietor of the land—was at that moment locked up in Ladysmith.

At dusk on 23rd January the attack started. 1,700 men formed the spearhead, most of them from Lancashire but some from Johannesburg, led by the gigantic Thorneycroft, whose volunteer regiment carried his name. General Talbot Coke, still hobbling about on a broken leg and replaced for that reason by Woodgate, watched them leave, ignoring, to their unsuspected, but ultimate, ruination, a pile of empty sandbags as they marched by. It was not long before a barking dog in danger of strangulation, was led off the hillside by a boy bugler, using a rifle pull-through as an improvised lead. Woodgate, no longer in the best of health, was being helped by his batman up the steeper sections of the slope. Finally, the first troops reached the summit. A Corporal Jeoffreys described the scene:

"There is a commotion in the rear and the clicking of bayonets tells that the second line is being formed. 'Advance . . . Down . . . Creep forward' and the front line are moving forward on their hands and knees within seventy yards of the enemy. Still no challenge. There is another commotion to the rear caused by the dropping of several picks and shovels by the overloaded Royal Engineers and immediately the challenge 'Wie's daar?' in front followed by a terrible fusillade."

Stunned by the sudden assault, the Boers of the Vryheid commando lost no time in fleeing in face of a shrieking wave of bayonet-wielding Lancastrians, but not before one of them had been transfixed by a huge subaltern of the Lancashire Fusiliers and "tossed into the air as if he were a stook of corn".

The British had taken the hill. The question for Woodgate and Thorneycroft was what to do next. The Royal Engineers began digging frantically into what turned out to be solid rock in an attempt

to provide an entrenchment. But there was no means of knowing what the outlook was from the top of Spion Kop, shrouded in mist at three o'clock in the morning. The British could not tell that they were on a three-acre triangular plateau with the south-western angle pointing towards Trichardt's Drift whence they had just come, and an easterly spur extending to Twin Peaks and Aloe Knoll—both soon to be occupied by Boers, as was Conical Hill along a narrow saddle to the north. It was not long before the disadvantages of this stony arena, on

Warren's force crossing Trichardt's Drift on the way to Spion Kop. The distant relations between Warren and Buller were another handicap which was never satisfactorily overcome.

which entrenching tools made almost no impression, became clear to them.

For three hours the British hacked at the solid earth and rocks and soon the soldiers were thinking of rest and the officers of the missing sandbags. When dawn came, their boomerang-shaped trench was long enough to accommodate the Royal Lancasters and the South Lancashire Regiment along the left-hand arm facing north-west, while the Lancashire Fusiliers shared 180 yards of the right-hand arm with Thorneycroft's mounted infantry. But the earthworks were pitifully shallow. At no point could a man secure cover except by lying prone, and, even then, he would be an easy victim of overhead bursting shrapnel. And when the mist lifted at 7 am Woodgate and Thorneycroft realized that they should have entrenched 400 yards further forward, where the ridge dropped sharply downwards—to the Boers and Louis Botha.

Woken up by the rifle shots and the cheers of the British on the summit, Botha performed a massive feat of leadership in the small hours of the morning, rallying and re-forming the dispersing Boer commandos. Haranguing and, in some cases, physically striking, would-be deserters, he sent Commandant Prinsloo, perhaps his most resolute subordinate, to take Aloe Knoll, the Germiston commando under Veldt-Kornet Albert to Conical Hill and Sarel Marais' men of Heidelberg to Twin Peaks. The Pretoria commando arrived from the Ladysmith perimeter and was at once dispatched up the northern slopes of Spion Kop and the men of Utrecht ordered to Green Hill. By 7.30 in the morning they were all in position. On the British side, General Woodgate was drinking tea on the summit of Spion Kop, while his troops were looking forward to a quiet day in the sunshine.

Shortly before eight o'clock, by which time there was more blue in the sky than cloud, the fusillade began. Boer riflemen firing from around an arc of 120 degrees were supported by two heavy guns behind Green Hill and another under Major Wolmarans of the Transvaal Artillery behind Conical Hill. The lounging British soldiery were shocked into a frantic scramble for cover, but they rallied equally quickly when their officers took charge and the mist mercifully descended once more. Woodgate himself reacted sharply, sending 200 men forward to the outer crest-line and Colonel à Court back down the hill to Warren with an appeal for artillery support and a show of strength by Lyttelton on the right.

By the time à Court reached Warren's headquarters at Three Tree Hill—his stumbling downhill scramble took only an hour and a half to cover the ground which the column had taken seven hours to climb— the situation on the summit had sharpened into a desperate close-quarter conflict. At 8.30, when the mist finally lifted, the Boers attacked once more—this time many of them a good deal closer than before. As the ebb and flow of hand-to-hand battle developed on the crest-line it was mainly the long-distance enfillading fire from both flanks and the shelling which decimated the British and the withering volleys downhill and spirited bayonet charges which dispatched the advancing Boers.

One of the first casualties was Woodgate himself, who was mortally wounded at about 8.30, and command then passed to Colonel Crofton of the Royal Lancasters, the next senior officer on the spot. The signal as received by Warren quite erroneously conveyed rather more than the sad news about his colleague: "Reinforce at once or all is lost. General dead."

Some believe that the signaller had added his own appreciation of the situation, but since he was blown to bits soon afterwards the facts will probably never be known. Certainly Warren's reaction showed that he took it seriously, for he replied: "I am sending two battalions and the Imperial Light Infantry are on their way up. You must hold on to the last. No surrender."

So more men poured up the hill into the Boer artillery's target area, with Major-General Coke to command them. But Coke's broken leg had not improved much since the day before and it was 5.30 in the afternoon before he reached the summit, having, some say, had a snooze on the way. In the meantime, it was becoming clear to Buller, the only general on either side whose location afforded a view of the whole battle area, that the man of the moment was Thorneycroft. This massive figure, something over twenty stone, was plainly identifiable through Buller's powerful telescope, galloping from one position to another, encouraging, urging, commanding. At 11.40 Buller drew Warren's attention to this in a signal: "Unless you put some good hard fighting man in command you will lose the hill. I suggest Thorney-croft." Warren immediately heliographed to the summit to this effect, but, unfortunately, no one thought of informing Coke that he had been superseded.

Buller's opinion was more than justified an hour or so later when the Lancashire Fusiliers, almost totally bereft of officers, began to crack. "The Lancs are giving in," wrote Corporal Jeoffreys, and this collapse on the right of the British position was described by yet another member of the same regiment—Thorneycroft's Mounted Infantry. In a letter to his parents, Benjamin Walker spoke of:

"a crowd of Lancashires who lay with their heads rolled up in their arms, laying flat on the ground, not daring to lift their guns to shoot, shaking and trembling with fear."

With as much speed as sheer physical weight and a twisted knee would permit, Thorneycroft charged towards the Boer leader who had come forward to accept the surrender of the shattered Lancastrians. "Take your men back to Hell, sir," he bellowed. "I'm in command here, and I allow no surrender." But he was too late and 150 Fusiliers went off to captivity and, no doubt, some dishonour. Minutes later, however, Thorneycroft recovered his composure and part of the lost ground, when the newly-arrived Middlesex Regiment joined him. Together with his own Mounted Infantry and a company of the more stout-hearted Lancastrians, they drove the Boers over the crest-line in a headlong bayonet charge.

For several hours the carnage continued in attacks and counter-attacks, where death and destruction were personally meted out by small groups locked in close-up combat. The one incident apart, the British never wavered and neither did the Boers withdraw. "Individual acts of heroism and cowardice of soldiers and burghers alike were all swallowed up in the monstrous confusion of this struggle," wrote Oliver Ransford. And no confusion was more acute than that which

Bringing in the wounded from Spion Kop. At least 500 British soldiers and Volunteers died in this attempt to break through to Ladysmith.

disrupted the British chain of command on the summit.

With the loss of heliograph operators and the untimely death of signallers and runners struck down with vital messages on their lips, nobody knew for certain who was in charge. Was it Thorneycroft, the natural leader on the spot and Buller's nominee, or General Coke, still short of the summit and even more short of breath, or Colonel Crofton, who, though wounded by now, was still the senior officer participating in the battle? There were other contenders too—Colonel Hill, the newcomer in command of the Middlesex who outranked Thorneycroft, and Colonel Cooke of the Scottish Rifles, who outranked Hill! Disputes were, on the whole, subdued by common purpose, but the misunderstandings were never totally resolved.

The responsibility for this lay firmly on the shoulders of Buller and Warren. And there was another, and more serious, charge to be laid against the two generals. Coke had already grasped the point that it was madness to thrust more and more reinforcements on to Spion Kop to be mown down by Boer shot and shell. Yet neither Buller nor Warren took the obvious step of ordering a relieving attack elsewhere.

General Lyttelton, however, realized that the sorely-pressed Thorneycroft needed relief and so ordered the 60th Rifles to attack Twin Peaks, on the Boer left flank. The attack went well, but Lyttelton had to contend not only with the Boers but also with Buller, who savagely reprimanded his subordinate for using his own initiative. The result was that the British withdrew shortly after consolidating their victory. So ended the only serious attempt to assist the British force on Spion Kop by diversionary action.

In the meantime, the seemingly ubiquitous Winston Churchill had found his way to the top of Spion Kop in company with Captain Brooke of the 7th Hussars. On his climb to the summit, he found his path obstructed by a trail of wounded coming downhill:

"Men were staggering along alone, or supported by comrades or crawling on hands and knees, or carried on stretchers. Corpses lay here and there. Many of the wounds were of a horrible nature. The splinters and fragments of the shell had torn and mutilated in the most ghastly manner. I passed about two hundred while I was climbing up . . ."

The two men got back at sunset and Churchill told Warren what he had seen. He also somewhat imprudently delivered the general a lecture on the terrible example of Majuba Hill and what the reactions of the "great British public" would be in the event of defeat. "Who is this man?" shouted Warren. "Take him away and put him under arrest." But he eventually calmed down and gave Churchill a written message to take back to Thorneycroft.

It was well after dark when Churchill made his return journey uphill past the dead, the dying and those who had simply had enough. He eventually found Thorneycroft sitting on the ground, surrounded by the surviving half of his regiment which had "fought for him like lions and followed him like dogs". Warren's proposal to send up reinforcements of infantry, sappers, and gunners to continue the fight the following day had no impact on Thorneycroft. "The retirement is in process," he told Churchill. "Better six good battalions safely off the hill tonight than a bloody mop-up in the morning."

In fact, Thorneycroft had given the orders for withdrawal some time before, having won over Colonel Hill who was in favour of holding on. Coke, for his part, had received orders to report to Warren and, reluctantly, hobbled down the hill. In his diary he commented "I hold that he (Warren) should not have taken me away from my command at such a crucial moment." For Coke, too, would have been in favour of staying.

Warren himself was asleep when Churchill found him. "I put my hand on his shoulder and woke him up. 'Colonel Thorneycroft is here, sir' ". The battle of Spion Kop was over.

The tragic irony of Scion Kop lay in the kaleidoscopic jumble of judgements during the operation and in later analyses of the battle. On the British side, the only man, save Lyttelton, who made a decision worthy of a senior commander was Thorneycroft, and it was wrong, for hindsight proved, and military discipline demanded, that he should have stayed on the hill. And the officer with the most direct claim on his soldierly allegiance, Warren, was dramatically and deplorably unworthy of it. For eleven hours he failed lamentably to command or, worse still, to communicate adequately with his lieutenants in the thick of battle. While Thorneycroft demonstrated the full range of military virtues—except unswerving obedience—Warren showed none, and Buller, a monarch in abdication, did little to assist except comment, sometimes to the point, but always as it happened, disruptively. No gesture was more unhelpful than his obstruction of Lyttelton's highly commendable initiative in dispatching reinforcements to Thorneycroft and the 60th Rifles to take Twin Peaks.

For the débâcle of Scion Kop Lord Roberts blamed Thorneycroft, Buller blamed Coke, and Warren, to his credit, blamed no one in particular. Buller's sternest critic was Lyttelton. It was Churchill, the meddler, who made the most charitable and, perhaps, the most pertinent comment of all. "I was also sorry for the army."

As for the Boers, subsequent recriminations were prolonged and passionate, especially since the Boer commanders knew that they had come within an inch of defeat. Botha, however, spent the night reorganizing his commandos, persuading his men to reoccupy Twin Peaks. At dawn, two Boer scouts, who had gone in search of a wounded comrade, were seen on Spion Kop itself. As Deneys Reitz put it: "Their presence there was proof that, almost unbelievably, defeat had turned to victory—the English were gone and the hill was still ours."

For most of the night, Spion Kop had been left by both sides to the dead and the dying, and a terrible stillness, broken only by the groans of the scarcely living and of undiscovered survivors. The following morning, Britons and Boers met again, but with different faces—Lieutenant Knox, of the Royal Army Medical Corps, a young Indian lawyer called Ghandi, and the other imperial stretcher bearers mingling with their Boer counterparts, trophy hunting here and there, and scavenging tenderly among the dead for boots and clothing, but always compassionate when a still-living soldier or burgher was found.

At least 500 British soldiers and Volunteers had died and Ladysmith was still as far from relief as it had been the day before. Spion Kop was in Boer hands, though neither side really wanted it any more.

19 The Waiting Game

"Our lingering faith is growing small. 'Where's Buller?' is the weary call." ("Marking Time", *Ladysmith Bombshell*, January 1900)

For nearly three weeks, between the battles of Wagon Hill and Spion Kop, January 1900 was a bleak month for the Ladysmith diarists, with "no news of Buller" the most recurrent theme for the militarily-minded, while weather, food, and health became ever more pressing preoccupations for all. Pomeroy monitored food prices on the open market and sent his diligent manservant, Wickham, on occasional foraging expeditions, while Colonel Park spent much of his time with the journalists, collecting newspaper reports about his regiment's performance at Wagon Hill. Soon he and his fellow officers were to have a new problem which Park recorded in a letter to his wife:

"A small hole appeared this morning, for the first time, in the toe of one of my thick socks. Considering that I have worn them all day and often all night for four months they have done well."

Civilians under siege in Ladysmith. Whisky is being offered for sale at £6 a bottle—the London price was four shillings.

Packs of playing cards became almost as revered as ammunition, and

officers who could teach new games were much sought after, though Park himself stuck firmly to patience. Pomeroy was appalled to discover that a fellow officer and gentleman was cheating at Piquet— "he does it in the shuffling". Bella Craw went to equally desperate and—for a nicely brought-up young lady—most regrettable lengths to relieve the tedium. The 18th January entry in her diary read:

"I did an awful thing today which I am afraid I will many a time regret, and that is to have on my arm tattooed:

1899
LADYSMITH
PRO PATRIA
1900"

Football matches and bagpipe playing gradually went out of fashion as legs thinned down and breath shortened. By the end of January, the infantry's battleworthiness was dramatically reduced. As General Sir Frederick Maurice noted in his Official History, "Even the short marches entailed by the relief of the outposts were already as much as many of the soldiers could manage, and that often only with many halts for rests by the way."

For the Royal Navy contingent, boredom was linked with anxiety, as shell husbandry became Captain Lambton's main preoccupation. At the start of the siege, his total arsenal consisted of 300 rounds for each of the two 4.7s and 290 rounds for each of the four 12-pounders. Lieutenant Hodges, in command of the 4.7 gun at Junction Hill, estimated that he had fired about 60 rounds on the first day and 30 on the second. Thereafter, an average firing rate of two or three shells a day was all that Lambton would allow, and by the end of December it had dropped to one. At Cove Redoubt, on 23rd December, Lieutenant Halsey, commanding the other 4.7, obtained special permission to fire off a week's ration at Bulwana's "Long Tom". Three weeks later, at the battle of Wagon Hill, he had a field day with 28 rounds, but, by the end of January, there was scarcely 100 rounds of 4.7 ammunition left.

Above all, soldier and civilian alike waited and watched for news of the relief force. For days, there was silence and jokes in the homemade journal *Ladysmith Bombshell* testified to a diminishing sense of humour: "If the relief column takes a day and a half to march a yard and a half, how much longer will the price of eggs be 10/- per dozen?" White himself commented acidly in a letter to his wife: "Sir R. Buller is still coming . . . The only effect of the approach of his force we have yet felt is that we have been receiving many shells from the Field Battery guns captured at Colenso on the 15th December."

Then, Buller's heliograph started flashing once more on the horizon, with the news that battle was once more to be joined—at Spion Kop. On 17th January, he signalled:

". . . I somehow think we are going to be successful this time . . . Every man in this force is doing his level best to relieve you. It is quite pleasant to see how keen the men are. I hope to be knocking at Lancer's Hill in six days from now."

Slowly the rumble of the British bombardment intensified, and, as it did so, all eyes in Ladysmith turned towards the Tugela. Cove Hill and Observation West were favoured vantage points and at first light on 24th January, when General Woodgate's men were frantically hacking at the rocks on the top of Spion Kop, many pairs of friendly binoculars were turned their way from Ladysmith. Lieutenant Pomeroy was among those watching and later recorded the scene in his history of his regiment.

". . . to everyone's delighted surprise, wagons were seen to be moving off from the laager at the foot of the hill; then men were to be seen coming down hurriedly from the upper slopes, and soon horsemen and wagons, in a confused mass were streaming away from the hill. To all, the same idea occurred, though they hardly dared put it into words—'Buller must have gained possession of the hill, and that means Ladysmith is saved, and only just in time, for the provisions are almost run out, and we have about reached the limit of our endurance!'"

The hasty and the hungry could wait no longer and hurried downhill to breakfast and to break the good news to their friends. But they did not see—and neither could those who stayed, even with the most powerful field-glasses—the determined, vigorous and successful rallying operations being conducted by Louis Botha on the reverse slopes of Spion Kop.

Lieutenant-Colonel St. John Gore, commanding the 5th Dragoon Guards, remained all day with his adjutant on the hill. They noticed the pace and frequency of the northward-trekking Boer parties gradually decrease until suddenly his adjutant remarked, some time in the afternoon, "Hullo! they're coming back." By this time Pomeroy had joined them and commented:

". . . sure enough some of the horsemen were returning, almost as fast as they had left, while other little single figures were galloping wildly away from the hill. They looked like ants and, like ants, they stopped and communicated with the figures that were moving in the opposite direction to themselves, and ever the stream that was going towards the hill got stronger and stronger, and that which was moving away from the hill grew less and less. Soon the Colonel and adjutant mounted their horses and rode slowly down to Green Horse Valley to break the news to those below. That was the hardest day of the whole siege."

For the next two days, deprived of news from Buller, everybody in Ladysmith formed their own views on what had happened in the battle. Of them, none was more harassed by the silence than Gore, who had taken the trouble to watch. He wrote afterwards with some feeling.

"An almost unique situation. Everyone in the world has known what happened long ago, except ourselves, the interested parties, under whose very eyes the battle has taken place! They know in London, America and Australia. Every Boer around us knows. But we don't know. Thank Heaven we had duck for dinner tonight in our Mess."

St. John Gore was not the only commander to be depressed by the

Spion Kop set-back. When Buller's dispatch was finally received, Colonel Royston, commanding the Natal Volunteers over on the Klip river valley sector, "blew up" one of his officers in an outburst of frayed nerves. "I wish, Molyneux," he protested angrily, "you would stop whistling that beastly thing; you do nothing else but go about blowing off that wretched 'stable jacket' and creating despondency among the troops." Captain Molyneux apologized sheepishly and his fellow officers stood around in silent sympathy, embarrassed, bored, waiting.

At this stage neither surrender nor a break-out by the garrison seemed to be tenable propositions. Food was now the question of the hour. "I could feed the men another month, but not all the horses," White said in a signal, and then, a few days later, "By sacrificing the rest of my horses I can hold out for six weeks, keeping my guns efficiently horsed and 1,000 men mounted on moderately efficient horses."

The decision was made. White retained only one squadron of mounted men for each regiment; the remainder were issued with rifles and bayonets and sent off to join the infantry, their chargers being taken out beyond the defence perimeter and turned loose. For several days, while the Ladysmith command suppressed thoughts about horseflesh for humans as though it were cannibalism, abandoned horses galloped up and down the streets of the town, some fearfully lacerated by barbed-wire obstacles encountered in the stampede back to Ladysmith. Others found their way to their places in the cavalry lines and stood there, whinnying and waiting for the nose-bags which many a tearful trooper was able to smuggle along furtively, while officers deliberately looked the other way.

The fate of Ladysmith now lay in the hands of Colonel E. W. D. Ward. The notion that every crisis and time of stress produces its man of the moment was as true in that town as anywhere else. If December was General Hunter's month, with the successful sorties against the Boer big guns, and January belonged to Colonel Ian Hamilton, for his spirited defence of Wagon Hill, so Ward's administration of food supplies gave him a special claim to the February title.

For the cavalry, 10th February was the historic day when the first hundred of their mounts were selected for slaughter. A factory was established in the engine shed of the railway station to process the less palatable cuts of horsemeat into soup, jelly and sausages, awarded euphemistically the name "Chevril" after the famous brand name of Bovril. Slaughter cattle were converted into biltong and even neat's foot oil was extracted to lubricate weaponry. Indian corn was collected for crushing and grinding in the Natal Railway mills, and dairy cows requisitioned to ensure a supply of milk for the sick and wounded. But all Ward's efforts could not stop the death rate rising. A dozen people a day were dying from enteric fever.

Ward's role was ably summed up by White in his final dispatch from Ladysmith. "He is unquestionably the very best supply officer I have ever met, and to his resource, foresight and inventiveness the successful defence of Ladysmith for so long a period is very largely due." Private Bridgeford's laconic and informative postcard to his mother suggests that he did not entirely share the general's enthusiasm about Ward's control of the commissariat—but he had only one mouth to think of.

"Ladysmith, 19th February 1900
Our rations today consisted of:
1 lb. horse or mule flesh
¼ lb. mealie bread
¼ lb. mealie meal
1 oz. sugar
* oz. tea*
Yours etc."

Not only Ward's planning but individual resourcefulness and ingenuity also helped to keep the increasingly enfeebled garrison alive—although some believed that the introduction of laundry starch, as a thickening agent in the making of bread, killed more by gastric disturbance than it saved from malnutrition. A Natal Volunteer ran a successful one-man duck shoot for several days at dawn on the Klip river, until the Boers ambushed him. Another enterprising picquet got into the mealie fields of no-man's-land at night to return with nose-bags full of cobs, until in the end a ten-acre crop simply disappeared from under the noses of the Boer outposts. None was more ingenious than the man who built a light-proof compartment for his chickens in which he confined them in total darkness each morning after laying time and released them later in the afternoon. By providing the birds with two dawns per day, he secured a twofold harvest of eggs.

When people were not thinking about food, they were being

Siege bread, using laundry starch as a thickening agent, was, with "Chevril", a major part of the Ladysmith diet. (National Army Museum)

acquisitive about other things—hoarding, cherishing and hiding away some small, highly-valued comfort. "I still have a thin ring of soap clinging round the far corners of my pink Vinolia shaving soap box," wrote one of Colonel Royston's officers to his wife. Obsessive attitudes to scarce commodities brought with it the inevitable clash between self-indulgence and honesty, as demonstrated by Dr. Kay's diary:

"Matches are very scarce and candles are unobtainable. I received a visit from a friend, and directly he left I missed a box with nine matches in it; they were all I had. I accused him of taking them, but he denied it most indignantly; and although I was absolutely certain that he had, I had to be satisfied with his denial. I must confess that a few days later I stole from him a milk tin full of candle droppings, which he had been collecting for some time to make a candle. I procured a candle mould and so had four or five hours reading at night for my nine matches. I think I scored. This was my only theft but shortly afterwards my waterproof was stolen and I was rightly punished."

At a more professional level than one-time match stealers were those auctioneers and traders who made substantial profits by satisfying the hedonistic appetites of the more prosperous citizenry and rich army officers, some of whom seemed quite content to pay nine guineas for fifty cigars. Happily, not everybody exploited the opportunities for profiteering. David Sparkes, the store-keeper turned Carbineer officer, held his prices down to pre-siege levels, as did Stanley Sutton, an honest army contractor from Pietermaritzburg, who never lost his good name with the rank-and-file.

Throughout February, Ladysmith life pursued its miserable course—mounting sickness, rumours of Boer attacks, reassuring, palliative messages from Lord Roberts, horsemeat and shelling from Bulwana. In the distance, the rumblings of Buller's artillery, like a distant thunderstorm, seemed to increase and change position, but came no nearer, while in the foreground Midshipman Carnegie and the gunners on Caesar's Camp watched and harassed a German engineering party attempting to dam the Klip river, and so flood Ladysmith. African runners came in from the south with conflicting reports of Buller's progress and carried back private letters for posting in Pietermaritzburg at £1 a time. The going rate for mail into Ladysmith was higher; Mrs. Currie paid a £5 delivery charge for a letter to her husband, wrapped in silk-skin and concealed by an African postman inside his mouth. The letter took only four days to get through to Dr. Currie at Intombi Camp.

Buglers from the Carbineers, Indian signallers with semaphore flags and infantrymen with whistles were now giving alarm signals—twenty-one seconds worth—each time "Long Tom" opened fire, and soldiers crept out at night to place broken bottles and tin cans in front of the outposts to supplement the by-now reduced standards of vigilance among the sentries.

General White patted passing children on the head and kept their parents' spirits up by promising "lollies 'ere long", but his soldiers were rapidly looking less warlike. After weeks of waiting for Buller, his army, according to Donald Macdonald, "was the flabbiest, shabbiest and sorriest lot of human beings ever gathered together."

20 Breakthrough

"From the captured ridge we could look right down into Ladysmith, and at the first opportunity I climbed up to see it for myself. Only eight miles away stood the poor little persecuted town, with whose fate there is wrapt

Cavalry from Buller's relief force entering Ladysmith. The scraggy necks of the guard of honour from General White's beleaguered garrison contrast strongly with the robust look of the cavalrymen.

up the honour of the Empire, and for whose sake so many hundred good soldiers have given life or limb—a twenty-acre patch of tin houses and blue gum trees, but famous to the uttermost ends of the earth."
(Winston S. Churchill, Camp, Cingolo, 19th February 1900)

CAVALRY ENTERING LADYSMITH   COPYRIGHT

The Dorsets were the last battalion to stumble back across the pontoon bridge spanning the Tugela at Trichardt's Drift in pouring rain in the early hours of 27th January. The Spion Kop débâcle was behind them and there was a surprisingly cheerful General Buller to meet them, "riding hither and thither with a weary staff and a huge note-book," wrote Churchill. And though Lyttelton was disgusted—"I have lost all confidence in Buller as a general and I am sure he has himself"—he may well have been wrong in his estimate of Buller's self-esteem. There were those who attributed Buller's evident vigour and resumption of direct, personal command of the army to an almost pleasurable feeling about the failure at Spion Kop. It was as if he were reassured about his own fitness for command, now that Warren's standard of leadership was being questioned. Not least of those blaming Warren was Buller himself. In a note to Roberts he wrote: "I will never employ him in an independent command again." A few days' rest at Springfield camp, extra rations and the arrival of some reinforcements was enough to restore the soldiers' confidence in their general, and soon they were to be called upon to prove it—at Val Krantz.

Once more, Buller climbed to the top of Swart Kop with his telescope and scanned the Tugela heights. This time he looked not to the west and the Thabanyama range, where Dundonald had so nearly turned the Boer right flank ten days before, but instead turned to Val Krantz, directly opposite his observation point. He had no information about the hill apart from what he could see and the report that it was topographically similar to Swart Kop itself. Yet hill-storming strategy was to remain the method and Buller settled for Val Krantz as the key to Ladysmith. He issued the following order on 3rd February 1900: "It is the intention of the General Commanding to attack the extreme left of the enemy's positions and to endeavour to take the hill Val Krantz."

The plan went on to provide for a feint attack to be carried out on the British left flank by Wynne's 11th Brigade, to be followed by a serious, but still secondary, attack from Lyttelton's 4th Brigade across the pontoon bridge located in the centre of the British front. This was to be followed finally by the main offensive, an attack by Hildyard's 2nd Brigade and Hart's 5th Brigade on the right flank across a third pontoon, which was to be set up during the course of the preceding operations. Burn-Murdoch's 1st Mounted Brigade and Dundonald's 2nd Mounted Brigade were to wait their moment to sweep through to the plains beyond—and Ladysmith—once the ridge was taken.

For several days beforehand, sappers, sailors and gunners had been hauling their heavy ordnance up the steep southern slopes of Swart Kop. On the night before the attack they had in position twenty pieces of artillery, including a 4.7-inch naval gun and some naval 12-pounders. All Buller's troops were full of confidence. This time they were going to break through to Ladysmith.

Spirits were not so high on the Boer side, however. Louis Botha was enjoying some well-earned leave and Paul Cronje, Schalk Burger and Lucas Meyer were all resting within call of Commandant-General Joubert, north of Ladysmith. Ben Viljoen was in charge on Vaal Krantz, anxiously watching the assembly of Buller's forces in the valley below. Joubert evidently thought that Viljoen was becoming rather jittery—as well he might have been, having, as he later claimed, a mere 400 men to resist the army of 20,000 mustering on the other side of the Tugela. But, instead of the reinforcements he asked for, Viljoen received a solitary "Long Tom" and old Lucas Meyer, sent over from Colenso to deliver a pep talk on faith in the Lord.

Viljoen, who had had differences with Joubert before, was not the only commander on the Boer side to be handled firmly by his superiors that week. Joubert himself was goaded by President Kruger into a flurry of decisions, designed to pre-empt a take-over on the Tugela front by President Steyn's Free Staters. "I shall be very pleased, if your health allows it," wrote Kruger to Joubert with unaccustomed restraint, "if you will go and take command on the Tugela." Fortunately for Joubert's reputation—for he had little more than a month to live—Botha returned from leave to take charge. But not before Buller's batteries had opened their bombardment, finding their mark with a shell which shattered Ben Viljoen's rifle and blew four of his fellow burghers to smithereens in front of him.

So opened the battle for Val Krantz, a battle that went well enough for the British at first, even though the Boers were not deceived by the feint attacks and Buller allowed natural delays in the unfolding of the plan to dominate the course of the action. It was already four o'clock in the afternoon of 5th February before the anxious observers on Mount Alice saw the glint of the Durhams' bayonets and soon afterwards the reassuring signs that they and the Rifle Brigade were in possession of Vaal Krantz.

All this was fine as far as it went, even though Lyttelton, for one, was not at all enthusiastic about the acquisition of a feature which must have brought to mind the agonizingly fresh memory of Spion Kop and the fate of Woodgate's brigade on top of it. He could actually see the feature as he stood amongst the acacia thorn, the aloes and the gathering dusk. "Disposing his men to the best advantage along the rocky crest," wrote Maurice, "he ordered them to entrench, and the soldiers, weary as they were with the day's fighting, began a long night's toil to secure what they had won."

Once more, Buller's lack of purpose became evident. His subordinates soon realized that, if the way to Ladysmith was to be opened, the British attack had to be broadened to capture Green Hill and then Doornkop. Buller, however, was paralysed by the fear of a high casualty list. The next day, while Lyttelton held his position, he telegraphed to Roberts:

"After fighting all day yesterday, though with but small loss, I have pierced the enemy's line and hold a hill which divides their position, and will, if I can advance, give me access to the Ladysmith plain . . . but to get my artillery and supplies on to the plain I must drive back the enemy either on my right or on my left. It is an operation which will cost from 2000 to 3000 men, and I am not confident, though hopeful, I can do it. The question is, how would such a loss affect your plans and do you think the chance of the relief of Ladysmith worth the risk? It is the only possible way to relieve White; if I give up this chance, I know no other way."

Faced with what seemed to be an abdication of responsibility, cloaked under a request for advice, Roberts briefly replied:

"Ladysmith must be relieved, even at the loss you anticipate. Tell your troops that the honour of the Empire is in their hands and that I have no possible doubt of their being successful."

But neither instructions from Roberts nor encouragement from Warren, who spent his sixtieth birthday scrambling about on the top of Val Krantz, were able to galvanize Buller into a more vigorous policy. After a night of hard labour, followed by a day of intense bombardment, Lyttelton's brigade was relieved by Hildyard's at nightfall on the 6th. Hildyard's troops occupied the same sangars and trenches—deeper than those of Spion Kop—and suffered the same slight casualties, torrid heat and day-long gunfire as Lyttelton, before they, too, were withdrawn under cover of darkness the following night. The position had been deemed untenable and the battle of Vaal Krantz was over. Nothing had been gained save gunnery practice, consuming 10,000 rounds of ammunition, and a different way to Ladysmith had still to be decided on.

Withdrawal had been decided on at a meeting of the generals in Clery's tent at tea-time on 7th February. Of the men concerned, Buller, Lyttelton, Wynne and Clery were for retreat and Hart and Warren for continuing. The conference ended with champagne and a half-hearted endorsement of yet another plan—to attack yet another hill, Hlangwane, and so turn the Boers' left flank. But this had still to be worked out in full detail and, the following morning, the leading British columns were already on their way—back to the camp at Chieveley which they had left for Colenso nearly two months before.

Even the Boers seemed to know where they were going and said so tauntingly in a heliograph signal from Monte Cristo directed at the retiring British column. Churchill, for one, was glad to be on the move, having passed a chilly night sharing a single blanket with a restless fellow officer and, for Lord Dundonald, there was a personal surprise to relieve a little the disappointment of a backward march to base. Shortly before reaching the camp, he recognized a roadside pineapple vendor as his own cousin, the same officer who had demolished his bottle of vintage port under a wagon at Colenso. "I had to send him away again," wrote Dundonald, "the only thing that did him any good was his native drink, whisky."

Buller had once more to explain his failure and he did so in another unfortunate series of telegrams, principally to Roberts. In them, he blamed White for his inability to contain a larger force of Boers on the Ladysmith perimeter and even Roberts himself for diverting reinforcements to his own formation. Roberts replied urging a bold, but defensive, policy and this provoked a fervent appeal from Buller to be allowed to try once more. Betraying slight signs of exasperation, Roberts then ordered Buller to ascertain whether Warren, as second-in-command, agreed with his views. Warren duly complied:

"The matter involves an immense number of considerations and innumerable details, on which I may or may not share your views; but on the main and important subjects I think that my views closely coincide with yours."

There the matter rested for the moment.

Meanwhile, Buller's plan was taking shape. On 12th February he put in some solid work with his telescope on Hussar Hill, after the feature had been cleared of Boers by Dundonald's cavalry, supported by the Royal Welsh Fusiliers and some gunners. Then they all went back to Chieveley and soon the fully worked-out plan emerged. The idea was to take the ring of hills from Monte Cristo through Cingolo and Green Hill to Hussar Hill which constituted the true left flank of the Boer forces and round to Hlangwane. The possession of this hill would render the Boer positions around Colenso untenable and so open up the passage of the Tugela. The road to Ladysmith would be open. The attack was set for 14th February.

It was hardly surprising that the sight of Dundonald's cavalry and three brigades of infantry converging on Hussar Hill early that morning was enough to persuade the handful of Boers on top of it that a token resistance would be enough to satisfy honour. On arrival, Barton's brigade remained in possession and the others moved on— but not far, for Buller considered the weather too hot for further exertions. It was only Dundonald, the professional flank-man, who was eager to press on. "I made up my mind to use some discretion with regard to the orders I had received," he wrote. This exercise of discretionary power took the form of a wide and unauthorized sweeping movement to the east of the army's next objective, Cingolo, during the night of 16th/17th February. However, the manoeuvre nearly landed Dundonald in severe trouble the following afternoon when, after a difficult ascent with ponies being led through a wild confusion of rocks and scrub while dealing with Boer resistance, Dundonald and his forward troops came under fire from Hildyard's 2nd Infantry Brigade. The latter had just completed an even more arduous and hazardous day-light attack on the same feature from the other side.

The next day, 18th February, was marked by some good planning on Buller's part and, for him, an unusually adventurous deployment of four brigades simultaneously, together with supporting artillery, in the course of a single day's operations. Hildyard controlled the movement of his scattered battalions in the main attack on Monte Cristo with considerable skill, while the customary élan of Dundonald on the right flank ensured the safety of Hildyard's brigade from that quarter. The well-timed advance of Colonel C. H. Norcott (who had taken over the 4th Brigade from Lyttelton) on the Boers threatening Hildyard's left relieved pressure on his inner flank. Norcott, in turn, was ably supported by the movement of Barton's 6th Brigade on to Green Hill. At the same time the field batteries, the naval 12-pounders now on Hussar Hill, and the 4.7-inch naval gun further to the rear pounded the Boer positions with a torrent of lyddite. By the afternoon, most of the features surrounding Hlangwane had been occupied, and at eleven o'clock the following morning Barton's brigade reached the summit of Hlangwane itself—almost unopposed.

The Boers immediately began to retreat, evacuating Colenso and the southern bank of the Tugela. Changing his mood from pessimism to optimism, Buller was quite happy to let what he thought was a general retreat continue unhindered. As Leo Amery saw it, "Buller's only desire was to get to Ladysmith; the less he had to do with Boers on the way, the better." The greater part of 19th February was spent

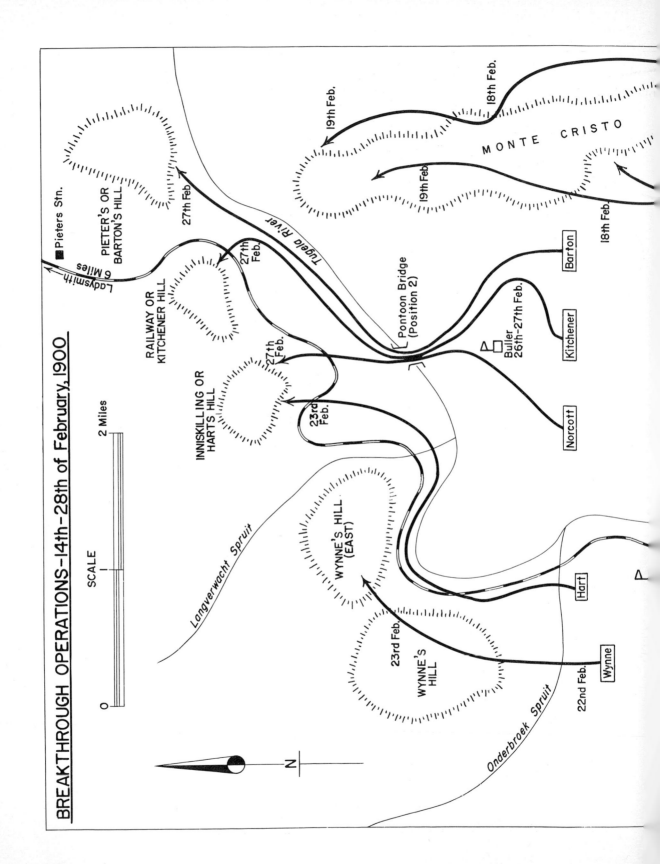

BREAKTHROUGH OPERATIONS—14th–28th of February, 1900

SCALE

2 Miles

0

Pieters Stn.

PIETER'S OR BARTON'S HILL

Ladysmith 6 Miles

27th Feb.

RAILWAY OR KITCHENER HILL

27th Feb.

27th Feb.

Tugela River

INNISKILLING OR HARTS HILL

27th Feb.

23rd Feb.

MONTE CRISTO

19th Feb.

18th Feb.

19th Feb.

19th Feb.

18th Feb.

18th Feb.

Pontoon Bridge (Position 2)

Barton

Buller 26th–27th Feb.

Kitchener

Norcott

Langverwacht Spruit

WYNNE'S HILL (EAST)

23rd Feb.

WYNNE'S HILL

Hart

Wynne

22nd Feb.

Onderbroek Spruit

N

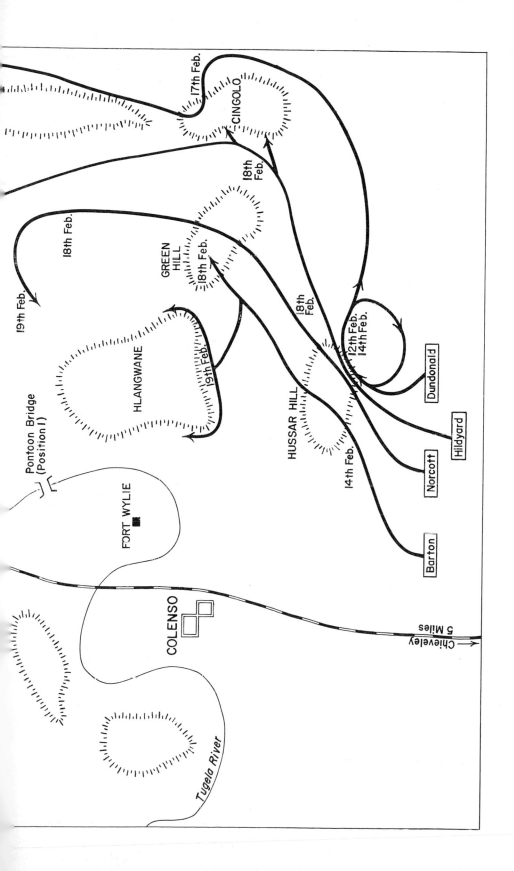

Pontoon Bridge
(Position I)

FORT WYLIE

COLENSO

Tugela River

HLANGWANE

GREEN
HILL

19th Feb.

18th Feb.

18th Feb.

18th
Feb.

CINGOLO

17th Feb.

19th Feb.

18th
Feb.

HUSSAR HILL

14th Feb.

18th Feb.

12th Feb.
14th Feb.

Dundonald

Hildyard

Norcott

Barton

Chieveley
5 Miles

203

entrenching and watching the northward trek of the Boers past Pieter's Station on the other side of the Tugela.

With the week's casualty list for the British showing less than thirty killed, it was so far, so good. But now Buller decided to wait for two days while he pondered the alternative routes to Ladysmith. At length, he decided to occupy Colenso, set up a pontoon bridge to the north-west of Hlangwane and advance straight along the road from Colenso to Ladysmith. Such was his confidence, he disregarded a signal from White—"We can detect no signs of enemy retreating; all indications point the other way"—and replied "I hope to be with you tomorrow night. I think there is only a rearguard in front of me". All the time, men and munitions were pouring across the Tugela into a position which Colonel à Court described ominously to Churchill: "We are getting ourselves cramped up among these kopjes in the valley of the Tugela. It will be like being in the Coliseum and shot at by every row of seats."

A Court's prediction was well founded. Under the inspiration of Botha's leadership and appeals from President Kruger, the Boer commandos had reorganized. Instead of a mere rearguard, Buller had to face 5,000 Boers well entrenched on the line of kopjes from Onderbroek Spruit to Pieter's Hill, and completely dominating the proposed British line of march.

But, although the harassment of the troops amassing on the west bank of the Tugela on 21st and 22nd February was quite severe, Buller still talked in terms of marching his entire army along the river valley to Pieter's Station and on to Ladysmith, with a battalion of Barton's brigade on the eastern side to deal with "snipers". However, this was quickly seen to be impractical and Warren eventually prevailed upon Buller to take one of the strong-points, later known as Wynne's Hill. No one appeared to realize that Wynne's Hill was itself flanked by another—also held by the Boers.

At 2 pm on 22nd February, Wynne led the 11th Brigade up the slopes of what turned out to be an irregular plateau with two main features, the whole corrugated by a confusion of minor knolls and ridges. The results were entirely predictable. By the evening of the 23rd, the 11th Brigade had suffered 500 casualties, including first Wynne, and then Crofton, as commanders. They had gained nothing except possession of the hill itself, a death-trap dominated by neighbouring Boer-held features. Buller's next move was to order Hart's 5th Brigade to take the next kopje in the row—Inniskilling or Hart's Hill.

Churchill stood with General Lyttelton on a convenient hilltop and watched the first mile of Hart's advance along the railway, the Inniskilling Fusiliers in front, followed by the Connaught Rangers, Dublin Fusiliers and the I.L.H. They were under fire before Churchill lost sight of them. Turning his telescope upwards to the Boer trenches on which 60 British guns were trained, he could see the slouch hats of the Boers amid the smoke and the dust and he watched with horror the carnage they inflicted with their deadly Mauser rifles:

"As the charging companies met the storm of bullets they were swept away. Officers and men fell by scores on the narrow ridge.
. . . The survivors hurried obstinately onwards until their own artillery

were forced to cease firing, and it seemed that in spite of bullets, flesh and blood would prevail. But at the last supreme moment the weakness of the attack was shown. The Inniskillings had almost reached their goal. They were too few to effect their purpose; and when the Boers saw that the attack had withered they shot all the straighter, and several of the boldest leapt out from their trenches and, running forward to meet the soldiers, discharged their magazines at the closest range."

Darkness fell. All night the living and the dead lay mixed together on the hilltop and all the following day too, with the opposing firing lines no more than three hundred yards apart. The dying and the wounded lingered on, untended without dressings, food or water. And the next night, too, they stayed until dawn on Sunday 25th February when common humanity prompted the agreement of a twenty-four hour truce for the stretcher bearers to perform their melancholy task. For the British, another 600 dead and wounded made the total for what had begun as a promising week up to 1,200. For hour after hour the staggering, lop-sided bearers lurched through the shiny mud, while Boer and Briton fraternized on the neutral ground. "We've all had a rough time," said one burgher who chanced upon General Lyttelton. "Yes, I suppose so," was Lyttelton's somewhat pensive reply. "But for us of course it's nothing. This is what we're paid for. This is the life we lead always—you understand?" "Great God!" said the Boer.

Buller, for his part, was pondering his next move. The first idea that came to him was to attack yet another hill. But he swiftly abandoned this for another plan—a plan which, this time, was going to work. Indeed, when it was explained to Lyttelton he tartly commented that it "appeared so sound that I doubted if they (the ideas) were his own."

The first step was to bring the army back across the Tugela, which in itself had the advantage of persuading the Boers that the British were once again withdrawing. The Hlangwane pontoon bridge was then dismantled after dark on 26th February and re-erected by the never-failing Major Irvine and his sappers in a new position near Monte Cristo. They were ready with a bridge a hundred yards wide by 10 am on the 27th.

There was once again an immense atmosphere of self-confidence in the air—the officers communicating a new-found faith in their commanding general and the men inspired by the news of Cronje's defeat at Paardeburg being passed along the lines. Also, it was Majuba Day—a memory from their father's war—which had to be avenged.

Barton's brigade was the first to cross Irvine's pontoon and turn smartly right, following the "TO LADYSMITH" sign erected by one of the sappers. Barton was to attack Pieter's Hill to be followed by Kitchener's brigade attacking Railway Hill; finally, Norcott was to take Inniskilling Hill, where Hart was still pinned down. All 91 guns, under Colonel Parsons, were instructed to keep up an all-out bombardment and special instructions to keep doing it until the last possible moment. What Botha had always feared had finally come to pass. The whole mighty British force was at last acting as one. Only the cavalry were mostly onlookers—Churchill among them. From his position, complete with rocks to sit on, shelter behind or on which to rest his telescope, the battlefield was "like a stage scene viewed from the dress circle."

The Royal Navy's 4.7-inch guns in action near Colenso. Working as a co-ordinated weapon, Buller's artillery deluged the Boer positions with high explosive.

By noon, Barton's 6th Brigade was in possession of Pieter's Hill and his Irish Fusiliers on the left began harassing the Boers on Railway Hill, which now came under total bombardment from Parsons' 91 guns. Small wonder that Kitchener had little difficulty in carrying the summit of Railway Hill, though this was more than Barton could say about holding Pieter's, where the Scots Fusiliers came in for withering fire from the extreme left of the Boer front. But they held firm and by 6 pm the third and last of the three hills to be attacked—Inniskilling Hill—was almost entirely in Norcott's hands.

From his vantage point across the Tugela, Churchill could still make out what was going on:

"There, painted against the evening sky, were the slouch hats and the moving rifles. Shell after shell exploded among them; overhead, in their faces, in the trench itself, behind them, before them, around them . . . Yet they held their ground and stayed in greater peril than was ever mortal man before. But the infantry were drawing very near."

Churchill was watching the East Surreys and the Rifle Brigade at that moment. He went on to pay tribute to an unknown Boer warrior,

probably from the Krugersdorp commando, who fell defending the ramparts to the end:

"At last the Dutchmen fled. One, a huge fellow in a brown jersey, tarried to spring on the parapet and empty his magazine once more into the approaching ranks, and while he did so a 50 lb lyddite shell burst, as it seemed, in the middle of him, and the last defender of Inniskilling Hill vanished."

A quiet descended—not total silence but the relative tranquillity of longer and longer gaps between each crash of gunfire. Somewhere on the top of Inniskilling Hill, a soldier—perhaps an Irishman—waved a helmet on the end of his bayonet. Then, from another part of the field, there came a small, solitary, tentative cheer, which seemed to seek confirmation. This quickly came. "Cheer answered cheer," said J. B. Atkins, "backwards and forwards across the river till all cheers became the same cheer, and Staff officers forgot that they were not as ordinary officers and threw up their helmets and shook hands with one another." The whole army was on its feet and all men knew there was to be no retreat that night. The battle of Pieter's Hill had been won.

Cavalry crosses Buller's pontoon bridge at its second position across the Tugela. This picture was probably taken on 27th February.

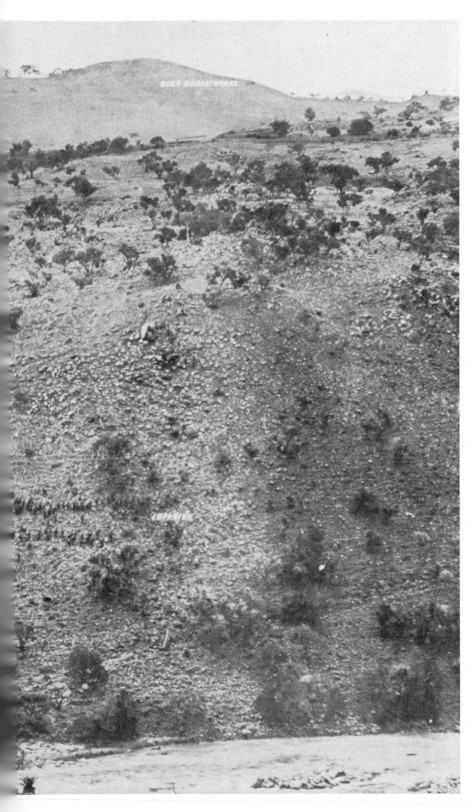

British infantry from Major-General Barton's 6th Brigade move up Pieter's Hill for the final battle for the relief of Ladysmith.

Dundonald's eagerness for a swift cavalry pursuit in the failing daylight was true to type, but neither the pleas of Warren and Lyttelton, nor even those of Barton, whose brigade had suffered nearly half the 500 casualties of the day's operations, could persuade Buller to exploit his success that night. "Retreating Boers are very hard to catch," he insisted, and considering his army had been committed to uninterrupted battle for two weeks, he may well have been right.

So the Boers were allowed to retreat unimpeded—exhausted by two weeks' incessant fighting, as well as being dispirited by the news from Paardeburg. Moreover, the ferocity of the elements was also let loose on them in their hour of anguish. H. J. Batts, in his *Pretoria from Within*, quotes one anonymous observer:

"The thunder was terrific, the rain was like an incessant water-spout, and the fearful lightning in its vivid play along the rocks and down the hillsides revealed thousands of men bedraggled and drenched, rushing as fast as they could, no one seemed to know where. Some were on horse-back, some in mule and bullock wagons, and many afoot all hurrying on, along mountain sides, over rushing rivers and sluits now turned into raging torrents . . ."

At first light on the following morning Dundonald's cavalry crossed the pontoon and set off in high spirits. They passed Kitchener's brigade and advanced on to Pieter's Station, where, to their astonishment, they were stopped. Not all the Boers had fled in the thunder and lightning of the previous night and it was well after midday before resistance finally subsided. But, by now, the thought in the mind of every horseman was who should be first into Ladysmith.

According to Dundonald's squadron rotation, it was Thorneycroft's day for advance duties, but Captain H. Bottomley of the I.L.H. now reminded his commander of a month-old promise to let his squadron be the first to enter Ladysmith. Colonel Burn-Murdoch, commanding the regular cavalry brigade (Royal Dragoons, 13th and 14th Hussars) on Dundonald's right, fortunately and rather sportingly declined to compete, and in the end it was Major Hubert Gough's patrol, scouting in the north, which unexpectedly found the way was clear. This patrol was a composite force of Natal Carbineers and I.L.H. and when Gough gave the word of command there was a wild race across the scrub to Ladysmith, the men shouting and cheering at the top of their voices.

After a frenzied mile of uncontrolled gallop, however, the race was halted, and Gough, Major Duncan Mackenzie of the Carbineers and Bottomley came to an agreement. For the final ride-in, each section would be made up of equal numbers from the two regiments. In this formation they set off once more in a headlong, but orderly, gallop, with Gough leading the way.

Dundonald was about an hour behind when he heard the news, and, leaving his main force near Pieter's Station, he, too, joined the race, bringing with him only his personal staff and Churchill, who later recorded the occasion in a letter home:

"Never shall I forget that ride. The evening was deliciously cool . . . The ground was rough with many stones, but we cared little for that. Beyond

the next ridge, or the rise beyond that, or around the corner of the next hill, was Ladysmith—the goal of all our hopes and ambitions during weeks of ceaseless fighting . . . Onward wildly, recklessly, up and down hill, over the boulders, through the scrub . . . We turned the shoulder of the hill, and there before us lay the tin houses and dark trees we had come so far to see and save."

The first startled eyes to spot the relieving cavalry were the sick and wounded at Intombi camp, many of them so weak that they had to support one another to fling their caps in the air. But there was no stopping now.

"They are Boers," said somebody to Colonel Frank Rhodes, standing on a hilltop in Ladysmith, watching the burghers' retreat.

"If they are," he replied, "they have become remarkably like our men."

The men in Caesar's Camp, however, had no doubts about who was approaching and, after a token challenge, the reply "The Ladysmith Relief Column" became the voice of deliverance for scores of scraggy soldiers, scrambling out of their trenches and sangars, shouting, cheering and running about like half-demented sports fans of a later generation.

At the Klip river crossing the troopers were intercepted by everyone who had heard the good news. There was a touch of impromptu ceremony in the helping hand from General Brocklehurst to a Carbineer sliding backwards on the muddy river bank, and the voices of men broke into a childish treble as they overtaxed their throats and lungs trying to cheer. Women laughed and cried alternately, while bewildered children looked down from the shoulders of those still strong enough to carry them.

All the way into the town, the cheering and the crowding continued as the more enfeebled and less promptly informed citizenry also joined in. "It was a scene never to be forgotten," wrote Gough, the man in the centre of it. "I suppose I have never felt such a scene, it was not much too look at. I felt at times more like crying than cheering."

Eventually, Gough found General White. Grey, stooping, emaciated, White was scarcely able to break through the yelling mass of citizens and soldiery to deliver, "in a voice trembling with emotion, but clear and soldierly for all that", his valedictory message:

"I thank you men, one and all, from the bottom of my heart, for the help and support you have given to me, and I shall always acknowledge it to the end of my life . . . Thank God we kept the flag flying."

But there was not much emotion from Gough's brother, Johnny, when the two men met. "Well, Hubert," said the four-month's beleaguered Gough, "How fat you have got!"

The dinner that night at General White's headquarters was as festive as horseflesh and ailing hosts could permit, but somebody, perhaps Colonel Ward, produced several bottles of champagne. Churchill, Gough, Mackenzie and all the senior Ladysmith commanders were there, but Dundonald slipped away to send Buller a simple signal. "Am in Ladysmith. Dundonald." And, though it was a day or two before the main columns of Buller's army marched in, the siege of Ladysmith was over.

21 A Reckoning

**"Even sober unemotional London found its soul for once fluttered with joy. Men, women and children, rich and poor, clubman and cabman, joined in the universal delight."
(A. Conan Doyle, *The Great Boer War*, 1903)**

John H. Bacon's view of the relief. White's comment was: "I thank God we kept the flag flying." (National Army Museum)

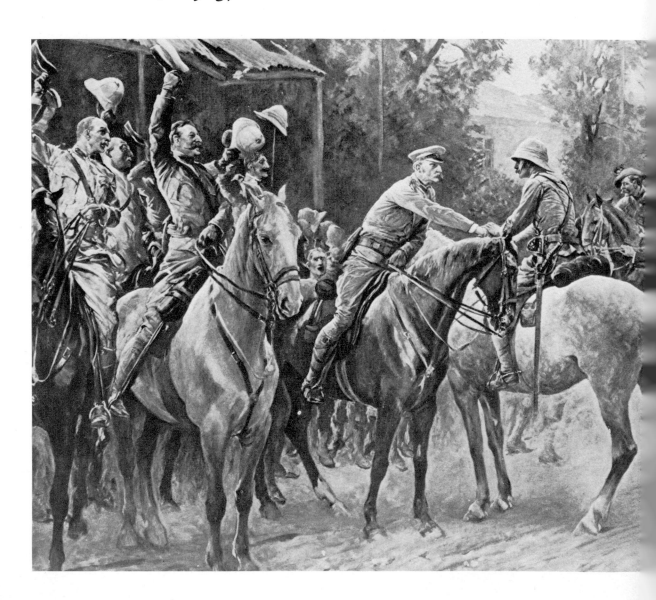

Neither White nor Buller, it seems, thought of sending telegrams to London as prompt and explicit as that of Lord Dundonald on arrival in Ladysmith. But there were plenty of journalists to pass on the news and the monarch's heir-apparent lost no time in dispatching a swift, if somewhat laconic, communication to the commanding general:

"To : Sir Redvers Buller, 1st March, 1900
Sincerest congratulations.
      Edward Albert."

It was hardly surprising that the taut, nervous tension of London's well-fed and Empire-minded public, or the high-spirited patriotism of undergraduates in Cambridge, exploded into an orgy of triumphal celebration which the haggard defenders of Ladysmith themselves could not equal. In the ancient university town, railings were torn down and barrows burnt, while traffic in central London was paralysed

by the throng of thousands of jubilant citizens. Carnivals in Pietermaritzburg and Durban, however, were ill-matched by the simpler and less hysterical largess of Buller's relieving troops, tossing, as they marched, plugs of pocket-worn tobacco and soggy biscuits to the men who welcomed them in. For the latter, it was relief from a state of siege. For the Britons in Britain the humiliation of imperial pride had been averted.

Nevertheless, on the day of the triumphal entry by the relieving force, Ladysmith tried to live up to the spirit of the occasion, and, in a military sense, the scene was totally British—though bereft of some of the pomp and panoply of a more fully equipped army. Colonel Park's disciplined Devons lining the route provided the distinctively English element. This contrasted with the tempestuous Irishmen, breaking ranks in joy—and sorrow, at the sight of the depleted ranks of their regimental comrades. And the noise of the cheering onlookers was dominated only by the sound of the bagpipes of the Gordon Highlanders.

Tiredness and malnutrition soon conquered exhultation and revelry, however. "An English frenzy has at best a short life," wrote Atkins, disappointed at the reception accorded him by passers-by the next day. "I have been greeted with as much ardour in the afternoon in London by a man with whom I had lunched two hours before."

The anguish of those who, the day before, had eagerly, but in vain, scanned the ranks of Buller's parading regiments for familiar faces would have been the more acute had they known of the frictions and tensions among their leaders on the saluting base.

White had already made his historic utterance about keeping the flag flying, but Buller had yet to give tongue. Neither man's biographer has recorded the exchanges between them when they first met in Ladysmith, but a marked lack of cordiality was observed by several eye-witnesses. Pursuit or non-pursuit was a theme on which the two generals were sharply divided, and which was most certainly broached at their initial encounter. White's own "flying column" was predictably defeated—not by Botha's retreating Boers—but by the effort of a four-mile march in which the infantry had as much difficulty staying on their feet as the horses had in dragging a few 15-pounders. Meanwhile, Buller refused to take any positive action, though many of the officers in his two mounted brigades looked on in frustration from their hilltop outposts at the chaotic Boer withdrawal. Deneys Reitz later confirmed their appreciation of what might have been done:

"In all directions the plain was covered by a multitude of men, wagons and guns ploughing across the sodden veldt in the greatest disorder . . . Had the British fired a single gun at this surging mob everything on wheels would have fallen into their hands, but by great good luck there was no pursuit."

Soon, the armies had moved on, the shelling had become no more than a recent nightmare and the war took a different turn. Within a month, Hamilton, Rawlinson and Hunter were far away, and, by 14th April, Sir George White was back in England. But the legacy of the siege remained, in the records of the town's scribes and diarists and in its effect on the eventual outcome of the war.

Whether Ladysmith should have been held or abandoned in favour of some other strongpoint within which, or from which, to defend Natal and the vital sea port of Durban continued to fascinate military historians long after the events themselves took place. There were at the time powerful advocates of the abandonment theory, including Lord Wolseley, Commander-in-Chief in London. But it was not a popular idea and would have met with considerable political resistance in Britain as well as in South Africa. For the majority, the question was not whether to defend Ladysmith, but where to take a stand—how far in front to hold the line. To most British military planners in 1899 the notion of abandoning Ladysmith would have been as unthinkable as a retreat from Woolwich.

What difference, then, did the successful retention of Ladysmith make to the course of the war? Spencer Wilkinson, in his *Lessons of the War*, rightly summed up the situation. "Sir George White's force," he wrote, "is the centre of gravity of the situation. If the Boers cannot defeat it, their cause is hopeless; if they can crush it, they have hopes of success." And, as the *London Weekly Times* put it, "Natal was the object on which the Boers had set their hearts ... their plan of campaign was framed from the very idea that they should have the territory from Majuba to the sea."

Defeat of the Natal Field Force would therefore have facilitated the capture of Durban and would, at the same time, have enhanced the prospects of substantial foreign intervention on the Boer side. The course of the war would have been dramatically different and the international political consequences quite unpredictable. Instead, whether by dint of British tenacity or Boer infirmity of purpose, Ladysmith was not abandoned and it was not overrun. As Churchill wrote from Durban shortly after the siege:

"The flower of the Boer army was occupied and exhausted in futile efforts to take the town and stave off the relieving forces. Four precious months were wasted by the enemy in a vain enterprise. Fierce and bloody fighting raged for several weeks with heavy losses to both sides but without shame to either."

From the Boer point of view, the main responsibility for this unsatisfactory state of affairs undoubtedly rests with Joubert. Had he prevented Yule's march to Ladysmith in the last days of October, he would have reduced White's forces by 4,000 men. His failure to close the ring around the town more speedily enabled the Royal Navy's big guns to join the garrison, thus providing White with artillery to match the Boer "Long Toms". And his consent to the establishment of the Neutral Camp at Intombi to house the sick and wounded may well have been the saving of Ladysmith.

Certainly, the Boers never had another chance to recover the momentum of their early initiatives. After Ladysmith, Lord Roberts' Grand Army pressed on. Kimberley had already been relieved, Bloemfontein and Mafeking were soon to follow, and, by June, the British had reached Pretoria. The British believed that the war was ended, and Roberts returned home, leaving Kitchener to wind up the campaign.

This was far from the case, however. The days of the set-piece battles were almost past, but the new generation of bold young Boer commanders refused to recognize formal defeat. With the introduction of guerrilla war by the Boers, and the consequent reprisals, "drives" and establishment of concentration camps by the British, the last of the "Gentlemen's Wars" was at an end.

Of the major figures who took part in the Ladysmith campaign, Louis Botha went on to become one of South Africa's greatest statesmen. Having come finally to recognize the hopelessness of guerrilla conflict, he was a leading architect of the peace treaty that ended the war and of the eventual Union of South Africa. When he died in 1919, spent by a lifetime of unswerving commitment to his country, Smuts unhesitatingly described him as "South Africa's greatest son".

It might have been better for Buller if he had never come to South Africa at all. Dundonald had observed during the campaign that, when he escorted Buller to vantage points across rough ground, the latter frequently stumbled over tufts of grass. Shortly after the relief, he commented on the change he found in the general since they had served together in the Sudan. "It is true, my dear Dundonald," replied Buller. "I am changed, and what changed me was the indoor life of that cursed War Office, the long hours day after day without exercise."

Advancing years, a deeply-held feeling for the welfare of the rank-and-file, and a sneaking sense of uncertainty of his own fitness for supreme command all plagued Buller throughout his unfortunate Natal campaign. He went home a sad, and ironically a defeated man, uncherished by most of his peers but revered to the end by his soldiers. He died in 1908, his only admirers of distinction being those who had known him when he was young.

For Sir George White, soldiering was over. After he recovered from the privations of Ladysmith, he was appointed Governor of Gibraltar. He retired from public life in 1905. Hunter, the successful leader of the Gun Hill sortie, Lyttelton and Dundonald all advanced in rank and reputation, though none surpassed in status Field-Marshal Lord Rawlinson of Trent. Ian Hamilton rose to command the ill-fated Gallipoli expedition of the First World War. Of the younger men, Gandhi—the Indian stretcher bearer from Colenso and Spion Kop— had not yet seriously entered politics, a career which Winston Churchill had already begun with a failure. All three of Lambton's surviving Royal Navy lieutenants became admirals.

For years, the siege was commemorated in annual dinners in London and Durban, but the occasion has long since lapsed. However, the battle zone remains much as it was, largely thanks to the efforts of a vigorous and dedicated, but tiny, Historical Society. Perhaps Winston Churchill, soldier, scribe and world statesman in the making, who was on the spot for much of the story, should have the last word: "The defence and relief of Ladysmith will not make a bad page in British history."

Bibliography

Amery, L. S.
Times History of the War in
South Africa, Low Marston &
Co., London, 1903.

Atkins, J. B.
The Relief of Ladysmith,
Methuen, London, 1900.

Barnard, Prof. C. J.
General Louis Botha op die
Natalse Front, 1899–1900,
A. A. Balema, Cape Town,
1970.

Moberly Bell, E.
Flora Shaw, London, 1947.

Blake, J. Y. F.
A West Pointer with the Boers,
Angel Guardian Press, Boston,
1903.

Boas, Guy
Sir Winston Churchill,
Macmillan, London, 1966.

Churchill, Randolph
Winston S. Churchill,
Vol. 1 (2 parts), Heinemann,
London, 1967.
Vol. 2 (3 parts), Heinemann,
London, 1969.

Churchill, Winston
My Early Life, Odhams,
London, 1958.

Colvin, Ian
A Life of Jameson, 1922.

Craw, Bella
Diary of the Siege of
Ladysmith, Ladysmith
Historical Society, 1970.

Crewe, Marquis of
Life of Lord Rosebery, 2
Vols., John Murray, London,
1931.

Cambridge History of the
British Empire
Cambridge University Press,
1936.

Davitt, Michael
The Boer Fight for Freedom,
Frink & Wagnalls, New York,
1902.

Deleage, Paul
Trois Mois chez les Zoulous,
Paris, 1887.

Conan Doyle, Sir Arthur
The Great Boer War, Thomas
Nelson & Sons, London, 1903.

Dundonald, Earl of
My Army Life, Edward
Arnold & Co., London, 1934.

Durand, Sir Mortimer
Field-Marshal Sir George
White, Wm. Blackwood &

Sons, London, 1915.

Fitzpatrick, J. Percy
South African Memories,
Cassell, London, 1932.

Garvin, J. L.
The Life of Joseph
Chamberlain, Macmillan,
London, 1934.

Gibbs, P.
Death of the Last Republic,
Frederick Muller Ltd.,
London, 1957.

Gibson, G. F.
Story of the Imperial Light
Horse, G.D. & Co., London,
1937.

Gore, Lt. Col. St. J.
Green Horse in Ladysmith,
Sampson Low, London, 1901.

Haldane, Gen. Sir Aylmer
A Soldier's Saga, Wm.
Blackwood & Son, London,
1948.

Hamilton, Ian
A Life of General Sir Ian
Hamilton, Cassell, London,
1966.

Hofmeyer, N.
Zes Maanden bij die
Commandos, Van Stockum,
The Hague, 1903.

Jeans, T. T., R.N.
Naval Brigades in the South
African War, Sampson Low,
London, 1901.

Kestell, J. D.
Through Shot and Flame,
Methuen & Co., London,
1903.

Kruger, Rayne
Goodbye Dolly Gray, Cassell
& Co., London, 1959.

Lindley, Sir Francis
Lord Lovat—a Biography,
Hutchinson, London, 1935.

Lockhard, J. G. and
Woodhouse, C. M.
Rhodes, Hodder & Stoughton,
London, 1963.

Macdonald, Donald
How We Kept the Flag Flying,
Ward Lock, London, 1900.

Maurice, Gen. Sir Frederick
History of the War in South
Africa, Hurst & Blackett,
London, 1907.

May, H. J.
Music of the Guns,
Hutchinson, London, 1970.

Le May, G. L. H.

British Supremacy in Southern
Africa, Clarendon Press,
London, 1965.

Black and White in South
Africa, Twentieth Century
Library, London, 1971.

Melville, Col. C. H.
Life of Sir Redvers Buller,
London, 1923.

McCourt, Edward
Remember Butler, Routledge
& Keegan Paul, London, 1967.

Meintjes, Johannes
General Louis Botha, Cassell,
London, 1970.
The Commandant General,
Tafelberg Uitgewers, Cape
Town, 1971.
De la Rey, Lion of the West,
Hugh Keartland,
Johannesburg, 1966.

Mouton, J. A.
Gen. Piet Joubert in die
Transvaalse Geskiedenis,
Archives Year Book, 1957.

Packenham, Elizabeth
Jameson's Raid, Weidenfeld &
Nicolson, London, 1960.

Park, Lt. Col. C. W.
Letters from Ladysmith,
Ladysmith Historical Society,
1972.

Patterson, Sheila
The Last Trek, Routledge &
Keegan Paul, London, 1957.

Payne, Robert
Life and Death of Mahatma
Gandhi, Bodley Head,
London, 1969.

Pearse, H. H. S.
Four Months Besieged,
Macmillan, London, 1900.

Pearse, Col. H. W.
The East Surrey Regiment,
Spottiswoode, Ballantyne,
London, 1916.

Pemberton, W. Baring
Battles of the Boer War,
Batsford, London, 1964.
Pen Pictures of the War,
Horace Marshall and Son,
London, 1900.

Pitchford, H. Watkins
Besieged in Ladysmith, Shuter
& Shooter, Pietermaritzburg,
1964.

Pomeroy, Maj. the Hon. R. L.
History of the 5th Dragoon
Guards, Wm. Blackwood,
London 1924.

Preller, Gustave
Lobengula, Johannesburg
A.P.B, 1963.

Ransford, Oliver
Spion Kop, John Murray,
London, 1969.
The Great Trek, John
Murray, London, 1972.

Reitz, Deneys
Commando, Faber & Faber,
London, 1929.

Schikkerling, R. W.
Commando Courageous, Hugh
Keartland, Johannesburg,
1964.

Seed, Jennie
The Red Dust Soldiers,
Heinemann, London, 1972.

Selby, John
The Boer War, Arthur Barker
Ltd., London, 1969.

Smuts, J. C.
Selections from the Smuts
Papers, Cambridge University
Press, 1966.

De Souza, C. W. L.
No Charge for Delivery, Books
of Africa, Cape Town, 1969.

Symons, Julian
Buller's Campaign, Cresset
Press, London, 1969.

Tatham, G. F.
Diary of the Siege of
Ladysmith, Ladysmith
Historical Society, 1970.

Viljoen, B
My Reminiscences of the
Anglo-Boer War, Hood,
Douglas & Howard, London,
1902.

Walker, Eric A.
History of Southern Africa,
Longmans, London, 1928.

Wallis, J. P. R.
Fitz, the Story of Sir Percy
Fitzpatrick, Macmillan,
London, 1955.

De Wet, Christian
Three Years' War, Constable,
London, 1902.

Wilson, H. W.
With the Flag to Pretoria,
Harmsworth, 1901.

Woodham-Smith, Cecil
The Reason Why, Constable,
London, 1953.

Woods, Frederick
Young Winston's Wars,
Sphere Books, London, 1972.

Index